D0368994

BROADCASTING

ROBERT E. SUMMERS

Professor of Communication
School of Public Communication
Boston University

Wadsworth Publishing Co., Inc.

AND THE PUBLIC

HARRISON B. SUMMERS

Emeritus Professor
Radio and Television
The Ohio State University

Belmont, California

**BROADCASTING
AND THE PUBLIC**

ROBERT E. SUMMERS
HARRISON B. SUMMERS

L.C. Cat. Card No.: 66–21452

Printed in the United States of America

5 6 7 8 9 10—74 73 72 71 70

PREFACE

When a medium of mass entertainment such as broadcasting claims the attention of millions of Americans for several hours each day, that situation should arouse the interest of all intelligent citizens. What kinds of programs do radio and television provide for the listening public? How do these programs influence listeners? What basic values does broadcasting offer, and what are its shortcomings? In particular, can the *product* of broadcasting be improved, and if so, how?

These are important questions to those who listen to broadcast programs and to all who are interested in the possibility of raising the standards of radio and television service. Those who attempt to find answers to these questions need, first of all, a broad understanding of the system of broadcasting we have in the United States. They must be aware of how that system works and of the many complex factors affecting the kinds of programs offered. To provide such an understanding of American broadcasting—both as a social force and as a form of business enterprise —is the purpose of this book. Major topics include coverage of the characteristics of the system itself, the directions in which broadcasting has developed over the years, the organization and operations of stations and networks, and the ways in which economic considerations affect those operations and the selection of programs to be put on the air.

Some of the major criticisms directed at the service provided by radio and television are presented, as are the efforts being made to meet those criticisms. Attention has also been given to the philosophies of regulation applied by government agencies, to the importance of broadcasting's activities in the area of public information, and to proposals for future improvement in station and network programming.

It has been our purpose in writing this book neither to condemn nor to defend the system of broadcasting that has developed in the United States. We are aware of its many values and of its shortcomings. Our intention has been only to provide, as objectively as possible, a wide background of information about broadcasting and the broadcasting industry that will enable each individual reader to make his own appraisal of this form of mass communication, which has become extremely important in our national life.

We want to express our appreciation to the A. C. Nielsen Company for authorizing the use of Nielsen data in several of our tables, to the many individual writers who have allowed us to quote some of the materials used in the final chapter, and to the editors of the *Bulletin of the American Society of Newspaper Editors*, the *Centennial Review*, the *Columbia Journalism Review*, *Fortune*, the *Journal of Broadcasting*, *Television* magazine, *Television Quarterly*, and *Variety*, for permitting the use of materials taken from their publications. Our special thanks go to Richard Goggin of New York University, Kenneth Harwood of the University of Southern California, Leo Martin of Michigan State University, Harold Niven, Assistant to the President of the National Association of Broadcasters, Paul K. Taff, Director of Program Operations for National Educational Television, M. C.

Topping of Oklahoma State University, and J. Clark Weaver of Florida State University, who were kind enough to read early drafts of the manuscript and whose suggestions and criticisms have been extremely helpful.

R.E.S.
H.B.S.

illustrations

CONTENTS

advertising and commercials ... the value of
criticism

tables

BROADCASTING AND THE PUBLIC

THE IMPORTANCE
OF BROADCASTING

At almost any hour from early morning until late at night, men, women, and children in millions of American homes are listening to the radio or watching television. At any given time during the day, the audience for broadcast programs includes 20 to 30 million; at night, the number runs as high as 50 to 60 million. The people of the United States spend hours every day being entertained or informed by radio and television.

In fact, in the more than 50 million homes equipped to receive television programs, the television set is in use for an average of at least five hours a day, 365 days a year. And people also listen to radio. Some radio set in the average home is in operation for well over an hour and a half a day; this does not include the time Americans spend listening to radio sets in automobiles, at the office or beauty shop, or anywhere else outside the home. These are figures reported by the A. C. Nielsen Company, one of the leading organizations in the field of radio and television audience research, and the Nielsen estimates are confirmed by those of other researchers.

These figures do not mean that every member of the family is listening to radio or watching a television program every second that the set at home is in use. The Nielsen figures deal with the use of sets, not with the numbers of individual listeners. But various other studies indicate that housewives devote an average of from. five to five and a half hours a day to television viewing or radio listening. Men are at home for fewer hours each day and do less listening; however, they spend an average of at least three hours a day with television or radio, including their out-of-home radio listening. School-age boys and girls are also exposed to broadcast programs for an average of some three hours each day—more hours in the course of a year than these same children spend in the classroom. It is safe to estimate that American adults are spending an average of from 25 to 30 hours a week—and children and teen-agers at least 20 hours a week—watching, listening to, or giving at least some degree of attention to materials broadcast on radio and television.

Twenty to thirty hours each week is quite a substantial amount of time. The figures become even more significant when compared with the amounts of time Americans devote to other sources of information and other forms of entertainment. Readership studies indicate that adults spend an average of perhaps 25 to 30 minutes reading newspapers every day, with not more than five or six hours a week devoted to reading books, magazines, and newspapers combined; children do even less reading than do adults. Attendance at motion picture theaters totals from 40 to 50 million paid admissions per week, which means that Americans spend an average of less than one hour each week at motion picture theaters. Another two hours per week would probably more than cover average church attendance and time spent at public lectures, at concerts, and at stage performances. And an additional hour or two per week would take care of the average American's attendance at spectator sports events as well as the time he devotes to actual participation in outdoor sports. Time required for all of these activities combined, from reading to playing golf, will average no more than ten or twelve hours each week, or roughly half as many hours as the average American spends watching television and listening to the radio. Radio and television have become extremely important elements in our national life, and elements that undoubtedly exert considerable influence on the interests, the tastes, and the standards of value of the average American.

Effects of Broadcasting

A study conducted in an Eastern city each year over a ten-year period shows the extent to which the introduction of television influenced the habits and interests of those who had access to the new medium.[1] Men and women in television-equipped homes reported that after they had purchased television sets they went much less often to motion picture theaters or to the legitimate theater; spent less time attending lodge meetings, club meetings, and social gatherings; and did less visiting with friends and neighbors. In addition, nearly half of the new owners of television sets stated that they devoted less time to reading books and magazines than they did before they had access to television programs. These changes in behavior patterns continued throughout the entire period covered by the study.

Effects on other forms of entertainment. Such changes in habit patterns, produced by the availability of home entertainment, have had striking effects on other elements in our national life. The rise in the popularity of radio in the late 1920s and early 1930s helped bring about the disappearance of vaudeville, the theatrical stock company, and the traveling tent theater. Both radio and television have contributed to the decline of the Broadway stage. Although in the decade from 1921 to 1930 there was an average of no less than 218 new productions on Broadway each year, in the period from 1956 to 1965 the average

---

[1] *The First Decade of Television in Videotown, 1948–1957.* Cunningham & Walsh, Inc., New York, 1957.

number of new offerings each year had dropped to 57, of which only 36 were new plays, the remainder being musicals or revivals. Motion pictures have been similarly affected; although from 1946 to 1948 paid admissions to motion picture theaters averaged approximately 90 million a week, average weekly attendance in 1964 and 1965 stood at only a little more than half that figure. It is significant, too, that since 1950 almost all of the small neighborhood motion picture theaters operating in that year, as well as many first-run houses in larger cities, have been forced to close their doors.

Television has had a decided influence on the popularity and the financial success of spectator sports. Most experts believe that the broadcasting of football and basketball games has stimulated interest in these sports and has helped produce an increase in the number of paid admissions to intercollegiate contests. Authorities in the field also attribute much of the recent popularity of professional football to the fact that many of the professional games are broadcast by television stations. Interest in golf and bowling has been greatly increased by the broadcasting of these sports; the same is true, although in more limited degree, with respect to sports-car racing, skiing, and ice hockey. But with boxing and baseball, the story is different. Small local boxing clubs have not been able to compete with television, and what was once the major source of boxing talent has all but disappeared. And with major-league baseball games available both on radio and on television, attendance at minor-league games has sharply declined, with the effect that only a few of the minor leagues have been able to survive.

Effects on newspapers and magazines. Broadcasting has had its influence, too, on the form and content of newspapers and large-circulation magazines. From the 1930s on, radio's greater speed in bringing information about important events to the public has forced American newspapers to make substantial changes in the materials provided for their readers. With almost no exceptions, newspapers have greatly increased their use of pictures; they have treated major news stories in more detail than can be provided in ordinary news broadcasts on radio and television; they have offered more syndicated articles by well-known columnists; they have greatly expanded their use of non-news feature materials, from "advice" columns to comic strips. Magazines, too, have been forced to modify their content. Since the short stories, once their most attractive offerings, have had to compete with dramatized "stories" on radio and television, practically all of our popular magazines have reduced their use of fiction in favor of more feature articles and human-interest materials.

Equally great has been the economic impact of radio and television on the printed media. Newspapers and magazines depend for most of their revenues on the sale of advertising; income from subscriptions and newsstand sales is rarely more than enough to cover costs of distribution. And competition of networks and stations for the advertiser's dollar grows more intense each year. In 1940, radio's revenues from advertising amounted to only a little more than 150 million dollars; today, national and local advertisers are spending two billion dollars a year for radio and television time, not counting the amounts paid for the production of programs. Much of that increase in advertising expenditures in broadcasting represents money that might otherwise have been spent for newspaper and magazine advertising. At least partly as a result of this competition from radio and television, many newspapers are operating on an extremely narrow profit margin, and the number of large-city daily newspapers is decreasing, year by year. Similarly, the loss of potential advertising revenues coupled with constantly increasing costs has forced several long-established mass-circulation magazines to suspend publication. The growing importance of radio and television has had a decided effect on newspapers and magazines, as it has on major forms of out-of-home entertainment.

Effects on politics. Broadcasting has had an influence on many other elements in our national life. Radio's ability to reach and to influence millions of people was evidenced in striking fashion in the "fireside chats" presented by President Franklin D. Roosevelt, which made it possible for him to calm the fears of a nation beset by bank failures, unemployment, and economic disaster. Presidents since Roosevelt have used radio and television to explain their philosophies of government to the American people, and to win popular support for measures presented to Congress. And naturally, broadcasting has become a major factor in national political campaigns—candidates can reach a far greater number of voters through a single appearance on a national television network than through all other agencies of communication combined. As a result, campaigns for national candidates in recent years have been conducted largely over television and radio, from the first announcements of candidates for party nomination until the night before the election in November. Even the national nominating conventions are now planned by party organizations to take advantage of the special opportunities created by broadcasting, with "important" proceedings such as keynote speeches, nomination of candidates, and actual balloting scheduled at hours when the largest numbers of radio and television listeners are available. Many political experts believe that the personalities of rival candidates, as they are brought to voters by television, are at least as important as the campaign issues in determining the winners of national elections.

Broadcasting and the Listener [2]

Radio and television not only affect many of the elements in our everyday life, but they also exert a direct influence on the individual listener and on listeners collectively. This influence must be considerable, if only because of the number of individuals reached and the amount of time during which they are "exposed" to radio or television. Radio sets are to be found in approximately 95 per cent of all American homes and in 70 per cent of the automobiles on our highways; in 1965, an estimated 93 per cent of all homes had television receiving sets—a considerably larger proportion of homes than had bathtubs or telephones, or than received daily newspapers. And as noted in

---

[2] Throughout this book, the term "listener" will refer to any individual giving attention either to radio or to television programs. Those who watch television also listen; in fact, attention studies indicate that very frequently television "viewers" do not watch the picture tube continuously, although they do hear and give some degree of continuing attention to the sound portion of the program.

earlier pages, the individual men, women, and children living in those homes spend an average of at least 20 to 25 hours each week listening to radio or television. To a much greater extent than any other agency of mass communication, broadcasting has an *opportunity* to influence the American public.

Furthermore, the listener to broadcast programs is usually *willing* to be influenced by what he hears or sees. Most of his listening is done in his own home; since he listens largely for entertainment, he is relaxed; his mental guards are down, and he listens more or less uncritically. The ideas offered in the programs he hears are not presented impersonally in print, but are conveyed by the voices of *people*—in most cases, people with whose voices and personalities the listener is already familiar and whom he tends to regard at least as acquaintances, if not as personal friends. In addition, the listener has a high degree of confidence in the reliability of the broadcasting media—of television in particular. This has been shown repeatedly in studies of listener attitudes. In one such study, conducted in 1964 by the Elmo Roper organization, men and women throughout the country were asked, "If you got conflicting reports of the same news story from radio, television, the magazines, and the newspapers, which of the four versions would you be most inclined to believe?" Of those reached by the Roper interviewers, 41 per cent would believe television in preference to any of the other sources; 23 per cent would accept the newspaper version, and 10 per cent would believe the account printed in a magazine.[3] Radio, overshadowed by television in recent years, still was considered most reliable by 8 per cent of the respondents; the remaining 18 per cent expressed no preference. This willingness to accept the ideas presented in television programs offers striking evidence of the extent to which broadcasting can influence listeners.

Listener Evaluations of Broadcasting

What *kind* of an influence do radio and television exert on their listeners? This is a most important question, but one about

---

[3] Results of the study published in *The Public's View of Television and Other Media.* Television Information Office, New York, March 1965.

which opinions differ widely. Some critics of broadcasting believe that radio and television programs leave much to be desired and that operators of networks and stations have failed to make effective use of broadcasting's tremendous potential as a force to raise the cultural standards of the American public. Most listeners, on the other hand, seem to be fairly well satisfied with the service that radio and television provide. In the 1964 Roper study already referred to, when men and women were asked their opinions concerning television's performance, 62 per cent of the respondents believed that television stations were doing either an "excellent" or a "good" job, as compared with 55 per cent who gave a similar rating to newspapers and only 47 per cent who had an equally good opinion of the activities of local governmental agencies. The public's general approval of broadcasting is indicated even more strikingly by the fact that television and radio sets are in use in the average home for a combined total of more than six hours a day. Of course, even the most enthusiastic listener to radio or television programs usually has some criticisms to offer, just as he can find things to criticize in his favorite newspaper or magazine or in our system of public education. We don't expect perfection in life; we can find shortcomings even in institutions and agencies which, on the whole, win our hearty approval.

Every listener makes his own personal evaluation of the things he hears on the air. Primarily, he forms judgments with respect to individual programs. Some programs he especially likes; they arouse his interest or entertain him, and he tries to listen to them regularly. Others he accepts as being moderately good or at least satisfactory; he will listen to them when more attractive programs are not available and will derive some pleasure from listening—but he makes no special effort to "catch" them. Still other programs fail to interest him at all; some of them arouse his active dislike. Rather than listen to programs in this third group, he will turn off his radio or his television set completely.

The listener makes his own evaluations of programs—or perhaps in the case of radio, of the stations that supply those programs—but on the whole, his evaluations are based almost entirely on the *entertainment* values of the programs considered and the extent to which he finds them attractive and interesting. Rarely does the average listener give much thought to the desirable or undesirable aspects of the *content* of programs—aside, of course, from those programs to which he listens for information—or to the manner in which the programs he hears may affect his attitudes or standards of value or tastes, or the attitudes and tastes of other listeners. If radio and television supply a substantial number of programs which, for him at least, have high entertainment values, then broadcasting is "doing a good job" and its weaknesses are of minor importance. But if he finds very few attractive programs and a large number of programs that he dislikes, then the listener tends to become critical of the entire broadcasting industry and of the service it provides the public.

Perhaps this tendency is logical and reasonable; most Americans think of radio and television primarily as sources of entertainment, like the motion picture or the theater. But entertainment is not the only factor that should be considered. Programs broadcast by radio and television stations exert some degree of influence on the tastes and attitudes of the listening public, and the nature of these influences must be taken into account. In many respects, at least, radio and television have had a wholesome effect on our society, especially in the widespread dissemination of information. The American public today is probably better informed than are any other people on earth, and at least some of the credit must go to broadcasting. But radio and television also have their weaknesses and imperfections. And it is the obligation of every intelligent listener to examine critically the programs radio and television offer and the functioning of our system of broadcasting, and when improvements are possible, to use what means are available to him to help correct the weaknesses he finds. Of course, he must be realistic in his appraisal; not all of the conditions that he may regard as shortcomings can be eliminated. Some of these conditions are the result of our commercial system of operation or of the prevailing economic or social climate, but others may reflect errors in judgment—and these at least can be corrected. To help broadcasting serve the interests of the American public more effectively, intelligent listeners should accept the responsibility of encouraging good elements in broadcasting and of expressing their disapproval of elements that fall short of the requirements of good taste.

2

SYSTEMS OF BROADCASTING

In every nation, institutions and organizations are shaped by the country's history, its geography, its economic development, its cultural patterns and traditions, and its philosophies of government. These factors have exerted a tremendous influence on the systems of broadcasting organization found in the various nations of the world. Throughout most of Europe, and in other countries where governments exercise a high degree of control over the lives and economic affairs of citizens, broadcasting is a government monopoly; radio and television stations are owned and operated by an agency of the government. In the United States, following our traditions of individual freedom and competitive enterprise, broadcasting facilities are owned by private individuals and are operated for profit, with a minimum amount of government control.

In Canada, Australia, and Japan, where traditions of monarchy still exist—although the governments are highly democratic—systems of broadcasting have been developed in which privately owned commercial stations compete for listeners with stations owned by central government agencies. In many Latin American countries that have adopted at least the governmental forms developed in the United States, national governments own only a few major broadcasting stations; a far greater number are privately owned and operated for profit. However, in these countries radio and television are sometimes subject to very direct control by government agencies, and in many Latin American countries, nearly all stations are owned by a few powerful corporations— a situation very unlike that existing in the United States. In every country, the system of ownership and control—in combination with cultural patterns, institutions, and philosophies of government—also exercises its own influence on the type of broadcasting activities undertaken and on the types of programs made available to listeners.

THE EUROPEAN SYSTEM OF BROADCASTING

This book deals with the system of broadcasting we have in the United States and with the factors affecting the types of programs provided for American listeners. The nature of radio and television programming in this country is, partially at least, a product of our system of broadcasting. For an understanding of the American system, it is helpful to compare some of its features with those of what can be called the European system of government ownership and control of broadcasting.

Strongly centralized government based on the institution of monarchy is the political inheritance of Europe. Even in countries highly democratic today, the tradition of centralization and government control remains. For example, most railroad and electric power systems throughout Europe are operated as government monopolies. In all European nations, the government maintains not only the postal system, but also the national systems of wire communication—telephone and telegraph. It is hardly surprising, then, that in these countries broadcasting—a form of *wireless* communication—was almost immediately taken over by the government and has been retained as a government monopoly. To be sure, the degree to which centralized control is exercised over radio and television programs varies widely from country to country. In the Communist nations of Eastern Europe, a member of a government ministry exercises direct supervision over every program broadcast. In countries with democratic governments, there is almost no interference by government officials with the day-to-day operations of broadcasting stations; however, programming activities are expected to conform to long-range policies formulated by government committees.

Characteristics of the European System

Allowing for minor—or occasionally major—variations, government-owned broadcasting systems in Europe are alike in five important respects. First, broadcasting facilities, including stations, network transmission lines, and usually studios and studio equipment, are owned by the central government. Second, the system is monopolistic; *all* broadcasting operations are conducted by a single government agency with no competition for the attention of listeners from privately owned stations, at least from within the boundaries of the country operating the system. Third, programming is highly centralized; practically all programs are originated in a "Broadcasting House" in the nation's capital and are sent out over telephone lines, coaxial cables or microwave relay systems for simultaneous broadcast by stations throughout the nation. In most European countries, no broadcasting originates at local stations; where local broadcasts are permitted, they make up an extremely small proportion of the average station's schedule. Fourth, broadcasting is essentially noncommercial; at least it is not primarily a business enterprise operated for profit, although a few countries allow paid commercial announcements on government-owned radio or television stations. Finally, a major portion (and in most countries, all) of the money used to maintain the government broadcasting system comes from a special tax levied on each household in which a radio or television receiving set is used.

Except for Spain, in which practically all stations are

owned by private commercial companies, every major nation of Europe has a broadcasting system with all or most of these five basic characteristics: government ownership, monopoly, centralized programming, noncommercial operation, and support from an annual tax on receiving sets. Programming is not centralized in West Germany, where broadcasting stations are operated by the separate states making up the German Federal Republic. In both West Germany and Italy, the policy of noncommercial operation is somewhat modified by the fact that government-owned stations accept a limited number of paid advertising announcements, but advertisers are not permitted to sponsor entire programs. In Great Britain, a commercial television service on government-owned but privately programmed stations operates side by side with the noncommercial television service provided by the government; British radio, however, conforms completely to the five characteristics of European broadcasting.

Direct government control systems.   Although European broadcasting services are in the hands of government agencies, the structure of organization and control varies from country to country. In all of the Communist countries—Russia, Poland, East Germany, Czechoslovakia, Rumania, Hungary, Jugoslavia, and Albania—broadcasting facilities are owned directly by the government, and broadcasting activities are under the immediate supervision of a government minister or of an administrative official directly responsible to a council of ministers. This system makes for immediate and complete control of all program content; in Communist countries, news broadcasts, propaganda broadcasts, and even entertainment programs conform rigidly to the current "party line." The same system of direct control by a government minister is found in Belgium and Turkey, although in Belgium, changes in the political complexion of the government seem not to be reflected in the content of programs broadcast. Outside Europe, broadcasting is under the direct control of a government minister in such countries as India, Pakistan, Israel, Iraq, and Communist China.

Government-corporation systems.   Many of the more democratic European countries have a form of broadcasting organization that makes radio and television much less subject to pressures from the political party in control of the government. In these countries, broadcasting facilities are operated by a corporation which, although government owned, is almost completely independent of the ministry in power. The officers and directors of the corporation are appointed on a long-term basis and continue in their positions regardless of political changes. This government-corporation system was first developed in Great Britain, where the organization in charge of broadcasting is the British Broadcasting Corporation (BBC). France, Denmark, Norway, and (with some modifications) Italy have the same general system. The Netherlands and Sweden have systems resembling in some ways the government-corporation structure of control. In both countries, stations and equipment are owned by the government, which also provides engineering services; programs, however, are produced by private corporations or associations, with programming operations subject to periodic reviews by a government committee. Outside Europe, the government broadcasting monopoly is administered by a corporation in Egypt, South Africa, and New Zealand. In addition, government corporations are responsible for broadcasts over government-owned stations in the "dual system" nations of Australia, Canada, and Japan.

Broadcasting in Great Britain

Great Britain exemplifies the workings of the European system at its best. Government-controlled broadcasting began formally in Great Britain in 1922, with the creation of the British Broadcasting Company. Technically, this was a private company; its stock was owned entirely by British manufacturers of radio receiving sets and equipment. Otherwise, however, the Company had all of the characteristics of the European system of broadcasting. It had a monopoly on broadcasting activities, programming was on a centralized basis, its operation was noncommercial, and support was provided by a government-imposed tax on radio receiving sets. In 1928, the British government took over the stock and facilities of the Company, reimbursing the private owners for the amounts each had invested. To replace the Company, the government created a new, government-owned agency, the British Broadcasting Corporation, which has had complete control over government broadcasting in Great Britain since 1928.

In theory, the BBC is responsible to the British government. Directors of the Corporation are appointed by the ministry in power; stations owned by the BBC are licensed by the Postmaster General, who legally has veto power over broadcast programs. In actual fact, however, the BBC is an almost completely independent organization. Directors are appointed for fixed terms and continue to serve regardless of changes in the party in power; policies are determined by the Corporation's board of directors; day-to-day operations are carried on without regard for political considerations, and the veto power of the Postmaster General has almost never been used. Operations of the BBC are noncommercial, being supported by a special annual tax imposed on owners of receiving sets.

British radio broadcasting.   Radio in Great Britain is a government monopoly, with all programs originated and broadcast by the British Broadcasting Corporation. Since 1946, the BBC has provided three separate radio program services, with each service carried over a separate national network of stations. The BBC Light Service specializes in light entertainment features; the Home Service offers a mixture of popular entertainment and more serious programs, including the BBC's principal news broadcasts, educational programs for in-school use, and some serious music; the Third Service presents a schedule consisting chiefly of classical music, serious drama, and talks—what the BBC describes as "a programme for the educated." The Third Service provides programs only during evening hours; in the daytime, the same network and station facilities carry instructional and "hobby" programs, and on weekends, play-by-play accounts of major sports events.

Television in Great Britain.   Television developed somewhat earlier in Great Britain than in the United States, probably because of our delay in deciding on engineering standards for the new medium. As early as 1936, a BBC station in London was pro-

Aerial view of BBC Television Center, Wood Lane, Hammersmith, London

BBC control room

BBC Studio 3 during a rehearsal

viding regular, daily television. This station continued operating until 1939, when war conditions made it necessary for the BBC to discontinue its television broadcasts. After the war, however, television developed less rapidly in Britain. Although the London station returned to the air in 1946, the BBC had only five television stations in operation by 1952, as compared with no less than 129 stations in the United States at the end of the same year.

Television created a serious financial problem for the BBC. Practically all its revenues come from a special annual tax on receiving sets, amounting at the end of the war to £1, or $2.80, for each home equipped with a radio set. Later, to pay the costs of increased television operation, the fee for a combined television and radio license was set at £4, or $11.20. However, one of the four pounds was an excise tax that went into the public treasury, so that after costs of collection and the £1 allowed for the providing of radio service had been deducted, somewhat less than £2, or $5.60, a year was available for the support of television. During the year ending in March 1953, the television tax was paid by set-owners in approximately 2.15 million homes, providing revenues for BBC television of only about $12 million a year—not a very impressive figure when compared to the 1952 gross revenues of $324 million reported by American television networks and stations. However, there was increasing demand in Great Britain for a second television service to give listeners a choice of programs, and this could not be provided with the money then available to the BBC.

The result was that the British government was forced to abandon, for television at least, two of the principles basic to a system of pure government ownership and operation of broadcasting: monopoly in broadcasting operations and noncommercial programming. In 1954, Parliament passed an Act creating, side by side with the BBC, a second government corporation, the Independent Television Authority. In conformity with the Act's provisions, the Independent Television Authority, usually referred to as the ITA, has constructed and provides all engineering services for a system of television stations, one in each major population center in Great Britain and Northern Ireland. These stations are leased by the ITA to private commercial companies or contractors; the contracting companies build and maintain their own studios, provide programs for broadcast, and sell commercial announcements to advertisers. For several hours each week most of the ITA stations are linked together for network broadcasting; at other times, stations are programmed independently with films or locally originated programs.

During the spring of 1964 the British government authorized a second BBC television service and provided for the construction of stations to carry the new network's programs. To finance the new network, the radio-television license fee was raised in 1965 to $14.00 a year. As a result, listeners in the larger cities of Great Britain have had access since April 1964 to three television services; two BBC noncommercial services, and a commercial service offered by the ITA stations. Needless to say, there is vigorous competition among the three services for audiences, with both BBC networks carrying a substantial proportion of entertainment programs. So since 1954, Great Britain has had a mixed or "dual" system of broadcasting for television. But as regards radio, the British government has held fast to all of the essential features of the European system of organization and control—government ownership, monopoly, centralized programming, noncommercial operation, and financing provided by an annual special tax on receiving sets.

Advantages of the European System

For those countries in which it is used, the European system of ownership and control offers several obvious advantages.

To begin with, the European system offers economy in programming. With a few exceptions, notably in Great Britain, programs are provided on a network basis only; a single program produced in national headquarters is carried by stations throughout the nation, instead of each station's having to provide its own programs. Money available for programming can consequently be spent to provide programs of better quality than would otherwise be possible. In addition, with only a single employer of broadcasting talent, there is no competitive bidding for the services of such personnel as writers, actors, producers, directors, and musicians; artists' fees and program costs are kept at a much lower level than is possible in the United States. The combination of monopoly and centralized programming also contributes to national unity; the influence exerted by radio and television is applied in exactly the same way, and through the same programs, in every section of the country.

The system of government ownership and control also allows broadcasting to be used as an instrument of culture and mass education to an extent not possible under a commercial system. The government broadcasting agency can present operas, concerts by major symphony orchestras, and dramatic programs using the classics of the theater; it can provide talks by educators, scientists, or leading literary figures. Programs chosen for their cultural or educational values actually do make up a considerable portion of the offerings of both radio and television in nearly every country using the European system of broadcasting. There is no pressure from advertisers who demand large audiences, and for the most part there is no competition for listener attention from programs with greater popular appeal. With broadcasting a monopoly, the listener tunes in the one program offered at any given time, or he doesn't listen at all.

Disadvantages of the European System

But in that same lack of choice on the part of the listener lies one of the weaknesses of the European system. In the United States, at least, we like to make our own decisions with respect to the programs to which we listen. We do not like to be told what we must do, or to have a government commission to decide what radio or television programs we may hear. But in countries where broadcasting is a government monopoly, the controlling agency decides what is to be broadcast, often with little regard for the preferences or interests of the listening public. Lord Reith, Director General of the British Broadcasting Corporation for more than twenty years, expressed the philosophy of the European system in these words: "It is occasionally indicated to us that we are apparently setting out to give the public what we think they need—and not what they want. But very few know what they want and very few what they need."

A second weakness in the European system is the lack of

stimulus to experiment with new programs and new program forms—a lack resulting from the absence of competition. It must be admitted that in some countries, notably Great Britain, improvements in production techniques for dramatic programs came at least as rapidly as they did in the United States. But European broadcasting has been conspicuously slow to develop new types of programs; until the end of World War II the only radio program forms in use in most European countries were those that had existed in the United States before 1930. Comedy variety programs, serial drama, quiz programs, situation comedies, audience participation programs, panel discussions—these forms of entertainment were not provided by European stations before 1945. Since the war, European broadcasting has borrowed heavily from the United States, and most of the program forms that have been used in this country are also offered by European broadcasting systems. But without competition between stations or networks for audiences, there is no particular *reason* for European broadcasters to experiment with new ideas or new forms in programming.

The introduction of commercial television in Great Britain has had a decided effect on the television programming offered by the BBC; the government system has been forced to compete for the attention of listeners by offering a substantial amount of the same kind of entertainment programming provided on television in the United States.

A third and serious shortcoming of the European system, at least from the point of view of those interested in democratic government, is the ease with which a government-owned system can be made an instrument of political propaganda. Hitler, after becoming Chancellor in 1933, made extremely effective use of radio to indoctrinate the people of Germany with his Nazi philosophies. In Communist nations today, radio and television are used primarily for propaganda in support of the particular party group currently in power. On the other hand, in the countries of Western Europe, there is little if any overt propaganda in support of government policies, although the opportunity to use broadcasting for such purposes is always present. The charter of the BBC, for example, provides that the British Broadcasting Corporation is required to broadcast "any announcement" requested by "any department" of the government. But even without *overt* propaganda on the government-owned broadcasting facilities, news broadcasters in most countries are probably somewhat cautious in their reporting of events that reflect unfavorably on the government or on the party in power. And although radio and television time is provided freely for speakers who support government policies, most European broadcasting systems—Great Britain is an exception—are less likely to provide time for speakers who are vigorous in their criticisms of current government activities. Even in highly democratic countries, there is always the possibility that the government-owned broadcasting facilities will become an instrument for direct or indirect propaganda in support of the party controlling the government.

THE AMERICAN SYSTEM

The system of broadcasting in use in the United States contrasts strongly with the European system. In this country, stations are owned by private individuals or private corporations, not by the government. A few stations are owned by tax-supported universities or by branches of state government; others are owned by municipalities or local school systems. But no station engaged in domestic broadcasting is owned or operated by the federal government, and stations licensed to municipal or state agencies make up only a small percentage of the total number in operation.[1]

Not only are nearly all stations privately owned and operated, but there is a high degree of diffusion of station ownership. In some countries with private ownership, such as Spain, Mexico, and Chile, 20, 30, or more important stations may be licensed to a single owning corporation. In the United States, by government regulation, no individual or company may own more than seven standard radio stations, seven FM stations, and

---

[1] Out of a total of 6,515 AM, FM, and television stations on the air in December 1965 and listed in *Broadcasting Yearbook* for 1966, only about 222 stations were owned by tax-supported state universities, local school districts, or other agencies of state or local government. All but seven of the 222 stations were operated on a noncommercial basis.

seven television stations. Consequently, the more than 6,000 commercial radio and television stations operating in this country at the beginning of 1966 were owned and controlled by nearly 4,000 separate individual owners or ownership groups. Although a few large companies own several important stations each, station ownership on the whole is widely diffused in the United States.

Centralized programming or centralized control of programming simply doesn't exist in our country. We have national networks, and these networks provide most of our outstanding programs, especially in television. But the three television networks are owned by three separate companies that compete vigorously with one another. Certainly they do not cooperate in the planning of their programs. Moreover, the three television networks supply only some 60 per cent of the programs broadcast by the nation's commercial television stations, and the four radio networks account for not more than 10 to 15 per cent of the program time of our commercial radio stations. Most programs broadcast in this country—both radio and television considered—originate locally, with each station determining for itself what programs it will produce and what network or syndicated programs it will put on the air. Certainly, there is no centralized control over programs in America of the type that exists in countries operating under the European system.

Next, American broadcasting is commercial. We do have noncommercial stations, nearly all owned by educational institutions, community educational associations, or religious groups; at the beginning of 1966 there were approximately 400 such stations, with the number of noncommercial FM and television stations steadily increasing. But these are decidedly in the minority; nearly 95 per cent of all American radio and television stations are commercial. These stations, like our national networks, depend for their revenues on the sale of time to advertisers. They receive neither appropriations from government nor funds from a tax on receiving sets. To survive in this country, broadcasting must operate on a commercial basis.

Finally, broadcasting in the United States is highly competitive. Stations compete both for advertising revenues and for audiences. To be attractive to advertisers, a station must first have listeners; to get those listeners, it must provide programs that can compete effectively with the programs offered by other stations. National networks compete with one another for advertising revenues, for outstanding programs, for the most popular entertainers, and for affiliations with the best stations available in each community. American broadcasting is decidedly competitive.

So, as contrasted with the European system, the American system of broadcasting also has five distinctive characteristics. Stations are privately owned; there is wide diffusion of ownership; there is no central planning of programs or centralized control over programs; stations are commercially operated; and there is a high degree of competition between stations and between networks.

Advantages and Disadvantages of the American System

Like the system of broadcasting used in Europe, the system that has developed in the United States has its advantages, and also its disadvantages. It cannot operate on any unified, predetermined plan; wide diffusion of ownership makes systematic central planning impossible. Lack of such planning has resulted, especially in the case of radio, in the construction of a far greater number of stations than are needed to meet the real needs of listeners—in fact, there are more stations than can be supported adequately by the advertising revenues available. Such an absence of central planning and control is uneconomic; there is tremendous duplication of effort by stations and networks; network competition for programs and for outstanding entertainers has forced program costs to levels far above those existing in countries with broadcasting monopolies.

Problem of cultural programs.   Another major weakness is found in the field of cultural programs. No one would argue that the American system allows full use of the potentialities of radio and television for raising our standards of literary and musical appreciation. Symphonies, complete operas, and dramatic programs of outstanding literary value are common in European broadcasting, but much less common in the United States. With relatively few exceptions, cultural programs in this country attract small audiences. As a result, the advertiser who wishes to reach the greatest number of listeners possible is not usually interested in sponsoring such programs. Lacking advertiser support, cultural progams tend to be crowded out of the schedules of American networks and stations by programs with stronger mass-entertainment values.

Listener influence on programming. The situation with respect to cultural programs illustrates a feature of the American system considered by some to be an advantage, by others a disadvantage. In this country, each individual listener selects from a considerable variety of programs those that satisfy his own special interests and tastes. On a larger scale, the public collectively selects the programs that best satisfy the public's collective tastes. If substantial numbers of listeners tune in a particular program each week, the program remains on the air. But if a program fails to attract a reasonably large audience, that program will usually be dropped, and networks and stations are not ordinarily much inclined to introduce other programs of similar type. By listening or not listening, the public in effect votes for or against continuation of each program offered, and for or against the scheduling of other programs of the same general type. In other words, the listeners themselves determine collectively the kinds of programs that stations and networks will offer. In a European system, the public gets programs that those who control a government agency think that listeners "ought to have"; in the system used in this country, listeners get the programs that they themselves *want*, or at least programs that are attractive to major segments of the total listening public.

Whether this feature of the American system is an advantage or a disadvantage is a matter of individual opinion. It does result in the broadcasting of fewer cultural programs, and critics of broadcasting charge that radio and television cater to the tastes of the mass audience while ignoring the interests of intelligent minorities. But good or bad, our method of selection of broadcast programs is essentially the same as the method used to select our state and local officials, our members of Congress, and the President of the United States himself.

Discussion of public issues. Perhaps the greatest advantage of the American system of broadcasting lies in the very fact that it is a system of private ownership, with programs free from government control. True democracy demands an informed public, and broadcasting has become the most important agency through which the public may be informed. Under a system of government ownership, information is not always provided on a two-sided basis. At its worst, broadcasting may be used as an agency for out-and-out government propaganda; at its best, the broadcasting organization can hardly be expected to take positions highly critical of government policies. But here in the United States, broadcasters do not depend on the government for support; they are as free to criticize as they are to commend, and they take full advantage of that freedom. Radio networks provide commentary programs, some of which are highly critical of the party in power. Television networks schedule several programs each week dealing with national affairs; in some, government spokesmen are called upon to answer the frequently embarrassing questions posed by a panel of interrogators; in others, analyses of government proposals are presented in documentary form, with as much attention given to weaknesses as to possible values. In addition, owners of many stations use their facilities to present editorial opinions that may be critical of actions of the local or national government as often as they may be favorable.

The possibility of free discussion of vital public questions, and the resulting wide dissemination of information on issues of importance, is one of the major advantages inherent in the American system of broadcasting.

THE AMERICAN SYSTEM AND PROGRAMS

In the system of radio and television that exists in the United States, programs do not conform to any central "master plan." No single agency of government, or of the broadcasting industry itself, decides what programs will be offered or the general types of programming that should be provided at any given time. Nor is the decision—in the long run, at least—one made by network officials, by program directors of stations, or by advertisers. Programs, to be successful, must win the approval of listeners; the listening public makes the final decision concerning each individual program, or programs of any given type.

Changing Patterns in Programming

But even though listeners determine the fate of individual programs, other factors enter into the total programming situations. The *kinds* of programs provided by networks and stations change, and change tremendously, with the passing of time. Radio stations once offered listeners a wide variety of types of programs: serious drama, variety shows, quiz programs, popular orchestras, comedy programs, broadcasts of sports events. Today, most radio stations offer few programs other than recorded music and short, capsuled news summaries; some also provide broadcasts of baseball games and other sports events; others offer various types of talk programs to provide a change of pace.

In the short history of network television, we have witnessed the rise and the decline of half a dozen program types. For example, during the winter of 1948–49, national television networks devoted from 12 to 14 hours of *evening* time each week to broadcasts of sports events such as basketball, boxing, wrestling, and bowling. Today, no sports events whatever are scheduled on a regular basis at night by any of the three national networks, and although baseball, golf, and football are used extensively on Saturday and Sunday afternoons, the networks offer no broadcasts of wrestling or boxing matches. In 1950 and 1951, network schedules included more than 20 hours of evening variety programs each week; ten years later, only about six hours a week were devoted to programs of this type. During the early 1950s, anthology dramatic programs using different actors and different situations each week were among television's most popular offerings; in recent years, the anthology dramatic form has almost completely disappeared. We have seen the rise and later the decline in the popularity of audience quiz programs, of "private-eye" detective dramas, of "international spy" adventure stories, of "gangster-type" crime dramas and of "adult Western" programs, to name only a few. In recent years, on the other hand, evening schedules of television networks have shown a marked increase in the number of situation comedies, of hour-long medical or "courtroom" dramas, and of tongue-in-cheek "spy" dramas, with some trend toward an increase in the use of dramatic series with social-problem themes.

Reason for Changes

These constant changes in the types of programs offered for the approval of listeners are characteristic of American broadcasting. We had such changes in radio in the days when radio was the dominant form of broadcasting; we have the same type of changes in television today. The question is, *why* do these continual changes take place in the types of programs offered on radio and television? Even a casual analysis of the situation shows that the types of programs provided by networks or by stations at any given time are the result of a variety of different factors—technological advances, changes in economic conditions, changes in the structure of the broadcasting industry, and changes in the preferences of the listening audience.

The organization of national radio networks in 1926 and 1927, for instance, made possible the offering of much more expensive and elaborate programs than could be provided by a single station; without networks, the comedy variety programs that attracted millions of listeners during the 1930s would never have been included in station schedules. The musical programs presented by nationally known orchestras and vocalists and the major dramatic programs with Broadway or Hollywood stars in featured roles would also have been impossible without the networks. The economic depression of 1933 and 1934, attended by bank failures and drastic reductions in expenditures of local advertisers for radio time, forced many stations throughout the country to accept programs featuring self-styled astrologers or programs inviting listeners to "send in their dollars" to stations in return for real or imagined benefits. Refusal of national press associations to sell their news services to radio stations during the middle 1930s practically drove local news programs off the air; adjustment of the difficulty a few years later, combined with public concern over the threat of this nation's involvement in the war in Europe, resulted in a tremendous increase in the use of news programs both on station and network schedules.

In more recent years, two factors have largely shaped the type of programming offered by radio stations throughout the country. First, the rapid development of television after 1950 brought with it an abrupt decrease in the amount of network programming available to radio stations, making it necessary for radio outlets to provide local programs to fill from 80 to 90 per cent of their daily schedules. And second, competition from television combined with a tremendous increase in the number of radio stations on the air brought about substantial reductions in average station revenues. With more hours to fill each day, and with limited revenues, radio stations were forced to turn to the lowest-cost program material available, with the result that most radio stations today offer a schedule consisting largely of recorded music.

In similar fashion, changes within the broadcasting industry have had their effects on the types of programs offered on television. For example, the development of the image orthicon camera tube, one requiring far less light than did the tubes used in earlier cameras, led to greatly expanded offerings of televised baseball, football, and other outdoor sports. Excessively high costs of network television programs placed sponsorship of complete programs out of the reach of most national advertisers. This forced networks as well as stations to present programs on a "participating sponsorship" basis, with advertising messages for a number of different sponsors included within each broadcast. This, in turn, has encouraged the scheduling of network programs 60 or 90 minutes long, and the presentation by networks of motion picture features that can include the commercial announcements for as many as thirteen or fourteen advertisers. The tremendously heightened interest in color television on the part of both broadcasters and advertisers around 1965 has resulted in more extensive network use of programs that particularly lend themselves to use of color—variety programs, Westerns, and adventure programs in exotic settings.

Two factors in particular seem to have an important and continuing effect on network television programs. One is the tendency of broadcasters to copy successful programs developed by others. Let one new program be introduced with a fresh idea or different "twist" that catches the fancy of the American public, and within another year or two, network schedules will include at least half a dozen other programs exploiting that same basic idea. A highly popular *$64,000 Question* brings other big-money quiz shows into being; a successful *Gunsmoke* creates a vogue for "adult" Westerns; a situation comedy like *Bewitched* starts producers looking for other comedy vehicles using a theme involving fantasy. So network television, like network radio before it, is characterized by programming trends; every successful new program leads to a new trend in programming.

The other basic factor in programming operates in exactly the opposite direction. Every program and every program idea, no matter how great its popularity when first presented to listeners, tends sooner or later simply to "wear out." It loses its freshness and novelty; after a time it loses the outstanding ability it once had to attract and hold the attention of listeners. And when the public will no longer listen, the program is taken off the air. Program *forms* wear out, no less than individual programs; when a program form has lost its power to attract, programs using that form disappear from station and network schedules. Before the war, almost every radio station had a daily "man-on-the-street" interview program; dropped at the beginning of the war, they largely failed to reappear. Around 1948 or 1950, most radio stations scheduled telephone quiz programs, but the telephone quiz idea ran its course, and today such programs are carried by only a few stations. What became of the once-popular television network programs featuring puppets or marionettes? Or of the wrestling programs so extensively used in the early days of television? Or of costume-type adventure dramas? Or of programs dealing with crime-solving exploits of private detectives, or the more realistic police dramatizations for which *Dragnet* was the inspiration? Dozens of other illustrations could be offered. Program forms, like individual programs, wear out; as they lose their ability to attract and entertain listeners, they are dropped from network schedules and must be replaced by something new.

Presumably in countries using the European system of broadcasting, listeners also tend to lose their original enthusiasm for some of the types of programs presented by government stations. Novelty wears off in Europe no less than in the United States. But in most European countries, the public has little to say about the types of programs provided, and so changes in program forms take place less frequently than in the United States. The broadcasting system itself has a very definite influence on the types of programs provided for listeners.

3

THE DEVELOPMENT OF
AMERICAN RADIO

Broadcasting in the United States did not become an important agency of mass communication overnight. Like other forms of communication and entertainment, it developed slowly, and after nearly half a century broadcasting is still changing.

For several years before 1900, scientists had experimented with the transmission of wireless signals. In 1901, Guglielmo Marconi succeeded in sending a signal in Morse code across the Atlantic Ocean, and in the next few years, wireless was increasingly used as a means of point-to-point communication. In 1910, radio had so far developed that Congress passed a law requiring installation of wireless equipment on certain passenger vessels sailing under the American flag. In the same year, Lee deForest, who had earlier invented the audion tube, which made possible the transmission of music or of the human voice, put on the air what was possibly the first *broadcast*—the voices of opera singers Enrico Caruso and Emmy Destinn from the backstage area of the Metropolitan Opera House in New York. For the next half dozen years, various types of program materials were transmitted by other experimenters; following our entry into World War I in 1917, however, the government took over all wireless installations and brought experimentation with radio temporarily to an end.

When radio transmitters were returned to their private owners early in 1920, equipment manufacturers and amateur radio enthusiasts renewed their experiments with the broadcasting of radio programs—talks, vocal music, or music from phonograph records. These transmissions, like the deForest experiment in 1910, were early forms of *broadcasting*—the dissemination of radio signals intended for reception by the general public, as opposed to point-to-point communication by wireless. Most historians consider that *regular* broadcasting in the United States began on November 2, 1920; on that date station KDKA at Pittsburgh reported the Harding-Cox presidential election returns by radio and inaugurated a regular daily program service. By January 1922, a number of other stations were also broadcasting regularly, and radio was beginning to be recognized as an agency of mass communication.

THE NONCOMMERCIAL ERA

During 1922, interest in radio increased tremendously. By the end of that year, licenses had been issued to 666 stations,[1] and receiving sets were in use in nearly a million American homes. The new medium had little resemblance to the agency of entertainment and information it was to become even half a dozen years later. Equipment was primitive; most stations operated with power of no more than 10 to 50 watts; only a very few stations were broadcasting on a regular daily basis, and those provided programs for only two or three hours each

---

[1] *The First Decade of Broadcasting.* Broadcast Pioneers, New York, 1958.

day. During those early years from 1920 to 1922, American radio was nothing more than an interesting novelty.

Early Radio Stations

Between 1923 and the end of 1925, the Department of Commerce issued an additional 766 licenses, bringing the total number of stations authorized to more than 1,400. Not all of this number, however, actually went on the air, and many surrendered their licenses within a few weeks or months after the authorizations were issued. The 1925 Annual Report of the Department of Commerce indicates that only 571 stations were actually operating at the end of that fiscal year. Even the stations that stayed on the air had financial problems; until the late months of 1925, radio was almost completely noncommercial, and operating costs had to be borne by station owners themselves. Perhaps 30 or 40 of the "big" stations of the period were relatively well financed; these were outlets licensed either to major electronic companies that manufactured radio receiving equipment, or to insurance companies, large-city department stores, or major newspapers, which received advertising value from the operation of their stations. But most of the early radio stations were small-time affairs, licensed to local radio repair shops, hardware stores, small daily newspapers, sometimes to operators of ballrooms or local motion picture theaters, frequently to private individuals who were simply "interested in radio" or who wanted the satisfaction of presenting their ideas over the air. Up to the end of 1925, licenses had also been issued to no less than 153 schools and colleges and to 71 local churches or other religious organizations. These smaller stations frequently operated for only an hour or two each week, often on a completely irregular basis. While owners of major stations provided budgets of several thousand dollars a year for their broadcasting operations, the annual expenditures of smaller stations were usually limited to a few hundred dollars. Even this was more than many licensees could afford; throughout the period, scores of stations surrendered their broadcasting licenses each year, to be replaced by other small stations.

In spite of the limited service available to listeners, the

radio audience continued to grow. During 1923, the number of receiving sets more than doubled; by the late autumn of 1926, an estimated 5.5 million families owned radio sets. Practically all of the radio receivers produced before the autumn of 1925 were battery sets, using one "wet" storage battery similar to those used in automobiles, and two smaller dry cells; "plug-in" alternating-current receiving sets were not yet in general use. Each set was equipped with a pair of earphones, allowing only one person to listen at a time. Tuning was a complicated operation, requiring accurate adjustment of three tuning dials to bring in the signal of any desired station. Reception was usually marred by static or by interference from signals of other stations. But primitive or not, these early sets did bring in programs provided by broadcasting stations, and during evening hours they could pick up stations hundreds of miles away.

Early Radio Programs

Radio programs of the early 1920s reflected the conditions existing at the time—equipment was primitive, listening conditions were unsatisfactory, and in particular, almost no money was available to be spent on programs. Since radio was non-commercial, radio stations had no outside sources of revenues; what money a station owner was willing to spend usually went for improved technical equipment. So for programs, station operators depended on materials that could be provided without cost: talks and amateur musical recitals. Some of the larger stations did provide programs of other types, such as remote pickups of band concerts or sometimes of concerts by symphony orchestras; many also placed microphones in hotel dining rooms and broadcast dinner music by string ensembles or small orchestras. And of course some stations in larger cities experimented with broadcasts of baseball and football games or boxing exhibitions. But for all stations, talks and musical recitals accounted for at least 90 per cent of all programming.

THE RISE OF COMMERCIAL RADIO

If programs were to be provided on anything but an amateur-talent basis, stations had to find outside sources of

KTRK in Houston, Texas

NBC's Burbank (Calif.) color studios

White Columns, home of WSB, Atlanta, Georgia

The dramatic exteriors of television studios reflect the glamor of the medium while masking the warehouse-like character of the studios inside.

revenue. The money might come from a government-imposed tax on receiving sets, following the precedent already established in Great Britain, or it might come from sale of time to advertisers. Use of the first method would involve either government ownership of stations or at the very least a high degree of government control over privately operated stations; neither seemed consistent with our theories of democratic government. So following a series of conferences arranged by the Secretary of Commerce, the idea of government support was definitely discarded; broadcasting stations were left to finance themselves by the only other alternative available to them, the sale of time to advertisers.

Possibly the year 1927 can be designated as the one in which American radio became really "commercial"; it was the first complete year of operation of permanent commercial radio networks. For some years before 1927, however, a few stations had operated on what was at least partially a commercial basis. Station WEAF [2] in New York broadcast advertising programs as early as the autumn of 1922; other broadcasters followed WEAF's example, and by the winter of 1924–25 a number of advertisers in large cities were using radio on a regular once-a-week basis. But sponsored programs made up only a small proportion of the total program offerings even of major large-city stations. During a typical week in January 1926, station WJZ, one of the two or three leading stations in New York City, broadcast a total of 123 programs, of which only six were presented on time paid for by advertisers. Radio was becoming commercial, but through 1926 no station had advertising revenues large enough to pay ordinary costs of station operation.

However, the fact that even a few programs were sponsored had a decided effect on owners of radio outlets. If advertisers were willing to pay stations to carry their advertising messages, then broadcasting might in time become a profitable business. So by 1925 or 1926 station owners had a dollars-and-cents reason to spend money for improved equipment and to increase the power of their stations, in the hope of making their operations attractive to advertisers.

---

[2] Now using the call letters WNBC; WEAF later became the key station of the NBC Red Network.

Station Licensing

Prior to 1926, broadcasting stations operated under authorizations granted by the Department of Commerce and issued on the basis of a 1912 act of Congress, which required licenses for stations engaging in point-to-point radio communication. When hundreds of applications for *broadcasting* licenses were filed in 1922, the Department, in an effort to hold interference to a minimum, adopted the policy of specifying for each new station the frequency that station might use and the hours during which it might stay on the air. In 1926, however, a federal court held that the Department of Commerce, under the Act of 1912, had no power either to require stations to broadcast on assigned frequencies or to limit their hours of operation. The result was chaos; stations changed frequencies at will and broadcast whenever they chose, regardless of conflicts with signals of other nearby stations using the same frequencies at the same time. Interference became such a serious problem that Congress was forced to take action. The result was the Radio Act of 1927, creating a Federal Radio Commission and giving the regulatory body authority to specify in each broadcasting license the frequency to be used, the hours during which the station could operate, and the transmitter power permitted.

The newly created Commission took immediate steps to correct the situation. Many of the stations that had held Department of Commerce licenses were taken off the air entirely. Those remaining were forced to comply with the Commission's restrictions on frequencies, power, and operating hours. By the end of 1928, broadcasting licenses issued by the Commission were held by 620 stations; 325 of the total shared time with other stations using the same frequency and located in the same general area, while the remainder were authorized to operate on a full-time basis. Among stations on the air during the autumn of 1928 were 53 outlets owned by colleges or universities, seven operated by public school systems, and 49 others licensed to churches or other religious organizations. Practically all of the educational or religious stations were part-time operations, on the air for only two or three hours a day.

Most broadcasting stations licensed before the end of 1922

used power of 100 watts or less. Between 1925 and 1927, many stations—a majority of those still on the air in 1928—made increases in the power used by their transmitters, to enable their signals to be heard over larger areas. By 1925, most of the larger stations broadcast with power of from 1,000 to 5,000 watts. In 1927, WGY, the General Electric outlet in Schenectady, became the first station to operate with power of 50,000 watts—the maximum permitted for standard AM stations today. When the Federal Radio Commission announced a general reassignment of stations to new frequencies in 1928, power increases were authorized for some 200 stations; ten major stations were licensed to operate with power of 50,000 watts, and 17 others to use power of 10,000 watts or more. However, in December 1928, approximately 150 stations were still broadcasting with power of less than 100 watts and some used as little as five watts or ten watts of power.

Improvements in Equipment

At the same time that operating power was being increased, stations were making improvements in transmitting equipment and in studio facilities. Many stations built studios large enough to allow the origination of programs by full orchestras; some also made provision for the seating of studio audiences of as many as a hundred people. Typical of the improvements in equipment was the replacement of the early carbon microphones by more effective types; by 1930, velocity or "ribbon" microphones had become standard in all but the smallest stations.

Equally important were improvements made between 1925 and 1929 in home receiving sets. New sets offered for sale in 1925 and 1926 had much improved circuits, which lessened static and interference problems. By 1926, too, the earphones of earlier years were being replaced by loudspeaker systems, allowing the entire family to listen at the same time. Most sets sold after the summer of 1927 were built to use alternating current so that a receiving set could be plugged into any regular electric outlet in the home; in cities, at least, cumbersome batteries were no longer needed. Another major improvement was the introduction, around 1927 or 1928, of single-dial tuning, replacing the three-dial system required on earlier sets. All of these modifications encouraged family listening; instead of merely attempting to tune in distant stations, people increasingly were listening to the programs that stations offered.

Development of Networks

With stations operating more efficiently, with improved reception and resulting increases in total listening, conditions were favorable for the next bold experiment in the development of radio—the establishment in 1926 of the first permanent radio network. The idea of linking stations together by telephone lines for simultaneous broadcasting of programs was nothing new; as early as January 1923 the first recognized "chain" broadcast had been presented over facilities of WEAF in New York and WNAC in Boston. Five months later, a program originated by WEAF was carried over an experimental network that included WGY in Schenectady, KDKA in Pittsburgh, and KYW in Chicago. By 1924 network broadcasting had so far developed that during the winter of 1924–25 and again during the following season two different groups of stations were operating on an informal network basis; stations in each group broadcast programs simultaneously three, four, or five evenings each week. One of these informal networks had WEAF, then owned by the American Telephone & Telegraph Company, as its New York originating station; the other was under the leadership of WJZ, also in New York, and owned by the Radio Corporation of America. Most of the stations in each group were owned by electronics companies.

The success of these informal networks or chains of stations led to the incorporation in November 1926 of the National Broadcasting Company, a wholly owned subsidiary of the Radio Corporation of America created for the express purpose of engaging in network operation. The new company inaugurated service on November 15th, 1926, with programs fed by telephone lines to a group of 20 stations making up what was to be known as the NBC Red Network. Originating station for the chain was WEAF in New York, which RCA had purchased from A.T.&T. a few weeks earlier. On January 1, 1927, six weeks after the

start of NBC-Red, the NBC Blue Network [3] commenced operations, with WJZ serving as its New York key station. For the
first few weeks this second network group consisted of only five
stations, all in cities in the Northeast or North Central states,
as were the stations making up the NBC Red Network. During
1927 service from both network groups was extended to several
stations in Southern or Southwestern states.

In September 1927 a second company, now called the Columbia Broadcasting System,[4] entered the network field, providing service to another group of stations. The first CBS program
was fed to 16 affiliates, more than half of them located in cities
having NBC stations. During 1927 none of the three networks
had lines extending further west than Omaha or Kansas City
in the Plains states or Dallas in the Southwest, although NBC
was establishing a Pacific Coast network with affiliates in major
cities from Seattle to Los Angeles. Coast-to-coast network service
was inaugurated by the NBC Red Network in December 1928;
within a few months, both NBC-Blue and Columbia were also
linked up with stations on the Pacific Coast.

Programs before 1930

Before the winter of 1924–25, practically all programs presented by radio stations fell within the broad categories of talks,
musical recitals, and remote pickups, with some stations providing music from phonograph records. During the middle 1920s,
as larger studios became available, several of the more important
stations began to provide more elaborate types of programs.

---

[3] The Blue Network continued as a part of the National Broadcasting
Company until February 1942, when it was formally organized as a separate
corporation. In October 1943 the new company was purchased by a group
headed by Edward J. Noble. The Blue Network name continued to be used
until June 1945, when the corporation was officially designated as the
American Broadcasting Company.

[4] The company was originally incorporated as the United Independent
Broadcasters. Prior to the network's inaugural program, the company was
purchased by the Columbia Phonograph Company and given the name
Columbia Phonograph Broadcasting Company. In 1928, the network com-
pany was sold again, and in January 1929 it officially became the Columbia
Broadcasting System.

Four or five stations in the Middle West and South developed late-night programs using a loose variety form. Others scheduled programs featuring local dance orchestras. A few—WGY in Schenectady in particular—experimented with dramatic programs presented by amateur actors; materials used were in most cases one-act plays written for production in theaters. A new form for radio was the program featuring a "song-and-patter" team, borrowed directly from vaudeville. Several such teams of entertainers traveled from station to station on a sort of organized "circuit" basis, each team remaining not more than a week or two in any one city. During 1927 and 1928, a few stations carried weekly or daily variety programs on a semisponsored basis; an advertiser paid the costs of presenting the program, which carried his advertising messages, but no payment was made for station time. The earliest sponsored programs for which advertisers paid for both station time and production costs were usually straight talks. However, for a year or more before the establishment of permanent networks, many stations in large cities were presenting weekly sponsored musical programs, usually featuring small orchestras or novelty musical groups.

When national networks were organized, it was natural that their schedules should include a number of the programs already being presented on the networks' key stations in New York, usually programs featuring musical organizations. In addition, several elaborate new programs were developed, some paid for by sponsors, others provided by the network company on a sustaining basis.[5] During January 1927, the weekly schedules of the two networks operated by the National Broadcasting Company included a total of 22 hours of evening programs, of which 16 hours were sponsored. Among the programs presented by advertisers were a one-hour variety program, an opera broadcast by the Chicago Civic Opera Company, a concert by a symphony orchestra, twelve hours of popular or concert music, and two half-hour talk programs. Evening sustaining programs included a two-hour symphony program, a 60-minute musical

---

[5] A sustaining program is not sponsored and contains no advertising announcements; consequently it brings in no revenue to the network or station. In most cases, production costs of sustaining programs are paid by the station or network presenting them.

comedy, two hours of concert music, a 30-minute hymn program, a religious talk, and a 15-minute commentary on Washington politics. Daytime programming was limited to four hours of sustaining religious programs on Sunday afternoons, and three 15-minute, sponsored cooking talks on weekday mornings. There were no dramatic programs, no daily news broadcasts, no audience participation programs.

As the number of network programs increased during the next two years, music continued to dominate evening network schedules, and daytime offerings consisted entirely of various types of talks. However, a few new program forms were introduced. By the winter of 1928–29, evening programs included a minstrel show, two programs featuring comedy patter teams supported by popular orchestras, and seven or eight dramatic offerings. Patterns of network programming were beginning to show the types of changes that were to characterize the next decade.

Revenues from Advertising

Although during the middle 1920s some stations carried sponsored programs, station advertising revenues were small. During 1926, all radio stations combined probably received no more than $200,000 from sale of commercial time. But after permanent networks had come into being, expenditures for radio advertising showed a rapid increase. In 1927, radio's revenues from sale of time totaled $4.82 million; in 1928, the figure had reached $14.1 million; and for the year 1929 network and station revenues totaled approximately $26.8 million, of which all but $7.6 million went to network companies. Probably by the end of 1929 the two network organizations were on a fairly sound financial footing. But the same could not be said of individual stations, whether network affiliates or independents. With annual station revenues averaging only about $12,000 per station—in addition to whatever payments were made by the networks to their affiliates—it is doubtful whether more than 80 or 100 of the 618 stations on the air at the end of 1929 had revenues great enough to cover costs of operation. Broadcasting promised a bright future, but in most cases the operation of a radio station was not yet a profitable undertaking.

THE DEVELOPMENT OF AN INDUSTRY

However, by the beginning of 1930 the foundation had been laid for what was to become an important American industry. Stations provided program service for listeners from coast to coast; national networks had been organized; radio had proved itself an effective advertising medium; and most important of all, people were listening to the programs that networks and stations were providing. From 1930 until this country's entry into World War II in December 1941, radio found itself in a period of phenomenal expansion, becoming probably the nation's most important source of entertainment, an increasingly used vehicle for the carrying of advertising, and in the later years of the decade a highly significant source of information for the people of the United States.

The Expanding Audience

Radio's possibilities as an advertising medium were naturally dependent on the number of prospective buyers of advertised products who could listen to broadcast programs. From 1930 to 1941, the number of radio-equipped homes increased steadily. In 1930, homes with radio receiving sets had reached a total of nearly 12 million—more than double the number reported four years earlier. In 1935, almost 23 million families had access to radio; by 1940, there were nearly 30 million receivers installed in listeners' homes, and more than seven million automobiles were equipped with radio sets. As the number of radio homes increased, the amount of listening done by members of family groups was also becoming greater. In 1930, the average radio set was probably used no more than an hour or two a day, partly because networks and many stations offered only a limited amount of daytime programming and partly because the number of outstanding evening programs was still decidedly small. But by 1940, average listening per home had increased to at least three or four hours each day; more good programs were available, stations were operating on a full-time basis, and people had developed the habit of depending on radio as their major source of entertainment. In 1940 any evening network program of average quality attracted an audience of from four to six million families, while such favorites as the *Jack Benny Show* or the *Edgar Bergen and Charlie McCarthy* program had listeners each week in nine or ten million American homes.

Network and Station Revenues

As radio listening increased, so did network and station revenues from the sale of time to advertisers. As shown in Table 1, the industry's total revenues doubled over the five years

TABLE 1

REVENUES OF RADIO NETWORKS AND STATIONS FROM SALE OF TIME—1930 TO 1945 (IN THOUSANDS OF DOLLARS)

	For calendar years			
	1930	1935	1940	1945
From sale of time by networks	27,694	39,735	73,789	133,973
From sale of time by stations				
national spot	—	13,805	37,140	76,696
local advertising	12,806	26,074	44,757	99,814
Total net time sales for the year	40,500	79,614	155,686	310,483

From annual reports of the Federal Radio Commission and the Federal Communications Commission.

from 1930 to 1935, and almost doubled again between 1935 and 1940. Almost equally important was the fact that throughout the period a constantly increasing proportion of the industry's revenues from advertising went directly to stations, instead of to network companies. National advertisers, during the early 1930s, began to divert some of their radio advertising dollars to what has become known as *national spot advertising*, buying time for programs or in some cases for commercial announcements directly from stations in the areas or "spots" in which special advertising coverage was desired. Use of national spot advertising continued growing, and local merchants kept increasing expenditures for local radio advertising, so that starting with the year 1935, station revenues from sale of time exceeded the amounts spent each year for network advertising.

The Station Situation

For several years after 1930, the number of radio stations remained practically unchanged. The economic depression and bank failures of the early 1930s resulted in a serious drop in local advertising and in station revenues. At the same time, operating costs increased, in part because new engineering standards announced by the Federal Radio Commission required stations to install additional and improved equipment. Nearly all stations lost money; some were forced off the air. And although a number of new stations had received authorizations, only 605 radio stations were in operation in January 1935, as compared with 620 to which the Radio Commission had assigned frequencies in the autumn of 1928.

However, after 1934 the economic situation improved, and from 1935 to 1940 the number of stations steadily increased. The 1940 issue of *Broadcasting Yearbook* shows a total of 754 stations within the continental limits of the United States on the air in January of that year. Although in 1928 more than half of all stations shared time with others in the same general area, only 90 operated on a time-sharing basis by 1940; however 97 others in 1940 had licenses for broadcasting during daylight hours only.

As shown in Table 2, increases in station power during the 1930s more than kept pace with the increase in the number of stations. In 1928, ten stations had been authorized to use maximum power of 50,000 watts. In 1935, a total of 27 were in the 50,000-watt category, and another was blanketing half the nation with full-time power of 500,000 watts—the highest power ever used by a standard AM station in the United States.[6] Five years later, the number of 50,000-watt stations had increased to

---

[6] For nearly five years between 1934 and 1939, station WLW in Cincinnati was licensed to operate experimentally with power of 500,000 watts. At the end of its period of special authorization in 1939, the station returned to its earlier power of 50,000 watts.

39, and an additional 140 stations used 5,000 watts power or more.

The amount of power used is a matter of considerable importance to standard AM radio broadcasting stations. Although power is not the only factor determining a station's coverage, high-powered stations serve substantially larger areas and provide stronger signals in their home communities than competing stations with less power; as a result, they usually have con-

TABLE 2

RADIO STATIONS IN VARIOUS POWER AND OPERATING TIME CATEGORIES, 1928 TO 1940

Stations using daytime power of	November 1928 (authorized)			February 1935 (on the air)			February 1940 (on the air)		
	Full time	Share time	Day only	Full time	Share time	Day only	Full time	Share time	Day only
500,000 watts	—	—	—	1	—	—	—	—	—
50,000 watts	8	2	—	22	5	—	34	5	—
5,000 watts[1]	35	30	—	26	14	4	114	12	14
1,000 watts	36	49	—	119	38	19	89	26	30
250 watts	65	131	—	79	55	18	270	21	41
100 watts[2]	151	113	—	85	75	20	60	26	12
Totals	295	325	—	332	187	61	567	90	97

[1] Power classifications of 5,000, 1,000 and 250 watts include a few stations authorized to use power somewhat higher than the amounts given; for example, a few stations using 10,000 or 25,000 watts power are included with those with power of 5,000 watts.

[2] This category also includes some stations broadcasting with less than 100 watts power.

Figures for 1928 from the *Second Annual Report* of the Federal Radio Commission; those for 1935 and 1940 from listings in *Broadcasting Yearbooks* for those years.

siderably larger audiences than other stations in the area. This in turn makes the high-powered station more attractive to national advertisers, so at least in the case of AM radio stations, increased power generally results in larger total revenues and substantially greater profits.

Networks

The economic depression of the early 1930s had little real effect on the two national network companies. The nation's major advertisers were becoming more and more convinced of the effectiveness of radio advertising; as a result, network revenues continued to increase in spite of the depression. As shown in Table 1, network revenues from advertising expanded considerably over the period from 1930 to 1935, and almost doubled between 1935 and 1940. In 1934, the two network companies already in the field were joined by a third, the Mutual Broadcasting System, originally consisting of only four stations, WXYZ in Detroit, WOR in New York, WGN in Chicago, and WLW in Cincinnati. In 1936, Mutual added already existing regional chains in New England and on the West Coast, and the new network became an active competitor with NBC and CBS in the sale of time to national advertisers.

By 1930, approximately 130 stations were affiliated with NBC or with CBS, including all of the stations licensed for the use of 50,000 watts power. At the beginning of 1935 NBC's two networks provided service to 89 stations, CBS had contracts with 96 outlets, and Mutual still included only its four original stations.[7] By January 1940, a total of 386 stations were affiliated with networks, including all 39 of the 50,000-watt stations and 116 others with power of 5,000 watts or more. Most stations without network connections were stations with limited power or outlets operating on a part-time basis.

As the size of networks increased, so did the number of programs provided for affiliated stations. In January 1930 the three then-operating national networks offered a combined total of approximately 60 hours of sponsored programs each week, including seven hours of daytime programming. Five years later, the four national chains supplied a total of nearly 125 sponsored hours each week to their affiliates; about 80 hours represented sponsored evening programs, and the rest were programs broad-

---

[7] At this time WLW in Cincinnati, broadcasting with 500,000 watts power, was a member of the Mutual network; however the station also carried both NBC-Red and NBC-Blue programs and occasionally, by transcription, programs from the CBS network.

cast during the morning or in the afternoon. In January 1940 the four networks combined carried sponsored programs totaling 156 hours a week, including 87 hours of daytime programs. Time devoted to sponsored evening programs decreased somewhat between 1935 and 1940, but the increased number of affiliates meant that each program was broadcast by a larger number of stations and that network revenues from sponsored programs were correspondingly greater.

The figures given refer only to *sponsored* programs provided by the various networks for their affiliates. In addition, schedules of each network included a substantial number of *sustaining* programs, which individual stations could broadcast or not broadcast as they wished. For example, in January 1940 the four networks supplied approximately 40 hours of evening programs and 80 hours of daytime programs each week on a sustaining basis— three-fourths the number of hours devoted to commercial programs. Many of these sustaining network offerings were inexpensive presentations of talk or light music provided simply to fill gaps in the networks' schedules. But others were programs of considerable importance, produced each week at network expense. During the early months of 1940, for example, the networks' sustaining offerings included 18 hours of serious music each week—a broadcast of a complete opera as well as concerts presented by ten of the nation's leading symphony orchestras. Also carried by the networks without sponsorship were several religious programs, four or five weekly discussions of important public issues, a farm information program six days a week, a few educational programs for children of school age, and about 30 news and commentary broadcasts each week.

The Expanding Industry

With four coast-to-coast networks, more than 700 commercial stations, and revenues from sale of time totaling more than $150 million a year, radio by 1940 had become a major business enterprise. Equally important, it had become a very complex business involving a wide variety of special services beyond those provided by networks and stations. To secure network time, and in many instances to develop and produce programs for their clients, the major advertising agencies were forced to create special radio departments. News-gathering agencies originally established to provide a wire service for newspapers expanded their activities to serve broadcasting stations.

Scores of new enterprises came into existence, some to act as sales representatives for stations in dealing with national advertisers, some to provide libraries of transcribed music for the use of broadcasters, some to develop and produce "package" programs to be carried on network schedules, and some to provide transcribed programs for use by stations on a syndicated basis.[8] Music-licensing agencies were established to collect royalties from networks and stations for use of copyrighted music; research organizations were set up to provide information concerning the number of listeners reached by sponsored network programs. Radio had its own national trade association, the National Association of Broadcasters (NAB), and most states had their own associations of broadcasters. And, of course, as the industry's revenues increased, unions were organized to represent network and large-city station employees of almost every type, from actors to musicians and from writers and directors of programs to technicians and engineers. Administrative personnel and those engaged in sale of station or network time were not represented by unions.

Industry Problems

The development of radio into an important industry brought new problems into being for operators of networks and stations. One such problem involved the use by broadcasting stations of news from the wires of national news-gathering agencies—the Associated Press (AP), the United Press (UP), and the International News Service (INS). Disturbed by the increasing number of news programs carried by stations and networks during the early 1930s, publishers of newspapers determined to cut off the supply of news materials used on such programs. Pressure was exerted on the three news services; the result was that in

---

[8] Functions performed by many of the most important components of the broadcasting industry are discussed in more detail in Chapter 5.

1933 the three news agencies announced that they would no longer accept radio stations or networks as subscribers, and that the news materials they provided could not be used even by stations owned by newspapers. The following year, a compromise arrangement was worked out between broadcasters and the news services under which a newly created organization, the Press Radio Bureau, would supply a limited amount of headline news each day to broadcasting stations, which in turn were required to advise their listeners to read local newspapers for complete details. The arrangement did not satisfy the radio industry; networks moved in the direction of setting up news-gathering organizations of their own, and many stations subscribed to a newly created news service, Trans-Radio, which undertook to provide national news for the exclusive use of radio stations. Within two or three years, UP and INS gave up the fight and again made their services available to networks and stations. In 1939, AP formally withdrew restrictions on the use of its news on radio, and a year later activities of the Press Radio Bureau came to an end.

Another problem for broadcasters involved royalties to be paid for the use of copyrighted music. Even before radio became important in the economic field, holders of music copyrights had been organized in the American Society of Composers, Authors and Publishers, or ASCAP, to collect royalties from theaters, ballrooms, and producers of motion pictures for public performance of music. When radio became a commercial undertaking, ASCAP issued licenses allowing stations to broadcast music in return for payment of annual fees usually based on station revenues. As revenues of stations increased during the 1930s, license fees also increased. In 1937, ASCAP officials announced that when existing contracts with radio stations expired in December 1939, the new contracts would call for annual payment of license fees equal to five per cent of total station revenues. At this, the broadcasters rebelled. The NAB was authorized to set up a new licensing agency to provide music for radio use. The new organization, Broadcast Music, Inc., or BMI, came into existence in 1939; it entered into contracts with a number of composers and music-publishing firms designating BMI as licensing agent for the music they produced. However, very little BMI music had become available by the end of December 1939 when the

ASCAP contracts expired; for several months during 1940 networks and stations were forced to depend primarily on music in the "public domain" for the programs they presented—music on which copyrights had expired and which was not under ASCAP control. The competition provided by BMI ultimately forced ASCAP to moderate its demands, and since 1941 most broadcasting stations have had licensing contracts with both organizations.

A third problem faced by broadcasters in the late 1930s involved relations with the most powerful entertainment-industry union of the period, the American Federation of Musicians. To make work for its members, the Federation in 1937 announced its intention of requiring broadcasting stations to employ as regular staff members a number of union musicians, the number employed by each station to be determined by a quota arrangement based on the station's annual revenues. The following year, contracts were signed with most stations, putting the union's demands into effect. Networks and recording companies were forced, under threat of strikes, to refuse program service to any station failing to meet the union's requirements. The contracts with the union were declared illegal by the United States Department of Justice, so upon their expiration in 1940 they were not renewed. However, the pressures on networks and recording and transcription companies continued, so even without contracts stations found it expedient to employ their previously assigned quotas of union musicians. Finally in 1946 Congress amended the Communications Act, specifically outlawing any use of threats to require any broadcasting station licensee to employ "any persons in excess of the number . . . needed to perform actual services."

An event of major importance to the broadcasting industry was the enactment by Congress of the Federal Communications Act of 1934, replacing the Federal Radio Commission with a new seven-member Federal Communications Commission as the regulatory body for radio. The new agency was granted substantially the same powers over radio that had been exercised by the Radio Commission; in addition, the Communications Commission was given the responsibility of regulating interstate wire communication by telephone and telegraph.

Of importance, too, was the reorganization in 1938 of the

National Association of Broadcasters, making the organization a much more powerful and influential representative of the broadcasting industry. In 1939 the NAB adopted a new and much more vigorous industry Code of Ethics, setting up rigid standards with respect both to program content and to advertising and creating a Code Compliance Committee to insure station adherence to provisions of the code. From the late 1920s to 1935, the NAB code had related only to "fairness" in advertising; in 1935, provisions were expanded to include some aspects of programming; the 1939 code was expanded even more, and included among other things specific limits on the time that might be devoted to advertising in any broadcast program.

Network Programs, 1930 to 1941

If radio's economic development during the 1930s was impressive, the advances made in network programming during the period were little short of spectacular. Broadcasting had become an important advertising medium; if network advertising was to be effective, programs carrying advertising messages had to capture the attention of large numbers of listeners. Networks were forced to develop more attractive programs than the talks and musical offerings provided during the first ten years of radio's history. With advertisers willing to pay the bills, money was not a limiting factor. So beginning in 1929 and 1930 radio entered an era of program experimentation, invention, and development without parallel in any other period in the history of broadcasting, or of any other branch of the entertainment industry. Within six or seven years more than a dozen new program forms appeared on network schedules—new at least to radio, since some were borrowed from the theater, the motion picture, or the vaudeville stage. In fact, almost every type of program used on television today, from variety to situation comedy and from quiz shows to documentaries, had its broadcasting genesis in the radio developments of the 1930s.

A stimulus to program experimentation was the tremendous success of the *Amos 'n' Andy* series, first scheduled on the NBC Blue Network during the season of 1929–30. The combination of comedy, excellent characterization, use of the same leading characters in a continuing dramatic series, and effective use of radio's ability to stimulate the imaginations of listeners brought *Amos 'n' Andy* a tremendously large and loyal audience; during its first two seasons on the air, it is estimated that the program was heard each evening in more than half of all radio-equipped homes.

Variety and music.   Almost as attractive to listeners were radio's new variety presentations. An early form of variety had been introduced on NBC's schedules before 1930; each week's broadcast offered a different general type of material, from short dramatic sketches to debates between Congressmen. Closer to present-day forms on television were (1) a vaudeville type of variety, first introduced in the autumn of 1930 and using a different lineup of "guest" acts from vaudeville each week, and (2) the comedy-variety form, built around a featured "name" comedian and one or more permanent secondary characters, which appeared a year later. By the winter of 1933–34 more than a dozen comedy-variety shows were presented by national networks each week, featuring such established comedy stars as Eddie Cantor, Al Jolson, Will Rogers, Ed Wynn, and Fred Allen, along with a comparative newcomer named Jack Benny. Other variety forms introduced during the early 1930s included the "barn dance" or "country and Western music" type of program, the form of daytime variety used in the Blue Network's *Breakfast Club* (which started its long network run in the autumn of 1932), and the "amateur contest" form, of which the *Major Bowes Amateur Hour* was the most successful radio example.

No really new forms appeared in the field of musical programming, although by 1934 or 1935 the novelty musical groups of early network days had disappeared, their places taken by popular dance bands. A substantial number of concert-music programs were carried during the 1930s, but the form used was essentially that of the concert hall, transplanted to local and network radio in the middle and later 1920s. One new idea did make its appearance in the field of popular music with the introduction of the program *Your Hit Parade* in the autumn of 1935; in each broadcast, the *Hit Parade* program presented instrumental or sometimes vocal versions of the "top tunes" of the week. Possibly this program was the inspiration for the "top 40" concept of formula program so widely used by radio stations in the late 1950s and early 1960s.

Dramatic programs. Broadcasts of dramatic materials became increasingly popular during the 1930s as network program fare. Radio's first dramatic offerings were anthologies, using a new situation and a completely new set of characters in each broadcast. The earliest network anthology series was *Collier's Hour,* first presented in 1927–28 and using dramatized adaptations of short stories appearing in current issues of *Collier's* magazine. But the dramatic anthology had by far its greatest success in the *Lux Radio Theater* program, which started a run of more than 20 seasons on network schedules in the autumn of 1934. The anthology idea was also used in a number of programs of the detective or adventure type, from *Empire Builders* and *True Detective Mysteries,* both carried on network schedules as early as 1928 and 1929, to the *Warden Lawes* series, *Gangbusters,* and *Famous Jury Trials,* all introduced several years later.

However, only a very small proportion of radio's dramatic programs during the 1930s and later were presented in anthology form. Far more successful were the new types of programs introduced during the 1930s; these programs, like *Amos 'n' Andy,* used the same leading character or characters in each broadcast in a series—situation comedies, adventure programs, crime-detective programs, late-afternoon "action" programs for children, and certainly women's daytime serials. Showing the prevalence of imitation in programming is the fact that although 30-minute situation comedies were offered in the late 1920s, the phenomenal success of the 15-minute *Amos 'n' Andy* caused network companies to offer situation comedies only in 15-minute serialized form until the pattern was broken by the introduction of *The Aldrich Family* in 1939. And although evening crime or adventure dramas—*Sherlock Holmes* in 1930 and the highly successful *Lone Ranger* starting in 1934—were presented as 30-minute programs, the 15-minute serial idea dominated late-afternoon "action" programs for children throughout the 1930s. But serials reached their greatest importance in daytime dramatized "stories" presented for women listeners—programs presented in 15-minute episodes, five times a week, and usually with a woman character in the leading role. Interestingly enough, the earliest "daytime serials" for women were presented in early evening hours— *Myrt and Marge, The Goldbergs,* and *Clara, Lu and Em,* all introduced during the 1931–32 season.[9] But serial stories for women, once introduced as daytime features, rapidly dominated daytime network schedules; by the beginning of 1940 no less than 57 different serials were being presented five days a week, all but four of them carried either by CBS or by NBC's Red Network.

Other types of programs. Most of the program forms used on radio or later on television were direct borrowings from other and older agencies of entertainment: musical programs from the concert stage, the recital hall, or the ballroom; variety programs from the vaudeville stage or from the Broadway revue; anthology drama from the legitimate theater; serial drama from the action-suspense two-reel serials presented in motion picture theaters. The continuing dramatic series used on radio and presenting the same leading characters in each broadcast was probably an adaptation of a similar form used in motion pictures, especially in Western shorts and occasionally in full-length family dramas. But one category of radio programs that developed during the 1930s was original with radio and had no counterpart in any other medium of entertainment—the group of programs involving audience participation and depending largely on human interest values to hold the attention of listeners. Some of these programs were simply interviews with "ordinary people"; others, like *Professor Quiz* or *Old Time Spelling Bee,* both introduced during 1936–37, made use of a contest or quiz element and were the forerunners of the "game shows" extensively used on daytime television in recent years. Still others were presented for comedy values; *Truth or Consequences,* first broadcast in the autumn of 1940, made use of various "stunts" by people selected from the studio audience. A variant on the audience-participation idea was introduced in 1938 in *Information, Please;* the program

---

[9] *The Goldbergs* had been carried on network evening schedules during the two preceding seasons, but as a once-a-week, 15-minute program, presumably not using serial form.

used a quiz format with questions directed at a permanent panel of "celebrities"; it was the first of the "panel shows," which were later to become popular on television.

Along with entertainment features, radio networks offered news and commentary programs. Such programs had been included on network schedules from the beginning of network operations in 1926. However, the programs of Frederick William Wile, H. V. Kaltenborn, and David Lawrence were presented only once a week. They were limited to commentary concerning events in Washington and other capitals and made no attempt to provide up-to-the-minute coverage of the day's news. Network news broadcasting in the strict meaning of the term dates from the autumn of 1930, when NBC's Blue Network scheduled a 15-minute, early evening news series five times a week featuring Lowell Thomas; CBS followed with a similar program a year or two later. News, however, did not become a really important part of network service until the late 1930s, when events in Europe created an intense interest in national and international affairs and when the ending of the Press-Radio war increased the availability of news materials for use both on networks and stations. One important innovation was the introduction on CBS during the 1931–32 season of the *March of Time,* a weekly 30-minute program dramatizing some of the major news happenings of the week. This program, modeled after the newsreels shown in motion picture theaters during the 1930s, was radio's first documentary series and was the forerunner of the broadcast documentary programs used on television today.

As might be expected, the introduction of a wide variety of new program forms combined with changing economic and political conditions brought about significant changes in the makeup of network schedules during the period from 1930 to 1940. As shown in Table 3, music decreased in importance; there was a continuing increase in the use of variety programs and in various types of dramatic offerings; and in 1939–40, twelve hours a week were devoted to quiz and audience-participation programs, forms not yet developed in 1930. Introduction of the daytime serial form during the early 1930s was followed by a tremendous expansion in the use of such programs to the point where they practically filled the daytime schedules of at least two of the four national networks. And the threat of American involvement in the war in Europe stimulated interest in news

TABLE 3

HOURS PER WEEK DEVOTED TO VARIOUS TYPES OF NET-
WORK RADIO PROGRAMS, 1930 TO 1940

(During a typical week in January in each of the seasons
indicated)

	Season 1929–30	Season 1934–35	Season 1939–40
Evening or Sunday-afternoon programs			
Variety, all types	8.0	21.0	21.0
Serious music	17.5	16.5	13.0
Popular music	33.5	37.0	22.0
Quiz programs	—	—	8.0
Human-interest programs	—	1.5	4.0
General drama	4.5	8.0	10.0
Informative drama	0.5	1.5	3.5
Comedy drama	3.0	2.5	5.0
Action, crime, mystery drama	1.5	9.0	10.5
Women's serial drama	—	3.0	—
Sports events	—	—	1.0
News, commentary	1.5	4.5	14.5
Miscellaneous talks	6.5	12.5	19.0
Daytime programs			
Variety, all types	—	10.0	12.5
Popular or serious music	6.5	21.5	22.5
Human-interest programs	—	1.0	1.5
General drama	1.5	1.5	—
Informative drama	—	—	4.0
Comedy drama	—	3.5	1.0
Women's serial drama	—	12.0	75.0
Children's programs	3.5	8.5	7.0
News, commentary	—	—	3.0
Miscellaneous talks	12.5	24.0	11.5

Figures compiled from newspaper program listings for the
weeks indicated and from programs listed in reports of
national rating services; the table includes both sponsored
and sustaining programs.

and public affairs; by the beginning of 1940, networks were devoting more than 17 hours each week to news and commentary programs and presenting seven programs a week for discussions of important public issues.

Local Programming

Development in local radio programming was less spectacular than that on the network level; however, new forms were introduced and steady progress was made, especially after 1935 when stations were no longer seriously affected by the depression. Many of the program forms introduced on network schedules were originally developed by local stations; stations in turn "borrowed" many of the ideas made popular by the networks. By 1940, station programming was highly diversified. To begin with, station schedules included a wide variety of network offerings; more than two-thirds of all stations had network affiliations, and were devoting from eight to ten hours a day to network-originated programs. In addition, a number of syndication companies had been organized to provide non-network musical programs, complete dramatic programs, and even daytime serials for station use. Network affiliates in 1940 devoted an average of perhaps an hour a day to the broadcasting of transcribed programs provided by these syndication concerns; non-network stations, of course, made considerably greater use of syndicated materials.

Almost half of all station hours in 1940, however, were used to present locally originated programs. Nearly all stations carried several hours of "live" music each week; as a result of demands of the American Federation of Musicians, practically every station employed a few staff musicians on a regular basis, and used these musicians to present organ recitals, music by small orchestras, or in some cases fairly elaborate local variety programs. Many stations serving rural audiences scheduled "live" programs of country and Western, or "hillbilly," music. In addition, nearly all stations made considerable use of recorded or transcribed music. Most stations subscribed to a transcription library service; the music "library" included from three to five thousand selections ranging from semiclassical and operetta music to novelty numbers and old familiar hymns, and most programs of recorded music were built from selections in these libraries rather than from recordings of current popular numbers. Around 1936 or 1937, many stations developed local amateur contest programs presented once a week; by 1940, however, most of these amateur programs had disappeared from local schedules.

Practically all stations depended heavily on the use of "talk" programs. Nearly every station had its "women's program" director who conducted a daily homemakers' program. Almost all stations that reached farm audiences had full-time farm program directors who presented farm market reports and other information of interest to farmers. Many stations had special programs for children, often combining storytelling and the singing of children's songs. A considerable number of radio outlets scheduled regular weekly programs developed in cooperation with local civic, educational, or women's groups. Interview programs were popular; perhaps half or more of the stations operating in 1940 carried a daily "man-on-the-street" program, in which a staff announcer interviewed passers-by from locations on downtown streets. Many stations also had regular programs that offered an opportunity for studio interviews with local leaders or with important visitors to the community. Of course, on Sunday every station broadcast at least one locally originated religious program and often one or more transcribed programs provided by national religious organizations.

News by 1940 was a staple in local offerings. Most stations scheduled at least three local news programs each weekday, in addition to the network news and commentary programs. A relatively small number of stations broadcast play-by-play accounts of local sports events on a regular basis; network commitments made such broadcasts difficult for affiliated stations except on Saturday afternoons. A few stations offered local weekly quiz programs; some also attempted locally produced dramatic programs, usually in cooperation with schools or colleges. In spite of the development of numerous new program forms on networks, stations for the most part depended on talks and musical programs to fill the time not required for network presentations, but these local offerings were of more varied types than those carried ten years earlier.

Prewar Television

Although public attention was centered on radio during the 1920s and 1930s, the foundation was already being laid for a new form of broadcasting that after the war was largely to replace radio as a source of home entertainment. As early as 1923, Vladimir Zworykin secured a patent on an experimental iconoscope tube using the principle of electronic scanning. Two years later, Charles F. Jenkins made the first wireless transmission of a motion picture—the earliest real "television broadcast" in this country—using the mechanical scanning method he had developed. In 1928, the General Electric Company broadcast the first television drama. Three years later, the Zworykin method of electronic scanning was being used in regular broadcasts by an experimental television station in New York owned by RCA. By 1937, 17 television stations were operating under experimental licenses; in 1939, the RCA station in New York presented regular daily broadcasts from the New York World's Fair and also experimented with television pickups of major league baseball and of a college football game. In 1940, a television station in Chicago broadcast portions of the Democratic national convention, held in that city; in addition, remote pickups were made from the Republican national convention in Philadelphia, with televised materials carried by coaxial cable to New York and broadcast by the RCA experimental television station.

Commercial television was introduced in 1941. In that year, the Federal Communications Commission issued orders fixing technical standards for visual broadcasting and establishing the channels on which stations might operate. In addition, the Commission announced that it would grant licenses for stations desiring to broadcast on a commercial rather than an experimental basis; the beginning of commercial operation was set for July 1, 1941. Between July and November, five stations were granted commercial licenses: WNBT, now WNBC-TV, in New York, the former RCA-owned experimental station which had been transferred to NBC; WCBW, now WCBS-TV, also in New York, a CBS station; WPTZ in Philadelphia, owned by the Philco Corporation; WRGB, the General Electric Company's station in Schenectady; and WBKB, owned by the Balaban and Katz motion picture theater interests, in Chicago. Other television stations continued under experimental licenses.

Although these five stations held commercial licenses, their operation during 1941 was only nominally commercial. WNBT in its first week of broadcasting in July had only four sponsors; from July through December the station took in less than $7,000 from its sale of time to advertisers. Other stations had even smaller commercial revenues. The reason was obvious: fewer than 10,000 television receiving sets were in existence even at the end of the year, and the audience which could tune in any television program was much too small to have commercial significance. With the entry of this country into the war late in 1941, commercial operation was practically abandoned; stations simply marked time, broadcasting for only a few hours each week until normal conditions returned and regular operation could be resumed.

RADIO DURING THE WAR

During World War II, both industry and the American public were subject to wartime restrictions. Like most other forms of economic activity, broadcasting was directly affected by wartime conditions. Manufacturers of electronic equipment shifted entirely to production of materials used by the armed forces; private broadcasting stations were unable to secure new transmitters or technical equipment, and no new receiving sets or replacement tubes were produced for civilian use. In spite of shortages, there was some increase in the number of operating radio stations; by December 1945 approximately 940 stations were licensed and on the air. The number of radio homes also increased from an estimated 30.8 million in 1941 to almost 34 million in the autumn of 1945. Presumably some of the sets in the added homes had previously been second sets in the homes of relatives. In many of the 34 million radio-equipped homes, however, receiving sets were not in working condition by 1945, since in most communities radio tubes and other replacement parts were not available.

A major change in the network situation took place early in 1942. Complying with the "duopoly" order of the Federal

Communications Commission that prohibited operation of more than one national network system by a single company, NBC turned over its Blue Network system to a separate corporation, which was later sold to a new group of owners. The new company ultimately became the American Broadcasting Company (ABC), while what had been known from 1926 to 1942 as the NBC Red Network remained as NBC, with no color designation.

Revenues from Advertising

In spite of the war, revenues from the sale of time to advertisers increased tremendously. As shown in Table 1, advertising revenues doubled between 1940 and 1945; of the approximately $310 million received by stations and networks in 1945, more than 43 per cent went to the four national networks and another 24 per cent represented "spot" advertising placed on stations by national advertisers. The increase in radio advertising was in part a result of a wartime shortage of newsprint that made it necessary for most newspapers and magazines to limit the number of pages in each issue and consequently the amount of advertising carried. Another highly important factor was the wartime federal tax structure, which imposed a tax of as much as 90 per cent on excess profits of corporations. Companies earning high profits from war production could, as a result, buy broadcast advertising at an actual cost of only ten cents for each dollar's worth of radio time; the remaining 90 cents would otherwise go to the government in taxes. Other factors undoubtedly contributed to the expansion in radio advertising as well, but no matter what the cause, during the war years radio networks and stations enjoyed the greatest period of prosperity that broadcasting had ever known.

Wartime Programming

Naturally, the war had its effect on programs. No major new program forms were introduced, but the fact that the nation was at war was strongly reflected in the content of programs offered, especially at the network level. A number of variety-program series were presented on a regular basis with servicemen as participants: *The Army Hour* and *Meet Your Navy* were typical titles. Service bands appeared each week on network schedules. Quiz shows and audience-participation programs had Army and Navy enlisted men as participants, almost to the exclusion of civilians. Documentary or informative dramatic programs dealt with activities of the Air Force, the Service of Supply, and various other military services; "plot" dramatizations made extensive use of wartime themes. All entertainment programs, whether carried on network schedules or locally produced, carried "war messages" provided by the Office of War Information and the War Advertising Council urging listeners to conserve fats; to save copper, tin, and aluminum; to enlist in the various women's auxiliary military services; to contribute to the Red Cross or the United Service Organizations; or to buy government War Bonds. At the same time, certain types of material were excluded from the air by broadcasters on the basis of guidelines provided by a government-established Office of Censorship; the ban covered information concerning troop movements, dates on which convoys were to sail, figures concerning production of war materials and supplies, even information concerning weather conditions. In addition, broadcasters were urged to take all possible precautions to see that unknown or unauthorized persons did not have access to microphones. As a result of government restrictions, all weather broadcasts were discontinued, as were interview programs of the "man-on-the-street" type and programs of recorded music in which either "request" numbers were played or in which numbers used were "dedicated" to friends of listeners who suggested such dedications.

War conditions also produced changes in the extent of use of programs of certain types on network schedules. In January 1941, the four networks devoted approximately 13 hours each week to news and commentary programs, all but five of these hours on a sustaining basis. Four years later, news accounted for a total of 34 hours a week—as much time as was used to present evening dramatic programs—with nearly 18 hours of the total sponsored. Almost equally dramatic increases were made in the areas of informative drama and of serious music; advertisers whose companies were engaged in war production showed a strong interest in sponsorship of "prestige" programs, with the result that by January 1945 networks were carrying nearly five hours of sponsored informative drama each week and more than 15 hours of advertiser-supported concert or classical music, including four weekly broadcasts by symphony orchestras.

As the war continued, however, network schedules also reflected the need of listeners to forget for a time the problems of everyday living, accounts of battles in faraway places, and the tragedy of casualty lists. Programs offering escape increased both in number and in popularity. Time devoted to evening comedy variety increased from four and a half hours to eight hours per week between 1941 and the beginning of 1945. Situation comedy programs showed a similar increase, most of it after 1943. And evening "thriller" dramatic programs—Westerns, adventure stories, crime programs not related to the war situation—jumped from nine hours a week in 1943 to nearly 15 hours in January 1945, although "problem" dramatic offerings decreased in nearly the same ratio.

Other changes in network and local station schedules were also taking place, some of which were to continue in the years ahead. By the start of the 1945–46 season, the war had ended. But for the American radio industry, new and critical problems were ahead.

4

BROADCASTING
SINCE 1945

At the close of World War II, radio occupied an enviable position, both as an important and growing industry and as an influential American institution. Between 1940 and 1945 radio's revenues from sale of time to advertisers had practically doubled, reaching $310 million in 1945. Even more important, radio enjoyed the confidence and approval of the American people to a degree rarely attained by any other institution in the nation's history. When listeners in a nationwide study in 1945 were asked about agencies that they felt were doing an "excellent job," a "good job," a "fair job," or a "poor job," 82 per cent of the respondents from coast to coast expressed the opinion that radio stations were doing either an "excellent" or a "good" job.[1] In

[1] Paul F. Lazarsfeld and Harry Field, *The People Look at Radio*, University of North Carolina Press, 1946.

comparison, churches received a similar vote of confidence from only 76 per cent, daily newspapers from 68 per cent, public schools from 62 per cent, and local government agencies from 45 per cent. Further, four out of five of those questioned believed that radio was "generally fair" in presenting both sides of public issues; only 39 per cent expressed a similar feeling with respect to newspapers.

But radio after the war was confronted with serious problems, problems that were to produce revolutionary changes in programming and in the structure of the broadcasting industry itself.

THE POSTWAR ERA

Most historians of radio and television accept the year 1952 as marking the end of the era of radio dominance in American broadcasting and the beginning of the age of television in the United States. There were, of course, television stations and television networks before 1952, but that year the Federal Communications Commission ended its 42-month-old "freeze" on the licensing of additional television stations, and permitted new stations to come on the air. Moreover, in 1952, the combined annual revenues of the national television networks were for the first time greater than those of the four long-established radio networks.

Radio was a thriving and expanding industry during the years immediately following the end of the war. Receiving sets could again be purchased by the public, and the demand was tremendous; during 1947 alone, nearly 20 million new radio sets were produced by American manufacturers. By 1952, radio receiving equipment was available in an estimated 46 million homes (almost 97 per cent of all homes in the United States); at least half of the families in America owned two or more sets. Revenues from sale of time increased steadily in the postwar years, from $310 million in 1945 to $453 million in 1950—a gain in five years of nearly 50 per cent. In 1952, revenues of radio networks and stations reached a total of $473 million; radio revenues were still increasing, but at a less rapid rate than in earlier years.

Radio Network Problems

Networks in the postwar period were providing service to a constantly increasing number of affiliates. By 1952, NBC and CBS were serving from 180 to 190 stations each; the American Broadcasting Company had approximately 275 affiliates; Mutual had contracts with nearly 400 stations. In addition, a fifth network company, the Liberty Broadcasting System, had been organized in 1946 and three years later was providing a limited program service to some 300 stations. But radio networks were hard hit by the rapid expansion of television after 1948. National advertisers shifted their accounts from radio to the newly organized television networks. As a result, the financially shaky Liberty radio network was forced to suspend operations in 1951, and the long-established radio operations of NBC, CBS, ABC, and Mutual showed serious drops in revenues. In 1948, radio network revenues from advertising totaled $141 million for the year; four years later, national advertisers spent only $110 million for radio network time, as compared with $138 million for time on television networks.

Contributing greatly to the radio network problem was a decline in listener interest in programs offered on radio, accompanying the greatly increased interest of the American public in television. Ratings [2] of radio network programs dropped sharply as new television stations came on the air. In January 1948, the ratings of the ten most popular programs carried on national radio networks averaged 24.9; in other words, each program was heard each week in an average of approximately one-fourth of all of the radio-equipped homes throughout the nation. But four years later, the ten most popular radio programs then carried on network schedules had average ratings of only 13.2— only a little more than half of the figure reported in 1948.[3] Listeners were shifting from radio to television; in the circum-

---

[2] A program "rating" is a figure representing the percentage of radio-equipped homes (or in the case of television, of television-equipped homes) in which, on a given date, sets are tuned to a specific program. A detailed explanation of the methods by which rating information is secured is given in Chapter 9.

[3] Averages in each case have been computed from rating figures reported in the national Nielsen Radio Index for the month indicated.

stances, it was inevitable that advertisers' interest in the use of network radio would decline.

Radio Stations

But while radio networks were suffering losses both in revenues and in public acceptance of programs offered, the situation of individual radio stations was, on the surface at least, more encouraging. The volume of advertising placed directly with stations rose from $176 million in 1945 to a 1952 total of $363 million. But the increasing prosperity of radio stations was more apparent than real, as a result of the tremendous expansion in the number of stations among which revenues had to be divided.

In January 1945, there were 933 standard radio stations on the air, practically all of which had earned very substantial profits during the preceding five-year period. Station operation was obviously a promising field for investors. The result was that following the war, when transmitters and technical equipment were again available, there was a rush to secure authorizations for new broadcasting facilities. Frequencies were available, since the Federal Communications Commission had modified its engineering requirements to reduce the mileage separation between stations assigned to the same channel. By the end of 1947, more than a thousand new stations had been authorized; by January 1950, a total of 2,086 standard-band radio stations were actually in operation; and by the beginning of 1952, there were 2,331 standard stations on the air with 70 others under construction.

At the same time, there was an equally impressive increase in the number of frequency modulation stations.[4] Frequency modulation was not new; as early as the summer of 1940, there were roughly 50 FM stations on the air, all operating on an experimental basis. Regular or nonexperimental frequency mod-

---

[4] "Standard" or amplitude modulation radio stations occupy frequencies between 540 and 1600 kilocycles; FM or frequency modulation stations are assigned to much higher frequencies and also use a different method of modulating the signals transmitted. The two types of radio stations are ordinarily referred to as "AM" or "standard-band" stations, and as "FM" stations.

ulation broadcasting was authorized by the Federal Communications Commission in 1941. Because of the war, however, there was little FM development during the next five years, although by the end of 1945 most of the existing FM stations held regular licenses. But following the war there was a rush for construction of new FM stations, partly at least as a result of the encouragement given to the new form of broadcasting by the Communications Commission and the fear of some broadcasters that AM broadcasting might be dropped entirely by Commission order, to be replaced by service provided by FM outlets. In any event, by January 1950, a total of 733 commercial FM stations were in operation, in addition to a number of noncommercial educational stations. Almost all of the new FM stations were owned by operators of AM facilities in the same communities and carried the same lineup of programs used by AM stations under the same ownership. Consequently, frequency modulation operations brought no additional revenues to their owners, and after 1950 the number of FM stations took a downward trend that continued for several years. Even so, at the beginning of 1952 there were 637 commercial FM outlets on the air, bringing the total number of AM and FM stations to nearly 3,000—three times as many commercial stations as the number in operation seven years earlier. Radio station revenues increased after the war, but the number of stations increased even more rapidly so that average income per station showed a marked decline.

Postwar Radio Programs

Only one really new program form appeared on radio networks in the years following the war: the "press conference" type of public affairs program, of which *Meet the Press,* introduced in the autumn of 1945, was the most important example. However, important modifications were made in forms already used. The success of *Break the Bank* in 1945–46 started a trend toward use of "big money" quiz programs. A year later, the audio-taping of the *Bing Crosby Show* marked the first network use of a radio series in which complete programs were produced and recorded in advance of the time of broadcast. In 1947–48, "disk jockey" programs were included for the first time on network schedules. Use of telephone calls to listeners as a feature of network quiz programs was introduced in the highly popular *Stop the Music* program in the autumn of 1948. And in 1950–51, the *Arthur Godfrey Digest* series on CBS inaugurated on network radio the use of recorded reruns of programs broadcast on earlier dates—a practice to become widely used on television networks a few years later.

Changes in network programming. Even more important were changes that took place in the relative use of various types of programs between 1945 and 1952. Sponsored variety and musical programs showed a sharp decrease, largely as a result of the shift of advertiser interest to television. Quiz programs were more widely used from 1946 to 1950 than in any other period in radio network history; by 1952, however, only three such programs were sponsored each week on evening network schedules. The number of "thriller" dramatic programs increased tremendously; in January 1952, no fewer than 53 "thrillers" were presented each week during evening hours. However, only half of this number were sponsored; since "thrillers" could be produced at a relatively low cost, they were used as sustainers to fill holes in network schedules created by the disappearance of sponsored evening variety and musical programs. The number of daytime women's serials continued to decrease, although in January 1952 more than 30 such programs were still carried by national radio networks. Replacing the canceled serials were daytime quiz and human interest programs; by January 1949, programs of these types filled 13 half-hour periods a day on network schedules. Light variety programs were also used during daytime hours; such programs as *Arthur Godfrey* on CBS and *Breakfast Club* on ABC occupied several hours of network time each week, and continued to hold their attractiveness for listeners. In fact, daytime network radio up to 1952 was not greatly affected by the competition of television; although evening radio network programs were rapidly losing popularity, the ratings of daytime programs showed only a slight decline, and the total number of sponsored hours of daytime network programs per week remained almost unchanged between 1945 and 1952.

Local radio programming. Local radio station programming, like that of radio networks, changed materially over the seven-year period after the war. The constantly decreasing number of sponsored evening network programs created gaps in schedules of local affiliated stations; in most cases, these gaps were filled by the least expensive and most easily produced kind of local programming available—recorded music. For a time at least, loss of evening network programs created no financial problem for stations; revenues from sale of spot announcements on these local platter shows were usually greater than the amounts networks had been paying the stations for the time used by canceled network programs. So stations affiliated with networks turned partly—increasingly as sponsored network programming decreased—to the use of recorded music, still depending on networks to provide a variety of programs of other types, especially during daytime hours.

However, the tremendous expansion in the number of radio stations meant that not all could secure network affiliations. A majority of the more than 2,300 AM stations on the air in 1952 operated as independents. These non-network stations were forced to provide programs locally to fill their daily schedules, and they naturally turned to the type of program material most readily at hand and the type that could be produced at lowest cost—recorded music. By 1952, radio stations fell, on the basis of the programming they offered, into two basic groups. One group, affiliated with networks, provided a considerable amount of variety in programs offered and used recorded music only to fill the portions of each day's schedule when network programs were not available. The second group, made up of independent stations, used recorded music all day long, almost without interruption. For these independents, program diversification of the type that had characterized almost all radio stations before 1945 was simply impossible; they broadcast "good" music, or "popular" music, or "Dixieland and jazz," or sometimes "country and Western" music—but their schedules were filled with recorded music.

Postwar Television

Television got off to a slow start in this country after the end of the war. Between 1941 and 1945, ten television stations had been licensed to operate commercially, but in January 1946 only six of the ten were actually on the air. At the end of 1945, not more than 10,000 television receiving sets were in existence, all produced before 1942, and since tubes and repairs were not available during the war period, few of these sets were still in working condition. During 1946, a few thousand additional sets were manufactured. But set production on any large scale had to wait until final decisions were made by the Federal Communications Commission concerning the channels to be used for television broadcasting. Originally, in 1945, 13 channels in the "very high frequency" (VHF) band had been set aside for commercial television operation; however, the same channels were also to be shared with the military and other nonbroadcasting services. Not until 1948 was the problem of channel allocations finally resolved; the Federal Communications Commission dropped channel 1 from the list to which television stations might be assigned, but reserved channels 2 to 13 in the VHF band for the exclusive use of television broadcasting stations. This allowed electronic companies to go ahead with the manufacture of television receiving sets; in 1948, a million receivers were produced, and more than 10 million additional sets were manufactured during the next two years. These early sets had very small picture tubes, usually only from seven to ten inches in diameter; some of the higher-priced sets, costing from $350 to $400 each, featured twelve-inch tubes. But receiving sets were available, and the way was open for the development of television as an agency of mass communication.

With very few receiving sets in the hands of the public, construction of new television stations was slow for several years following the end of the war. At best, the construction of a television facility was not too promising an investment. To build and equip a station cost its owners from $750,000 to $1.5 million; after the station was on the air, it had to operate at a loss until enough receiving sets were owned in the community to make the station attractive to advertisers. So in addition to the six stations operating commercially at the end of the war, only one new outlet was built during 1946, and ten others in 1947. But with uncertainties about channels finally resolved and receiving sets in production, 1948 saw more broadcasters willing to gamble on the future possibilities of television; 33 new facilities were added, so that by the end of the year a total of 50 stations were providing programs for viewers in major cities.

In October 1948, the Federal Communications Commission ordered a "freeze" on the processing of applications for new television stations, partly to permit the assignment of channel allocations for different communities throughout the nation, and partly to allow decisions to be made on requirements of color broadcasting and on the possible future development of educational television stations. The freeze lasted for nearly four years, until April 1952; during that period, no construction permits were issued for new television stations. However, at the time the freeze was imposed, 109 stations were operating or had been authorized; by the early months of 1952, all but one of the 109 stations had been constructed and were on the air.

Encouraging to owners of stations was the rapid increase, after 1948, in the number of television-equipped homes. By the end of 1949, receiving sets had been installed in an estimated 2.8 million homes; by January 1952, 15 million families were able to receive television programs. The new sets were better adapted for family viewing than those available even a few years earlier. By 1952, manufacturers were producing sets with 20-inch screens; picture quality was much improved; "locked-in" tuning was standard on all sets, greatly simplifying the process of bringing in a good picture. Prices of the new sets were roughly the same as those charged in 1948; most of the 20-inch sets manufactured in 1952 were sold at retail for from $320 to $350, although some with smaller picture tubes could be bought for $275 or less.

Television Networks

National radio networks were not organized until hundreds of radio stations were already on the air. With television, the situation was different; networks existed almost before stations. As early as 1945 and 1946 when fewer than a dozen commercial television stations were on the air, television networks were being organized by four different network companies. One of the four was headed by Allen B. DuMont, owner of one of the pioneer television stations in New York City. The other three concerns were companies already operating national radio networks: the American Broadcasting Company, the Columbia Broadcasting System, and the National Broadcasting Company. Each of the four television network organizations secured construction permits for network-owned stations in each of several major cities; in addition, the radio network companies urged their affiliates throughout the country to apply for television authorizations, and long before the new stations went on the air their owners had signed television affiliation contracts.

By 1948, each of the four television network companies operated an Eastern network linking together stations in cities along the Atlantic seaboard; in addition, ABC, CBS, and NBC had set up Midwestern networks to provide programs for television outlets in Chicago, St. Louis, and Milwaukee. In January 1949, the American Telephone and Telegraph Company completed a coaxial cable connection between New York and Chicago allowing Eastern and Midwestern networks to be linked together. In September 1951, A.T.&T. completed microwave relay facilities to the West Coast for television network transmission, so that programs originating in New York could be broadcast simultaneously by stations from coast to coast. However, not all affiliated stations in 1952 had physical network connections; in many cases, A.T.&T. lines had not been installed to link these stations with the cable or relay systems used by the various networks. Network programs for these "noninterconnected" stations were provided in the form of kinescope recordings—films made from pictures appearing on the kinescope or picture tube of a television receiving set—shipped by mail or express to stations using them.

The Television Industry

Television's rapid growth between 1948 and 1952 was stimulated by a number of conditions that had not existed during radio's early years. Radio in the 1920s was a new form of communication; its development as an advertising medium had to wait until receiving sets were available in millions of homes and until advertisers became aware of the advantages radio offered. Services essential to the growing industry were developed slowly;

even the *ideas* behind most of these services were completely new. But television was not, in any similar sense, a new undertaking. Television was simply an extension of radio, a somewhat different and perhaps improved form of radio broadcasting. The newly born television industry of the late 1940s was built on a foundation created by radio; its patterns of operation and most of its services had already been developed as parts of the radio industry. Of the 108 television stations on the air in the early months of 1952, 87 were owned by licensees of radio stations; three of the four television networks were operated by companies that owned established radio networks. Advertising agencies, station representatives, equipment manufacturers, program "package" production concerns, syndication companies—all of these already existed, and had only to extend their operations into the television field. Even the program forms used on television were forms already developed on radio.

Equally important, the financial support necessary for the establishment of television was provided in large part by radio. Profits earned by radio networks and major radio stations went into the development of television and the construction of television stations. When a new television station went on the air, it necessarily operated at a loss for several months or even years; the public bought receiving sets only *after* the station was on the air, and was making programs available. These losses, in most cases, were paid for out of earnings of radio stations whose owners had constructed the new television stations.

Television's development was at the expense of radio in other ways as well. Television was new, exciting; radio was already established. So network and station owners gave their first attention and devoted their energies to the new form of broadcasting; they largely ignored the needs of their radio operations. Advertisers were encouraged to shift their expenditures from network radio to television to help develop the new medium. Radio's most popular programs were moved to television networks—and no one bothered to develop interesting new programs or new program forms to fill the places left vacant on radio network schedules. In financing, in program development, in interest and attention, the broadcasting industry robbed Peter to pay Paul, and contributed directly to the decline of network radio and the drop in listener interest in programs that radio still provided.

However, television benefited from the situation, and the development of the new television industry was rapid, even though networks and stations were forced for several years to operate at a loss. In 1947, combined revenues of the 17 television stations on the air at the end of the year were less than $2 million; expenses were many times greater. The following year, television stations and networks had a combined operating deficit of nearly $15 million; in 1949, with more stations, the deficit was more than $25 million. In 1950, television stations collectively had revenues large enough to equal expenditures, but networks were still operating at a loss. Finally, in 1951, television operators were making money; networks reported net profits of $12 million on total revenues of $132 million, and the 92 stations not owned by network companies had revenues of $107 million, of which $31 million represented profits.

Early Television Network Programming

In programming no less than in finance, television owes a tremendous debt to radio. Practically all of the program forms used on television were first developed on radio. Not only program forms, but actual programs that had won popularity as radio offerings were moved over bodily from network radio to network television. During the first two years of television network operation, more than 20 of television's most popular programs were taken directly from radio network schedules— programs such as Arthur Godfrey's *Talent Scouts, Suspense, Studio One, The Life of Riley, Lights Out, The Goldbergs,* the *Fred Waring Program, Break the Bank, The Aldrich Family,* and the *Martin Kane* detective series. The use of programs already established on radio contributed in no small measure to television's early success in attracting loyal audiences.

But although television networks borrowed heavily from radio to fill their program schedules, television was a new medium, different from radio, and television producers were forced to learn from experience what types of programs the public would find most attractive. So between 1948 and 1952, network schedules changed tremendously from year to year. As has already been mentioned, in 1948–49, the first full season of network operation, more than 30 per cent of all sponsored evening network programs were broadcasts of sports events—basketball, boxing, bowling, and wrestling—perhaps reflecting the fact that during that season, a large proportion of television receiving sets were located in bars and taverns. A year later, however, with sets installed in a much greater number of homes, sports broadcasts accounted for less than five per cent of evening network hours. Emphasis had been shifted to early-evening children's programs, reflecting the greater use of television in the home. In January 1950, children's programs made up more than one-fourth of all sponsored hours between 6:00 P.M. and 11:00 P.M. on schedules of television networks; like sports broadcasts the previous year, however, they retained their position of importance for only a single season.

Network programming in 1950–51 was strongly influenced by the early successes of such variety shows as the *Milton Berle* program and Ed Sullivan's *Toast of the Town;* in January 1951, no less than 24 hours on evening schedules were devoted each week to the presentation of sponsored variety programs. But once again, after one season programming patterns were changed. Most of the network variety shows involved the use of vaudeville acts, and the supply of such "acts" was quickly exhausted. So by January 1952, time devoted by national networks to evening variety shows had dropped to 15 hours a week, and the number of variety programs decreased even further in later years. Replacing variety as the dominant form in 1951–52 were dramatic programs; during that season anthologies, "thrillers," and comedy dramatic programs filled nearly 40 per cent of the networks' evening schedules.

Local Television Programming

From 1945 to 1952, television stations provided a substantial amount of local programming—a larger proportion than in later years, when network offerings had been increased and when large numbers of syndicated programs were available. With station revenues limited, the need was for programs that could be produced at a low cost. So stations experimented with various types of disk-jockey programs—usually with little success, since use of recorded music failed to provide visual attractiveness. Nearly all television outlets scheduled news broadcasts; almost as widely used were programs of weather information, usually five to ten minutes in length; weather maps and other reports were better adapted to use on television than on radio. Most stations devoted from 30 minutes to an hour each day to home-makers' programs, usually originating from fully equipped kitchen sets. Another hour or more a day was used to present programs, often featuring puppets, for young children. Many television outlets had daily programs of "live" music presented by small vocal and instrumental groups; a few provided fairly elaborate variety programs, often using amateur talent recruited in the community; several had daily or once-a-week local audience participation shows. Probably a majority of the stations on the air before 1952 invested in "remote" broadcasting equipment—special trucks or buses, cameras, lighting and control equipment—to pick up local sports events or to broadcast portions of public meetings or other events. In most cases, the "remote" trucks failed to justify their costs and were little used after the first year or two the station was in operation.

Of course, even during the early years, stations made some use of syndicated filmed materials. Many of the two-reel comedies and short subjects originally produced for use in motion picture theaters were available to television stations. The success on television of some of the early motion picture Westerns—*Hopalong Cassidy* in particular—led to the filming and leasing to television stations of a number of adventure or Western series produced especially for television use. In addition, in 1950 a few old theatrical feature films were released for television syndication; by the winter of 1951–52, about 300 such complete features were available for broadcast. But network programs and syndicated filmed materials filled only a part of the broadcasting day; television stations in 1952 had to depend heavily on locally produced "live" programs.

BROADCASTING SINCE 1952

During the years since 1952 the same trends evident in the postwar period of broadcasting have continued. Television has grown steadily in popularity and in importance as an advertising medium; the position of radio has become increasingly less secure.

The Problem of Radio

The radio situation since 1952 has been filled with apparent contradictions. Radio has continued to grow almost at the same rate as in the years following the war. Sale of radio sets has continued at a high level; from 1960 to 1964 an average of 19 million units were sold each year. The number of radio stations has grown tremendously; by January 1966, more than 4,000 AM stations and 1,400 commercial FM stations were on the air. Industry revenues have also increased; as shown in Table 4, the estimated total revenue from sale of radio time in 1962 amounted to nearly $662 million, and the figure has been even higher since that year.

TABLE 4

**ANNUAL TOTAL TIME SALES OF RADIO AND TELEVISION NETWORKS AND STATIONS, 1950 THROUGH 1962[1]
(IN THOUSANDS OF DOLLARS)**

	For calendar years			
	1950	1954	1958	1962
Radio time sales				
By networks	134,898	83,684	46,519	33,954
By stations				
national spot	108,315	120,168	171,939	208,455
local	182,144	247,478	323,207	419,468
Total radio sales	425,357	451,330	541,665	661,877
Television time sales				
By networks	35,210	241,224	424,500	520,200
By stations				
national spot	25,034	176,766	345,200	539,500
local	30,385	120,131	181,300	242,800
Total television sales	90,629	538,121	951,000	1,302,500

[1] Figures represent gross billings, before deductions of commissions to advertising agencies and station representatives.

From annual financial reports released by the Federal Communications Commission covering the years indicated.

But even with this expansion, radio has found itself the victim of circumstances that have seriously injured many segments of the industry. As television developed, listeners have spent more time watching television and less time listening to radio. As this decrease in audience size became evident during the early 1950s, national advertisers shifted their advertising expenditures from network radio to television, and as the attractive sponsored programs disappeared from radio network schedules, radio listening declined still further. And although advertising revenues of stations more than doubled over the period between 1950 and 1962, the increased number of outlets to be supported by those revenues and lack of balance in the distribution of advertising money between strong and weak stations have created serious financial problems, in the years since 1958 or 1959, for half or more of the radio stations on the air.

Even greater difficulties have confronted the four national radio networks. As a result of television competition, the combined annual revenues of the four network companies dropped from an all-time high of $141 million in 1948 to only one-fourth that amount in 1962. The decrease in revenues of course resulted from the steady disappearance of sponsored programs from network schedules. First to go were the popular programs of the pretelevision era. The winter of 1955–56 found the four national networks providing a total of only 35 hours of sponsored evening programs each week; even these disappeared over the next few years, so that by 1960 only a few, long-established news programs still remained on evening schedules. Daytime programs lasted a few years longer; as late as the autumn of 1955, the four radio networks still had sponsors for some 70 hours of daytime programming each week. But even these daytime programs were soon to disappear; by 1964 or 1965 radio network service to affiliates was limited for the most part to headline-type news programs and short-talk features, with each network supplying an average of little more than two hours of programming a day to its affiliated stations.

As television replaced network radio as a source of attractive programs, the amount of time devoted to radio listening naturally decreased. Reports released by the A. C. Nielsen company show that in the spring of 1949, receiving sets in radio-equipped homes were in use for an average of roughly four and a half hours a day. By 1953, average use of such home sets had dropped to three hours a day, and by the spring of 1962 the time devoted to radio listening on plug-in sets in the home had decreased to an average of hardly more than an hour and a half a day. Nielsen figures did not include out-of-home listening in automobiles or other places, of course, or in-home listening to transistor or other battery-powered sets; allowance for such listening might add considerably to the figures reported. But there is no question that since the advent of television and the decline of network radio, the amount of in-home listening to radio has shown a striking decrease.

The decline in radio listening, competition from television for advertising revenues, and the tremendous increase in the total number of stations among which radio's advertising revenues must be divided have all contributed to the financial difficulties of many radio stations in recent years. Some radio stations still have substantial revenues from sale of time and still earn very satisfactory profits on each year's operation, especially those with high power and large-city locations. But half or more of all radio stations eke out a precarious existence by cutting program and operating costs to the bone and then either losing money on the broadcasting operations each year or earning at most a few thousand dollars. Obviously, the difficulties of such stations have had an effect on the quality of radio programming. So serious has the situation become that in 1962 the Federal Communications Commission attempted to deal with the problem of station overpopulation by ordering a partial freeze on the authorization of certain types of new AM broadcasting stations until more effective long-range policies could be formulated. The freeze, however, was by no means complete. New AM stations still came on the air at a rate of approximately 100 a year, and in July 1964 the FCC brought to an end its freeze on new authorizations.

Radio Network Programming

In the years since 1952, the type of programming provided by radio networks and stations has changed almost completely.

Networks have lost their once-popular evening entertainment programs; most had disappeared by 1955 or 1956. Daytime network programs lasted a few years longer; around 1956, radio networks were still offering affiliates some daytime variety shows, audience-participation programs, daytime serials, and sponsored religious programs on Sunday mornings. Most of these left the air during the next few years; by 1960, almost the only conventional programs remaining on daytime schedules were ABC's *Breakfast Club*, the *Arthur Godfrey* program on CBS, a program or two of light music or chatter, some paid religious programs on Sundays, and a considerable number of news programs, most of them five minutes in length.

One network innovation that has proved at least moderately successful is the program form used in NBC's *Monitor*, a weekend combination of recorded music, news, and short features. Both CBS and ABC also provide a variety of short features to their affiliates, usually to be taped from the network line and inserted in local programs of recorded music. But network schedules today include little that resembles the type of entertainment programming provided for radio listeners during the 1930s and 1940s.

Local Radio Programming

During the early 1950s, stations affiliated with national radio networks still depended on the networks for most of their important programs. But as network programs went off the air, stations filled their daytime as well as their evening schedules with local programs of recorded music—the same types of programs already widely used by nonaffiliated stations. A few well-established "old line" stations did attempt to preserve some degree of program variety by scheduling local talk programs, audience-participation shows, or even daytime variety programs. But these attempts were usually not long continued; by the late 1950s probably 80 to 90 per cent of all radio stations were filling most of their program time with recorded music, interrupted at intervals by short capsule news summaries either taken from network lines or provided by the station itself. But stations did differ both in the type of music used and in the general manner of presentation. Most stations played nothing but current popular music—the "top 40" tunes of the week. Others made heavy use of "standards," or numbers popular in earlier years; still others featured "country and Western" music. Some large-city stations used highly paid "personalities" as disk jockeys and included almost as much "disk-jockey chatter" as actual music in each program; others permitted only a minimum of talk by announcers. Many of the "top 40" stations tried to be different and to attract listener attention by using a variety of "gimmicks" —special sound effects to identify news programs or to accompany station identification announcements, "lucky number" give-aways, organization of teen-age "record hops," shrill-voiced announcers, elaborate contests used as station promotion.

After 1957 or 1958, however, at least the beginning of a trend away from "top 40" popular music became evident. Many radio stations throughout the country began to aim their programs at various special audiences. A considerable number advertised themselves as "good music" stations, filling their schedules with show tunes, old "standards," and sometimes semi-classical or even classical music.

Some broadcasters gave special attention to farm audiences; many of these made heavy use of "country and Western" music in addition to expanding the time used for programs of farm information and weather reports. A considerable number identified themselves as "Negro-appeal" stations, with much or all of their programming aimed at the interests of colored listeners. Many stations gave increased emphasis to broadcasts of sports events and described themselves as "sports stations." Others expanded their local and national news coverage, and broadcast several 15-minute or 30-minute news presentations each day while continuing to give five minutes of "news on the hour." A few stations in major cities became "all-news" stations, filling their entire schedules with news broadcasts or news commentary—with varying degrees of success. A somewhat larger number became "all-talk" stations; in addition, at least one station in almost every major market introduced daily "all-talk" programs ranging from 60 minutes to as much as four hours in length, including telephoned questions from listeners directed at speakers appearing on programs. By 1962 or 1963, a few stations were even experimenting with dramatic programs; one or two syndication companies were supplying stations with taped or transcribed dramatizations based on scripts of old network radio "thrillers" or of once-popular daytime serials. It is difficult to characterize the radio programming of the early 1960s except to say that it was in a state of experimentation and change.

Many stations, of course, continued to use the "top 40" formula—in large cities, with few exceptions, the "top 40" stations attracted the largest audiences. However, by the middle 1960s local and national advertisers were beginning to be impressed by reports of various research organizations that audiences of "top 40" stations were made up largely of teen-agers and children. A Chicago report by Mediastat, for example, shows that during June 1965 the highest-rated station, using a "top 40" formula, was heard by an average of approximately 120,000 individuals during each hour of the broadcast day, of whom only 60,000 were 18 years of age or older. The second most popular station, offering a varied type of programming, attracted an average audience of only 87,000 individuals—but of this number, 85,000 were adults.

The Expansion of Television

While radio was facing difficulties after 1952, television was experiencing a period of rapid development in number of stations, in size of audience, and in annual network and station revenues. In April 1952, the Federal Communications Commission ended its freeze on the licensing of new television stations, at the same time releasing an allocations table indicating the channels that could be used for commercial or educational television stations in each of about 1,300 communities. Since it was evident that the twelve VHF (very high frequency) channels already in use could not accommodate the number of stations that might be needed in the future, the allocations table provided for use by television of an additional 70 channels in the UHF (ultra high frequency) band. One channel in each of some 240 communities was reserved for use of noncommercial educational stations; the remaining allocations were for stations to be operated on a commercial basis.

TABLE 5

BROADCASTING STATIONS IN OPERATION ON JANUARY FIRST OF EACH OF SIX SELECTED POSTWAR YEARS

	On January first					
	1946	1950	1954	1958	1962	1966
Radio stations[1]						
Standard AM stations						
Commercial	913	2051	2487	3156	3653	4018
Noncommercial	35	35	34	39	40	32
FM stations						
Commercial	48	733	560	537	960	1446
Noncommercial	6	48	112	141	194	269
Television stations[1]						
On VHF channels						
Commercial	6	97	228	408	461	491
Noncommercial	—	—	1	22	44	61
On UHF channels						
Commercial	—	—	121	84	84	107
Noncommercial	—	—	1	5	18	44

[1] Number of stations in each case includes those licensed and on the air plus those operating with construction permits.

Figures supplied by the Office of Reports and Information of the Federal Communications Commission.

New television stations. By 1952, television was established as potentially a very profitable type of business enterprise; consequently when the Commission's freeze ended, there was a rush to secure authorizations for new stations, especially in larger cities in which VHF channels were still available. Within a month of the date on which the freeze was ended, no less than 521 applications for new stations had been filed with the Federal Communications Commission, with many applicants competing for the same channel in most of the larger communities. By the end of the year, 17 new stations, including UHF stations, had gone on the air. By January 1954, there were 356 commercial television stations in operation, and almost 300 others had been authorized.[5] Expansion was less rapid thereafter, since the more desirable VHF channels in larger cities were already taken. However, by the beginning of 1960 there were 525 commercial television stations on the air, and by January 1966 a total of 598 stations, 107 of which were operating on UHF channels.

Both revenues and net profits of television networks and stations increased tremendously in the years following 1952. In 1956, television revenues from sale of time and from other sources totaled $897 million, as compared with the $324 million received by networks and stations in 1952, only four years earlier. Profits earned in 1956 were approximately $190 million, before federal taxes. For the year 1960, the television industry's total revenues had risen to $1.27 billion, and profits were approaching the $250 million figure. By 1964, industry revenues had increased still further; reports of the Federal Communications Commission showed network and station revenues for that year of almost $1.8 billion, and total operating profits had skyrocketed to more than $415 million.

Not all television stations shared in the industry's growing prosperity. Nearly all of the stations that had gone on the air before 1952 showed consistently high earnings; all were VHF stations, and with few exceptions they occupied the choice, large-city locations. But a considerable number of the newer stations found conditions less favorable. Some had gone on the air in large cities as fourth or fifth stations, too late to secure network affiliations—with only three national networks after 1955, only three outlets in any one community could be network affiliates. Others were located in very small markets in which the advertising potential was limited, a few of them in small cities with populations of no more than 30,000 or 40,000. Especially acute was the problem of the new UHF stations. Many had been constructed in small, one-station markets; others were usually forced to compete with VHF stations located in the same com-

---

[5] At the beginning of 1954 there were also two noncommercial educational stations on the air; one of the two, however, discontinued operation before the end of the year, and surrendered its license to the Communications Commission.

munities, and the relatively limited coverage of UHF outlets combined with the fact that only a small proportion of television receiving sets before 1964 had UHF tuning placed the UHF stations at a serious disadvantage. In fact, of the approximately 190 UHF commercial television stations that had gone on the air between 1952 and 1964, only about half were still in operation in January 1965. So even the usually profitable business of operating a television station has not always proved profitable; some stations have extremely high rates of earnings, but a considerable number of others have had financial problems.

Network developments.   For the first few years after 1952, television stations received program service from four networks: ABC, CBS, NBC, and DuMont. But the DuMont network—and to a lesser extent the American Broadcasting Company—encountered problems. During the early and middle 1950s only a half-dozen cities had more than three stations; many important markets had only two. The result was that NBC and CBS "captured" the most desirable stations, leaving ABC with few primary affiliates except in three-station markets; DuMont was placed in an even weaker position. Since DuMont had never been able to offer many sponsored programs (and none of the big, outstanding "audience-pleasers" other networks were providing), DuMont was never able to secure more than a few stations that were willing to carry its commercial schedule. Naturally, lack of stations made it difficult for DuMont to find advertisers willing to sponsor the programs the network could present. During the winter of 1953–54, DuMont was scheduling hardly more than a dozen sponsored programs a week; a year later, the number had dropped to only three or four. So after the spring of 1955, the DuMont company gave up its network activities entirely, leaving only three television networks in the field.

In 1953, the competitive position of the American Broadcasting Company's network was improved when the company merged with United Paramount Theaters, providing a much-needed increase in operating funds. But even since 1953, the ABC network has been at a disadvantage in lining up primary affiliates, although the steady increase in the number of major cities with three or more commercial stations has allowed ABC to secure stations in most of the country's important markets. In recent years ABC's position has been further improved by the popularity of programs included in its evening schedules. During the autumn of 1964, the ABC network for the first time caught up with its rivals in the average number of homes tuned to its evening programs each week, and although charges for time are still considerably lower than those of the other two chains (as a result of its smaller number of affiliates), the American Broadcasting Company has won a solid position as a national television network.

Further to strengthen the financial position of the American Broadcasting Company, arrangements were completed in the autumn of 1965 for a merger of ABC-Paramount Theaters with the International Telephone & Telegraph Corporation, a $2 billion concern, subject of course to approval by both the Federal Communications Commission and the Securities and Exchange Commission of the federal government.

Color television.   The development of color television has been the occasion for another type of network rivalry. During the period of the television freeze, the Federal Communications Commission asked manufacturers of television equipment to demonstrate the color systems they had developed. In 1950, the FCC gave official approval to the system proposed by the Columbia Broadcasting network, involving the use of a revolving color-disk both on cameras and on receiving sets. Unfortunately, the CBS system was not "compatible"—programs broadcast in color could not be received at all on black-and-white receiving sets. As a result, equipment manufacturers made no attempt to produce receiving sets using the CBS color system, and in the autumn of 1951 CBS gave up its efforts to secure industry and public acceptance of its color technique. The Radio Corporation of America, meanwhile, had continued to work on its own color system—one using electronic scanning and producing color programs which could be received in color on special color sets or in black and white on ordinary receiving sets. In 1953, the Federal Communications Commission gave official approval to the RCA method of providing color, and in November of that year the National Broadcasting Company—a company owned entirely by RCA—fed an experimental program in color from New York to the West Coast. Since 1954, NBC has provided a substantial number of color programs each week, both "specials" and programs carried on a regular series basis. During the season of 1964–65, the network was making an average of from 35 to 40 hours of color programming available to listeners each week and during the autumn was even broadcasting football games in color.

But the season 1965–66 was the one which marked the real breakthrough in the use of color by networks. Encouraged by the presence of color sets by early 1965 in nearly 3,000,000 American homes and by research reports showing that ratings of color programs were 80 per cent higher in homes with color sets than in black-and-white-set homes, the National Broadcasting Company announced in the summer of 1965 that all but two of the programs on its evening schedule, as well as a majority of its daytime offerings, would be presented in color. The other two networks, which had made little use of color in earlier years, were forced to follow the NBC lead; CBS in the autumn of 1965 was presenting nearly half of the programs on its evening schedule in color, and ABC used color for a little more than a third of its evening offerings.

Television Network Programs after 1952

No entirely new program forms have appeared on network television since 1952. However, some partially new patterns have been introduced that were not previously used on network radio. One was the "talk variety" form, combining rather lengthy interviews or talk features with variety materials, introduced in 1952 and used on NBC's *Today* and *Tonight* shows. Others were "live actuality" broadcasts and filmed documentaries carried on a series basis: NBC's Sunday afternoon *Wide, Wide World* program, introduced in 1955, and the CBS *Twentieth Century*, appearing two years later, were the earliest representatives of these types. Another form new at least from the standpoint of emphasis was what might be called "satire variety"; the one example was the series *That Was the Week That Was*, a network feature for two seasons starting in 1963. In addition, a modification of the adventure drama form was borrowed from radio and first introduced on television network schedules in the autumn of 1955: the "adult" Western, usually dealing more with human problems than with adventure as such.

Major program trends. As might be expected, many important changes have taken place in the extent of use of programs of different types on network schedules; Table 6 gives an idea of the nature of the changes that have taken place in network programming. As shown by the table, nondramatic children's programs, sports broadcasts, and sponsored talk programs have disappeared entirely from evening schedules; anthology drama has been largely replaced by general dramatic programs of the *Ben Casey* type, using the same leading characters in each broadcast. Crime-detective programs and adult Westerns reached a high point of popularity around 1960; since that year, the number carried on network schedules has been considerably reduced. Major gains since 1960 have been registered by general drama (already mentioned), variety programs, "talk" variety— as represented by NBC's *Tonight* show and its ABC counterpart in 1964 and 1965, *After Dark*—and motion picture feature films, now a regular part of network evening schedules. Time devoted to news has also increased, with two of the national networks expanding their early evening news broadcasts to 30 minutes. Quiz shows, panel shows, and audience participation programs have shown a consistent drop in evening use since 1955, although continuing as popular features on daytime schedules.

One major change in television network programming not shown in the table is the extent of the trend toward longer programs. In January 1955, the four networks then operating broadcast a total of 129 sponsored programs per week between 7:30 and 11:00 P.M.; aside from sports broadcasts, 14 of these programs were 60 minutes in length, 88 were half-hour programs, and 22, including news broadcasts, were only 15 minutes in length. Ten years later, the three national networks scheduled three two-hour programs each week—all motion picture feature film presentations—one 90-minute Western, 49 hour-long programs, and 45 programs (most of them situation comedies) 30 minutes in length. Between 7:30 and 11:00 at night, 15-minute

TABLE 6

QUARTER HOURS PER WEEK OF SPONSORED PROGRAMS OF MAJOR TYPES ON SCHEDULES OF TELEVISION NETWORKS

	January 1950	January 1955	January 1960	January 1965
Evenings, after 6 P.M.				
Variety programs	38	48	20	42
"Talk" variety	—	—	30	64
Musical variety, light music	19	14	22	22
Anthology drama	26	56	32	4
Other general drama	4	6	2	24
Crime-detective-mystery drama	12	24	46	28
Action-adventure drama	2	6	20	20
Adult Western drama	—	—	66	22
Situation comedy	6	56	34	66
Theatrical feature films	—	—	—	24
Quiz, panel, or game shows	25	42	26	10
News broadcasts	11	24	11	26
Talks, forum discussions	7	7	—	—
Documentaries, informative drama	—	6	10	8
Play-by-play sports broadcasts	21	22	8	—
Children's programs, cartoons	24	19	6	10
Total quarter hours	195	329	333	370
Daytime, Monday through Friday				
Daytime variety or music	—	70	20	10
"Talk" variety	—	80	40	40
General drama	—	—	20	10
Women's daytime serials	—	85	90	90
Reruns, filmed evening programs	—	—	70	100
Game shows, panels, human interest	10	80	120	120
News, 15 minutes or longer	—	—	—	10
Talks, miscellaneous	50	25	—	—
Children's programs	10	35	25	20
Total quarter hours	70	375	385	400

Figures for 1955, 1960 and 1965 based on sponsored programs listed in national Nielsen Television Index for months indicated; those for 1950 on sponsored programs listed in New York TV Nielsen-Ratings for January 1950.

programs had disappeared entirely from network schedules. The trend toward longer programs was undoubtedly related to the decline in sponsorship of programs by a single advertiser and the increasing use of multiple-sponsored or "participating" programs.

A second major trend in network programming since 1952 has been the increasing use of programs produced on film, as compared with "live" presentations. Particularly has this been true in the case of evening dramatic programs. Of the approximately 60 sponsored dramatic programs carried on evening network schedules in January 1952 only 18 were filmed programs, most of them of the action-adventure type that could not readily be produced in television studios. By 1960, practically all evening dramatic programs were on film. In addition, in recent years many of television's variety and musical offerings have been filmed presentations; the remainder, along with daytime serials and many network "game shows" and audience participation programs, have been presented by means of videotape recording. The extent of the trend away from "live" production is indicated by figures quoted in *Broadcasting Yearbook* for 1966: during the 1954–55 season, 85 per cent of all network hours were used to present "live" programs; by the spring of 1965, "live" presentations accounted for only 24 per cent of the networks' weekly schedules, with the remaining time divided equally between filmed programs and those recorded on videotape.

Other programming features.   Four other features of network television programming since 1952 deserve special mention. One is the rise and fall of "big-money" quiz programs over the period between 1955 and 1958. Programs like the *$64,000 Question* achieved tremendous popularity during their first two years on network schedules, but audiences decreased rapidly, and programs of that type disappeared from the air after the discovery in the summer of 1958 that contests on some of the programs had been "rigged" in advance. A second feature has been the increased use of special programs. In 1954, NBC broadcast the first of a long series of color "spectaculars"—a one-time musical comedy, *Satins and Spurs,* starring Betty Hutton. For the next few years, both NBC and CBS broadcast elaborate "spectacular" entertainment programs on a regularly scheduled basis. Since 1957, such "spectaculars" have been dropped from regular schedules; however, each of the national networks has made frequent use of one-time entertainment "specials" featuring the top stars of Broadway, Hollywood, and network television. In addition, networks have made extensive use of documentary programs; during the winter of 1961–62, five or six documentaries were presented in evening hours each week on a regularly scheduled basis. Since 1962, the trend has been away from the presentation of such programs in regular once-a-week series; however, the national television networks have usually managed to schedule a hundred or more documentary programs each year, in most cases as one-time "special" programs.

A third important trend in network television programming has been the increased use of theatrical feature films in evening schedules. The trend started in the autumn of 1961 when NBC inaugurated a weekly *Saturday Night at the Movies* program; in 1962 ABC followed suit with a Sunday-evening program. By 1965–66, feature films were being scheduled on four evenings a week, and network companies were paying rental fees of from $500,000 to $750,000 per picture for the features presented. To insure a supply of first-run films for its programs, CBS in December 1965 arranged with Warner Brothers to finance production of ten new theatrical features each year, budgeted at from a million dollars to $1.5 million per picture; the films so produced were to be shown in motion picture theaters as well as on the network's programs.

A fourth conspicuous feature of network programming in recent years has been the tremendous increase in the broadcasting of sports events on Saturday and Sunday afternoons. Boxing and wrestling, popular as evening offerings in the early days of network television, have disappeared entirely as network features; indeed, no regular broadcasts of sports events have been included in recent evening schedules. But each of the television networks has filled several hours of Saturday or Sunday afternoon time each week with broadcasts of major-league baseball, of college or professional football games, and of professional golf and bowling tournaments, with a variety of minor sports ranging from curling to European sports car "rallies" thrown in for good measure.

Local Station Programming

The types of programs provided by individual television stations have reflected the changes in the availability of network and syndicated programs. Around 1950 or 1952, networks offered their affiliates a reasonably full schedule of sponsored evening programs but only a limited number of sponsored daytime shows. Stations as a result had to depend on local live programs and syndicated materials to fill half or more of their total broadcasting hours. But by the middle 1950s, network offerings had substantially increased; on weekdays during the winter of 1962–63, NBC was providing its affiliates nearly 13 hours of sponsored programs a day, CBS nearly twelve hours, and ABC approximately nine hours. Until 1958 or 1960, the supply of syndicated materials available to stations also increased; in recent years, however, few new filmed television series have been produced for syndication, and the backlog of theatrical feature films available for first-run showing by stations is rapidly becoming exhausted.

Surveys of station programming published in *Broadcasting Yearbook* for 1966 suggest the extent of changes that have taken place in the materials included in station schedules. In December 1953, network-affiliated stations were on the air for an average of 80 hours a week; of this total, 39 hours represented network programs, 14 hours were devoted to showings of theatrical feature films, 9 hours were used for other syndicated filmed materials, and stations produced nearly 17 hours a week of local live programs. In June 1960, average broadcasting hours had increased to 108 each week, of which 68 hours were used to present network programs. Use of syndicated filmed or taped programs had also increased to 28 hours a week; only 12 hours a week represented local programming. In June 1965, average hours on the air had increased to 119 each week, with 75 hours of network programming included in the schedule. Syndicated materials represented some 29 hours a week and an average of between 15 and 16 hours a week were devoted to programs produced locally.

So television stations in 1965 were still supplying approximately the same number of hours of local programming each week as during 1953 or 1954. And for the most part, there has been little change in recent years in the types of local programs provided. Nearly every station schedules at least two local news programs a day, Monday through Friday; many have increased the length of at least one daily news program to 30 minutes. Weather information is still important, and most stations offer separate sports news summaries once or twice a day. Some stations have farm information programs, usually scheduled before eight o'clock in the morning; a much larger number present daily "women's interest" local programs, although the "kitchen" programs of earlier years are no longer extensively used. Nearly all stations devote from 30 minutes to an hour of time a day to programs intended for younger children; clowns and puppets are still widely used, and many of the children's programs include short filmed cartoon features or other short filmed subjects. In recent years, a considerable number of stations have experimented with "live" locally produced daytime variety shows on a daily or weekly basis; a few others carry local ad-lib dramatic courtroom programs; a somewhat larger number carry programs featuring interviews with local people or with important visitors to the community. But the expansion in network programming, together with the fact that a considerable amount of syndicated material is available, has resulted in a reduction in the proportion of time, although not in the actual number of hours per week, devoted to local live programs on television.

5

THE BUSINESS OF BROADCASTING

Under the system of private ownership and operation of broadcasting stations that exists in the United States, broadcasting is a business undertaking. The licensee of a broadcasting station is a businessman. Like other businessmen, he naturally hopes to make a profit on his broadcasting operations; in any case, he must at least break even financially to stay in business. If radio or television stations fail to earn enough money to meet their expenses, sooner or later they will be forced to go off the air.

The business character of broadcasting is somewhat unusual in our economic society. Unlike other business enterprises, the broadcasting station "gives away" its primary product—programs—to be "consumed" by listeners who pay nothing whatever to the station for the privilege of listening to or watching the programs presented. The listener, as a result, is not really the broadcaster's "customer" at all, nor are broadcast programs the major commodity the station has for sale.

RADIO AND TELEVISION ADVERTISING

Advertising is the lifeblood of broadcasting. From advertising come practically all of the revenues needed to operate stations and networks and to pay the costs of programs that stations put on the air. The broadcaster's real customer is not the listener, but the *advertiser* who wishes to bring his wares to the attention of the public; the only commodity the broadcaster has to sell is *time*—time in the station's daily schedule. The advertiser merely buys the *use* of a station's or a network's facilities for specified periods of time, and uses the time he buys to bring his advertising message to the attention of listeners. Sometimes he buys sufficient time to present an entire program; more often, he buys only time enough for an advertising announcement one minute or less in length.

But a station's time is valueless unless that station has listeners. So the station presents programs to attract a listening audience. For practical purposes it might be said that the broadcaster is engaged in two separate enterprises: one, providing a free program service for the benefit of the nonpaying public, and the other, selling time in his schedule to advertisers to pay for this free service. Since each of these enterprises involves somewhat different procedures, it seems appropriate to examine them separately, looking first at the ways in which advertising is handled on radio or television.

Types of Broadcast Advertising

Some of the advertisers who buy time on networks or stations are big concerns, with products marketed in every part of the United States. Others are small, with operations limited to a single community. On the basis of the size of the area to be reached and the manner in which advertising time is purchased, broadcast advertising falls into three general classifications, all referred to in earlier chapters. First we have *network advertising*—advertising carried over the facilities of a network made up of a number of different stations linked together for the simultaneous broadcasting of the same program in a number of different communities. The second type of broadcast advertising is that known as *national* (or regional) *spot advertising*— that placed by a single advertiser on stations in a number of different markets, but not using network facilities. The advertiser using "national spot" may buy time for complete programs on the stations used or merely for the presentation of spot announcements. The term "spot" advertising comes from the fact that the advertiser selects the markets to be reached and the stations he wants to use, and so is able to "spot" his advertising in the particular areas where he thinks it will do the most good. Network and national spot advertisers are necessarily those big concerns whose products are distributed on a national or a regional basis. The small Main Street merchant who sells only to customers in a single city buys time only on his home town station; the advertising carried in his behalf falls into the third category, that of *local advertising*.

Local advertising is highly important in the radio broadcasting industry. In 1964, of a total of $764 million spent by advertisers for radio time, 64 per cent or nearly $489 million represented expenditures by local advertisers, as compared with 30 per cent spent by national spot advertisers and only 6 per cent spent for network advertising. However, a different situation exists in television. Advertisers spent approximately $1,549,000,000 in 1964 for time on television networks and stations—double the amount which went for radio time—and of this total only 19 per cent came from local advertisers. Network advertising accounted for 36 per cent of all sales of television time, and the remaining 45 per cent represented expenditures for national spot advertising.

Types of Program Sponsorship

Advertising time on radio and television may be purchased in units of varying length. Stations commonly divide the time they offer for sale into two classifications: program time, in units of five minutes or more, permitting the presentation of a com-

plete program, and announcement time, in units of two minutes
or less—usually no more than a single minute—suitable for the
presentation of a commercial message.

An advertiser who buys program time and presents an
entire program is said to "sponsor" that program. Three forms
of sponsorship are in fairly common use today:

Regular or single sponsorship—in which a single advertiser
pays the entire cost of presenting a program or a program
series.

Dual or alternating-week sponsorship [1]—in which two different advertisers share the costs of a program series, usually
with one paying the costs of presenting the program one
week and the other assuming the costs the following week.

Participating sponsorship—in which a number of different
advertisers "participate" in the sponsorship of a single program, the program including a separate commercial message for each of the advertisers involved.

In regular or dual sponsorship the advertiser pays the cost
of producing the program, as well as buying the time the program occupies on the station or the network schedule. In both
forms the advertiser is closely identified with the program he
sponsors. Participating sponsorship, in a technical sense, is not
really "sponsorship" at all; the advertiser does not pay the costs
of producing the program, but merely buys time for the presentation of one of the commercial announcements *within* the program. Program production costs, as noted earlier, are paid by
the station or network on which the program is carried.

During recent years there has been a decided trend away
from single sponsorship of programs. In the days before television, practically all radio network programs were presented on
a single-sponsorship basis; the same was true on network television during the early 1950s. But rising costs of programs and
increased charges for network time have produced tremendous

---

[1] Sometimes termed "split" sponsorship. There are many variations
of such "shared-sponsorship" arrangements. The "alternating-week" form
has been most prevalent in network television. A popular form in local
radio and television is alternate-day sponsorship of five-or-six-days-a-week
series such as newscasts, weather, and sports.

changes in patterns of sponsorship of television programs. Table 7 suggests the extent of these changes in evening network sched-

TABLE 7

EVENING TELEVISION NETWORK PROGRAMS WITH DIFFERENT TYPES OF SPONSORSHIP DURING THREE SELECTED SEASONS[1]

Type of sponsorship	Season 1951–52		Season 1957–58		Season 1963–64	
	Pgms pr wk	Total hours	Pgms pr wk	Total hours	Pgms pr wk	Total hours
Single sponsorship	81	46.0	51	29.0	8	5.5
Dual or alternating	6	4.0	45	23.0	25	13.0
Participating programs	6	5.5	9	8.5	42	43.0

[1] Only programs 30 minutes or more in length are included, and only those broadcast every week between hours of 7:30 and 11:00 P.M.

Figures compiled from network schedules in *Broadcasting* and *Sponsor* magazines.

ules. One reason for the decreased use of single sponsorship is obvious; in 1951–52, production costs of evening network programs averaged only about $28,000 for each hour of programming; in 1957–58 the figure was $70,000; in 1963–64 it had risen to nearly $120,000; and in 1965–66 costs per hour were nearly $137,000. Charges for network time had increased in proportion. In 1951–52 the one-time rate for a 60-minute evening period on the NBC network of 62 stations was a little less than $50,000; in 1965–66 the charge for an hour's time on NBC's full 201-station network had jumped to more than $145,000. With costs of program sponsorship so tremendously increased, only a few network advertisers can afford to carry the full load of presenting a network program, week after week; multiple sponsorship has been the only feasible method of dealing with the problem.

Almost all daytime network programs on television are also handled on a multiple-sponsorship basis. And trends in sponsorship on individual television stations have followed the same patterns as those on national networks. In radio, of course, participating sponsorship and participation programs were widely used even before the advent of television; aside from news broadcasts and occasional short features, few programs on radio stations today are sponsored by single advertisers.

Spot Announcements

The second category of time sales on radio and television involves the sale of periods of a minute or less for presentation of spot announcements. Originally, "spot announcements" referred to the commercial messages scheduled in station-break periods between programs; announcements within programs were simply "commercials" if the program was sponsored, or "participating announcements" if messages for several sponsors were included in the same program. In recent years, however, such distinctions are rarely made; a "spot" or "spot announcement" today may refer to any announcement sold independently of a program, whether inserted in a multiple-sponsorship program or in the "break" between programs.

Spot announcements come in a variety of shapes and sizes. On radio, those for local advertisers are usually "live" announcements read by a station announcer. National spot advertisers usually provide their spot announcements to stations in the form of "ETs"—electrical transcriptions, on disks—or recorded on audio tape. On television stations, spots for local advertisers may be presented "live" with the announcer on camera, or with the announcer unseen while pictures or printed words are thrown on the television screen. Some of the more important local advertisers have their commercial messages produced on film. Spot announcements used in national spot advertising campaigns are almost always produced on film, as are the great majority of the announcements used in television network programs. Most radio spots are 60 seconds—110 to 120 words—in length; however, much shorter announcements are sometimes used in connection with time signals or brief weather reports. Television announcements come in lengths ranging from ten seconds up to one minute; occasionally longer announcements are used, particularly on single-sponsored network programs. In recent years there has been widespread use of "piggyback" commercials—the inclusion in a one-minute filmed announcement of two segments, each advertising a different product produced by the same company. A popular form of television advertising used largely by local advertisers is the eight-second "ID" or station identification commercial; visual commercial material shares the screen with station call letters or the station's channel number. Sometimes spoken material is also included.

Radio and television stations are required by FCC regulations to give station identification announcements at regular intervals. To allow enough time for these identifications, the practice developed in the early days of network radio of shortening each network program by 30 seconds. Since the identification itself could be given in only a few seconds, this made time available for the inclusion, at each "chain break" or "station break," of a short spot announcement. All programs on television are similarly shortened, whether network presentations, filmed syndicated programs, or programs produced locally; the "station breaks" between programs are used to present spot announcements as well as station identifications. At certain times during the day and evening, television networks make 70-second "breaks" between programs, so that the affiliated station can insert a full-length 60-second spot as well as the usual 8-second ID announcement in the "break" period. Usually, however, the "break" between network television programs is either 30 seconds or 40 seconds in length; as a result, "station break" announcements are usually of the 10-second, 20-second, or 30-second types, depending on the number inserted in the "station break" period.

But both on radio stations and on television, the greatest use of spot announcements is *within* participating programs, and in these programs the 60-second commercial announcement is nearly always used. Aside from newscasts, almost all of the commercial programs on radio stations are of the participating-sponsorship type. Television stations offer many local or syndicated programs of types especially well adapted to the inclusion of participating announcements—homemakers' programs, children's programs, presentations of theatrical feature films, and broadcasts of sports events. These, like many of the longer variety and dramatic programs on network television schedules, are often referred to as "spot vehicles" or "spot carriers," since they are so well suited to the inclusion of spot announcements for a number of different advertisers.

No recent figures are available as to the proportion of total station revenues that come from the sale of spot announcements, and the amount derived from sale of program time. However, the Television Bureau of Advertising estimates that during the year 1961, nearly seven-eighths of all money spent for national spot advertising on television went for the purchase of spot announcement time. Only a small fraction of this total—possibly 11 per cent—represented expenditures for chain-break commercials. The remainder was spent for one-minute announcements placed in local participating programs. In local television advertising, as opposed to national spot, a somewhat larger proportion of money spent goes for sponsorship of complete programs; chain-break announcements are also more popular with local than with national advertisers. Television networks find sale of spot announcements their major source of revenue, since participating programs or "spot carriers" fill at least 80 per cent of the networks' evening schedules and from 90 to 95 per cent of all network daytime hours.

The National Advertiser

Although it is estimated that at least 13,000 business concerns market their products on a national or regional scale, not all of these companies engage in large-scale advertising. In 1961, approximately 400 companies bought time on national television networks; about one hundred of these concerns accounted for four-fifths of all expenditures for network advertising. In the same year, however, nearly 4,000 different companies engaged in national spot advertising on television, although not more than 1,500 of them spent as much as $20,000 each for television time. Two-thirds of all of the money spent for network television advertising goes for programs or announcements scheduled during evening hours. In national spot advertising, on the other hand, more than half of all expenditures go for advertising carried during the daytime.

Most of the money spent by national advertisers is used to promote the sale of low-cost, mass-consumption types of goods. The Television Bureau of Advertising reports that in 1962 more than $300 million was spent for network or national spot television advertising by producers of foods and grocery products; another $190 million went for the advertising of cosmetics and toilet preparations. Next in importance came drugs, tobaccos, and laundry products. Since many companies produce and market a wide variety of products, all of which must be brought to the attention of the public by advertising, a few major corporations spend fantastic amounts of money for television advertising each year. Procter & Gamble, the largest buyer of television time, spent nearly $150 million for television time in 1964 to promote the sale of more than 50 different brand items, from soaps and cleaning preparations to cake mixes and peanut butter.

Every national advertiser has a different marketing problem; he attempts to use broadcasting in the way best suited to his special needs and objectives. He is concerned with the problem of geographical coverage, to see that his advertising reaches every major community in which his product is offered for sale. Obviously the use of network time has many advantages. The advertiser is assured of full national coverage with a minimum of effort. On the other hand, if his product is not distributed equally throughout all sections of the country, the advertiser may find national spot advertising more satisfactory, although the problem of buying time on a large number of individual stations is much more complicated than that of buying a segment of time on a national network. The advertiser must decide which markets he wishes to reach, which station or stations to use in each market, and how much money he should spend on advertising on each of the stations selected.

Even when network advertising is used, there are a variety of factors to be considered. In 1965 or 1966, single sponsorship of an evening 30-minute television program on NBC or CBS would cost the advertiser approximately $140,000 a week —about $65,000 for production costs for the program, and slightly less than $75,000 for network time, after allowance for the usual discounts. On ABC, the weekly cost would be somewhat less, since that network could offer fewer stations. In a half-hour program, the advertiser would be allowed three minutes of time for commercial announcements; consequently, the cost would be in the neighborhood of $45,000 for each commercial minute. During the same season, the rate for insertion of a one-minute spot in an evening participating program would be somewhere between $35,000 and $60,000, depending on the popularity of the program; *Sponsor* magazine estimated the average cost of participating spots at between $40,000 and $42,000.[2] So the advertiser would have to decide whether to sponsor his own program, or to spend his money for announcements in network participating programs. Naturally, much would depend on what program or programs might be available for sponsorship, and in what participating programs spot announcement time was available for purchase. But whether he would finally decide to sponsor a separate program, to buy participations in a network program, or to use national spot advertising, the national advertiser who uses television must continually make decisions as to how best to spend his money.

The Local Advertiser

The owner of a business concern that serves only a single community does his radio or television advertising on a local basis. It is impossible to make more than a rough estimate of the number of local business establishments that buy local advertising time on radio or television each year, but the number must be close to half a million, scattered in markets throughout the United States. Some are regular, year-round advertisers; many others use the broadcasting media only during certain seasons of the year. Although some department stores and local drug or grocery chains spend substantial amounts of money for radio and television advertising, most local advertisers operate with decidedly limited budgets, especially as compared with those of companies that sell their products on a national scale.

But although the amount of money involved is relatively small, the local retail merchant must make the same basic de-

---

[2] Illustrating the variation in amounts charged for spot announcements in network programs, CBS during the autumn of 1965 received $60,000 each for one-minute spots in its Sunday afternoon broadcasts of National Football League football games; however, spots of the same length in pregame shows were sold for $27,500 each. One-minute announcements in the broadcast of the NFL championship game at the end of the season brought $110,000 each.

cisions as the national advertiser in his efforts to get the maximum results for the money he has to spend. He may sponsor a program or buy spot announcements; he may buy time on television or on radio; he may use two or three stations in his market or spend his money for time on a single station; he may spread his advertising budget fairly evenly over a 52-week period or concentrate his expenditures for station time during the month or two of each year offering the greatest sales potential for his products. He must also decide how much of his total budget should go for broadcast advertising and how much should be spent on billboards or direct mail or for space in the local newspaper. In one respect, of course, the local advertiser has a tremendous advantage over the concern that operates on a national scale: he has a first-hand acquaintance with the local market and a much more intimate knowledge of the relative values of the stations that serve the market, and as a result is usually able to plan his advertising more intelligently than the larger company located in a city a thousand miles away.

Many retailers, too, benefit from *dealer cooperative* [3] advertising allowances offered by national manufacturers of the brands the retailers handle. It has been estimated that as much as one-fifth of all local advertising on radio and television involves some dealer "co-op" plan under which a national manufacturer or a regional distributor pays a part of the cost of the time used by the retailer on the local station. A major reason for the widespread use of the dealer cooperative device is that most radio stations and almost all television stations charge a considerably higher rate for national spot advertising than the amount charged for an equal amount of time used by a local advertiser. Consequently, the national manufacturer of Brand X can secure the same advertising benefits at a considerably lower cost if station time to advertise Brand X is purchased by the local merchant who distributes the product instead of being

---

[3] Not to be confused with network "cooperative" or "co-op" advertising, in which network-produced programs are fed to affiliates over network lines with the express understanding that each affiliate is permitted to sell the program to a local advertiser, and to insert that local sponsor's advertising message in the program as it is broadcast locally. Each station that sells the program to a local sponsor is expected to pay the network a small amount to help pay the program's production costs; this charge is, of course, passed on by the station to the local sponsor of the program.

bought by the manufacturer himself as part of a national advertising campaign. Use of dealer "co-op" advertising also has the advantage of tying in local advertising efforts with national campaigns and of stimulating local retailers to do more advertising of the goods they have for sale than might otherwise be done. On the other hand, dealer "co-op" advertising has the disadvantage of being available to the local merchant only if he advertises in a certain way at a certain specified time, in most cases using advertising copy supplied by the manufacturer. Major users of co-op plans in television are manufacturers of automobiles and of home furnishings and appliances, but co-op arrangements are common to nearly every type of manufacturer of brand name merchandise.

The Machinery of Sales of Time

Every spot announcement or sponsored program, whether it is presented in behalf of a local advertiser, a national spot advertiser, or an advertiser using a national network, comes ultimately to the local television or radio station to be put on the air. The process of getting that spot or that program to the station follows one of four distinct routes, as indicated in Figure 1. Local time sales may be handled directly by the local advertiser and the station with no intermediaries involved; a member of the station's sales staff calls on the advertiser and sells him the time. Or, sometimes the local advertiser is a larger concern employing a local advertising agency to buy newspaper space or broadcasting time; in that case, the sale of time is handled through the advertising agency.

But the buying of national spot or network time is a more complex affair, involving many stations in a number of different cities. Almost all national advertisers employ large national advertising agencies to look after their advertising interests. Stations, of course, are not usually able to have their own sales employees call on national advertisers or agencies located in cities from coast to coast, and so each station employs the services of a national station-representative concern [4] to act as its

---

[4] Functions performed by advertising agencies and station representative companies are explained in greater detail later in this chapter.

sales representative in selling time to national advertisers planning national spot advertising campaigns. So in national spot
advertising, two intermediary organizations are used: an advertising agency representing the advertiser, and a station-representative company working on behalf of the station. If the
advertiser buys network time, the advertising agency deals with

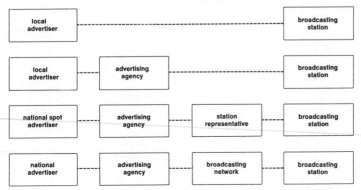

Figure 1. The four processes followed in the purchase of broadcast time.

the network organization, and the network in turn reserves the
necessary time on stations affiliated with the network. No station-
representative concern is involved, but there are still two intermediaries between the advertiser and the station that carries
the advertising message.

Selection of commercial programs.   Of course, the sale of time
does not complete the process of putting advertising on the
air. When a program is sponsored, the advertiser pays the cost
of station or network time; in addition, he also pays the costs
of producing the sponsored program. In local advertising or
national spot advertising, any locally produced, sponsored program is usually planned and developed by the station itself;
the station handles production, and the sponsor pays the bills
in addition to paying the costs of station time. In most cases,
syndicated filmed programs carried on television stations are
selected and contracted for by the station's program director;
then the station's sales staff tries to find an advertiser to sponsor
the program and pay costs of renting the film as well as the

cost of station time. When a local participating program is offered, whether a disk-jockey program on radio or a feature film series on television, the station selects or produces the program and pays all program costs; however, the rates charged for spot announcements are set at a level high enough to cover both costs of presenting the program and costs of station time, assuming that all or most of the available "participations" or spots in the program are sold to advertisers.

Network television programs are handled in much the same way as local commercial programs. The advertiser sometimes selects the program he wishes to sponsor from those offered for his approval by a network or by independent program-production agencies, pays a stipulated weekly amount to cover production costs, and merely buys time from the network company to put the program on the air. More often the network company makes the selection, or itself produces the program, and then tries to find an advertiser to sponsor the program and pay its production costs each week as well as the network's charges for time. The network participating programs or "spot carriers," which fill perhaps 80 per cent of every television network's evening schedules—as well as practically all of its daytime hours on weekdays—are always produced or selected by the network itself, and as in the case of local participating programs, production costs are borne by the network.

Commercial announcements.   One other element in broadcast advertising remains to be considered—the commercial announcement that carries the advertising message. In smaller communities, announcements for local advertisers are often written, without extra charge, by continuity departments of the stations over which the announcements are to be broadcast. This is especially true in the case of radio, where copy for the local merchant is read over the air by one of the station's staff announcers. But in larger cities and on national networks, advertisers supply the commercials at their own expense. Occasionally a television station will produce filmed or taped announcements for a local advertiser using its facilities; more often the copy is written and the announcements produced by a local advertising agency. In either case, production costs are paid by the advertiser. The program commercials and spot announcements used in network advertising and in national spot campaigns are always planned and written by advertising agencies, and in the case of television advertising, the actual filmed production of the announcements is either handled by the advertising agency itself or by a concern that specializes in producing filmed advertising materials. Naturally, the advertising agency is paid for the service it performs in the preparation of announcements used.

THE BROADCASTING INDUSTRY

In addition to networks and broadcasting stations, literally thousands of other business concerns are involved in the process of providing radio and television programs for American listeners. Many of these companies were organized during the late 1920s or early 1930s to meet the special needs of radio. Others were developed as parts of the motion picture industry and have broadened their activities to include functions related to television. Probably an even greater number have come into existence in more recent years to provide services connected with the expanding television industry. The business of broadcasting includes concerns engaging in specialized activities that range from the construction of antenna towers to the production and filming of commercial announcements.

Radio and Television Stations

At the base of the broadcasting industry pyramid, of course, are the radio and television broadcasting stations—the concerns actually broadcasting and delivering programs by wireless to the millions of homes with radio or television receiving sets. There are more than six thousand broadcasting stations on the air today—AM radio stations, FM stations, and television stations. Most are commercial, but about 400 are educational stations operated on a noncommercial basis. More than 70 per cent of the commercial FM stations are licensed to owners of AM stations in the same community, and a majority of these FM stations transmit, at least during some hours each day, the same programs that are broadcast by the AM stations with which they are associated. With these exceptions, every FM or AM radio station and every television station is a separate operating entity with its own staff of employees, its own equipment, and its own problems in attempting to provide programs for the community in which it is located.

Auxiliary television broadcasting services. A more complete discussion of the operations of broadcasting stations is provided in the following chapter. In addition to conventional broadcasting stations, however, several types of auxiliary services are currently being used to extend the coverage of television stations. In 1955, the Federal Communications Commission authorized the first "satellite" television station; ten years later, approximately 30 television "satellites" were in operation. These are regularly authorized stations, occupying channels allocated by the Communications Commission to their respective communities and using as much power as the amount used by other television stations. They are not required, however, to originate local programs or to maintain studios, although some of them do provide a limited amount of local programming. For the most part, the satellite merely reproduces the signal and the programming of a parent station located in a different community 80 or 100 miles away, thus increasing the effective coverage of the parent station, and bringing television service to communities too small to afford an independent television operation.

Since 1956 the FCC has also authorized the operation of "translator" stations. Translators pick up the signals of regular television stations and rebroadcast them on a different channel. They use very low-powered, inexpensive equipment; they maintain no studios and originate no program materials; they are not even required to have an engineer in attendance while on the air. Many translators are operated by regular television stations to extend the coverage of the parent station over a larger area. Others have been constructed by nonprofit groups to bring television service to small communities. Since 1963, more than 1,500 translator stations have been in operation—over 600 of them in the states of Colorado, Montana, Utah, and Wyoming alone.

A third type of auxiliary television service is provided by

"booster" or "repeater" stations. These are even less expensive to construct and operate than translator stations and serve substantially the same purpose of extending the coverage of a regular station over a larger area, or providing service in so-called "shadow areas" where reception is impaired by mountainous terrain. A "booster" station operates, usually with very low power, on the same frequency used by the parent television station; since the Federal Communications Commission in past years has allowed boosters to be used only by stations on UHF channels and very few UHF stations operate in mountainous areas, boosters are less widely used than translator stations.

Community antenna television services.   Another device for extending the area over which television service is available is the CATV, or community antenna television system. A CATV company erects a tall tower capable of picking up signals of television stations in cities from 60 to 100 miles away from the community in which the CATV system is located; frequently microwave relays are used to bring in programs from even more distant stations. The signals so received are fed to homes of subscribers by means of coaxial cables; for a monthly fee ranging usually from $4.00 to $6.00, subscribers can receive the television programs picked up by the CATV antenna. A typical CATV system serves from 800 to 2,000 homes, and offers viewers a choice of the programs supplied by from three or four to as many as a dozen different television stations. Originally, community antenna companies confined their operations to small communities with no local television stations. Starting in 1964, however, CATV systems were set up in a number of major cities in which the nature of the terrain or the number of tall buildings interfered with reception of the signals of local television stations. At the beginning of 1965, an estimated 1.78 million homes were receiving service from the approximately 1,600 CATV systems then in operation; several of the CATVs are located in cities with one or more local television stations. In some cases, two or more antenna companies serve different residential areas in the same city.

Most of the CATV companies have secured franchises from local city governments, and prior to 1965 no attempt was made by the federal government to regulate the antenna systems. Since CATVs do not "broadcast"—their programs are delivered to subscribers' homes by wire and not by radio—and since their activities are not interstate, they were considered as not falling within the area over which the Federal Communications Commission has jurisdiction. In fact, after making a special investigation of community antenna operations, the Commission in 1959 issued a formal report stating that, under the Communications Act of 1934, it had no power to regulate the antenna systems. But as the number of community antenna companies increased, the Commission became concerned with the effects of CATV competition on the economic well-being of television stations located in small one-station communities. As a result, in April 1965 the Federal Communications Commission adopted formal rules relating to the operations of antenna systems that receive television signals by use of microwave relay links—such relays of course being a form of radio transmission—and also announced its intention to control use of programs by other CATV systems. As a result, community antenna companies are now subject to some degree of regulation by the Federal Communications Commission.

Radio and Television Networks

Activities of national networks will be treated at length in the following chapter, but a distinction between the various types of networks may be made at this point. Technically, the term "network" refers to any group of radio or television stations linked together by telephone land lines or microwave relay systems for the simultaneous broadcasting of programs. However, the term is used more loosely to apply to any grouping of stations making possible the broadcasting of the same program or programs by all stations in the group, regardless of the method by which the programs are distributed. Accordingly, we find a variety of types of "networks" in the broadcasting industry: national networks, regional networks, special networks, or sometimes transcription or film networks.

National networks. By far the most important in volume of sales, in program service provided, and in influence, are the *national* networks. There are four national commercial network organizations, of which three are engaged in both radio and television network operation: ABC, the American Broadcasting Company; CBS, the Columbia Broadcasting System; and NBC, the National Broadcasting Company. The fourth national network company, MBS or the Mutual Broadcasting System, is concerned only with radio.

As Robert E. Kintner, former president of NBC, once remarked, a network is "nothing but programs and telephone wires." While this greatly oversimplifies the situation, a network company does no actual *broadcasting* of programs—at least not in its activities as a *network*; national network companies do own broadcasting stations, referred to as "O & O" or "owned-and-operated" stations. The network company's function is to create an organization of stations that will operate as a group and to provide facilities for linking those stations together for simultaneous broadcast of programs. For radio service, long-distance telephone lines are leased from the American Telephone & Telegraph Company to connect affiliated stations with network studios in New York, Washington, or other cities from which network programs are originated. For television, stations are linked together by coaxial cable or microwave relay systems, also provided by A.T.&T. Network programs are then "fed" over these wire or relay connections to the various affiliated stations, to be broadcast in each local community.

A listing of national networks would also include NET, or National Educational Television, the organization that provides programs to educational television stations, and the National Association of Educational Broadcasters, which supplies taped programs to educational radio stations. Neither is an "interconnected" network using telephone lines to link affiliates together for simultaneous broadcasting of programs; the filmed or taped programs provided by each organization are sent to member stations by mail or express.

Regional networks. In addition to national network organizations, there are at least 12 or 15 more or less permanent regional television networks and perhaps five times as many regional networks of radio stations. A few of these are actively functioning organizations that provide a regular—though usually limited—

program service on a year-round basis. Others are groups of stations operating as networks only when advertisers wish to secure coverage of a number of markets in a single state or even a portion of a state, Several are so-called "sports networks" or "baseball networks," active only during the baseball or football season; in 1965, a dozen such networks provided coverage of major-league baseball games to more than 100 television stations, while play-by-play accounts of the same games were carried by more than 650 radio stations comprising 19 regional radio networks. A few of the more important regional nets are parts of national network organizations; for instance, the Yankee radio network covering the New England states is a part of the Mutual Broadcasting System, and the CBS West Coast television network is made up of stations owned by or affiliated with the Columbia Broadcasting System. Because stations comprising these permanent regional groups are already linked together to form "legs" of national networks, it is a relatively simple matter for them to provide service for regional advertisers on stations in a specified area in the same way that the national network carries programs for national advertisers on stations throughout the country.

Special networks. Custom-built or "special" networks may be created at times for national or regional spot advertisers who wish to present a program in a particular group of cities where no permanent regional net exists to provide the service desired. Such special networks are set up in most states during political campaigns to carry programs in support of individual candidates for state office. Sometimes, too, stations join together in setting up special temporary networks to secure coverage of major news or sports events of particular interest to listeners in their respective communities. By sharing time charges and the expense of originating the program, it is possible for even the smallest stations to broadcast eye-witness accounts of events taking place in distant cities, although the cost of providing such accounts might be prohibitive for any single station.

Transcription and film networks. National networks, regional networks, even special networks are literally "networks" or "chains" of stations; the stations composing them are linked together by telephone line or microwave relay for simultaneous broadcast of programs. Transcription and film networks are technically not "networks" at all, since stations are not connected by telephone lines or microwave relay systems and since no simultaneous broadcasting of programs is involved. But the transcription and film network companies do serve groups of "affiliated" stations, primarily as central sales agencies through which sponsored programs may be placed with the various affiliated outlets—the programs being prepared in taped, transcribed, or filmed form and distributed to the stations by parcel post or by express prior to the time of broadcast. Only one regularly constituted commercial transcription network is in existence: the Keystone Broadcasting System, with more than 1,000 "affiliated" radio stations, located for the most part in small towns and agricultural areas throughout the nation. With the reduced importance of national radio networks, Keystone in recent years has received considerable attention from national spot advertisers interested in reaching rural listeners.

One television film network, National Telefilm Associates, was in operation for a few years, attempting to provide a limited quantity of filmed programming to affiliates in a number of major markets. But difficulties in clearing time for NTA programs on stations whose evening schedules were already committed to the regular national networks resulted in the failure of the project. Noninterconnected networks have been more successful in the educational field; the National Association of Educational Broadcasters, referred to in an earlier paragraph, inaugurated a taped program service for educational radio stations as early as 1950, and the foundation-financed National Educational Television organization provides several hours a week of filmed programs for use by noncommercial television stations.

American Telephone & Telegraph Company

Distribution of "regular" network programs is the special province of the long-lines division of the American Telephone & Telegraph Company and its associated Bell System companies. More than $200 million has been invested by A.T.&T. in program transmission facilities—coaxial cable connections, microwave relay systems, and special long-distance telephone lines—and the company collects annual rentals ranging from $36 million to more than $40 million from the three national television networks for carrying their programs to affiliated stations, plus an additional $8–10 million a year from national radio networks. Costs of cable or microwave interconnection are an important part of the television networks' expense of providing program service to affiliated stations, averaging approximately $6,000 per month for each television network affiliate.

Equipment Manufacturers

The manufacturing of equipment—receiving sets, transmitters, television cameras, technical equipment of a thousand different kinds—is a fundamental part of the broadcasting industry. The statement has been made that the rapid development of radio during the early 1920s was largely a result of the desire of manufacturers of radio receiving sets to create a market for their products. Certainly it is a fact that the technical excellence of radio and television today has been a result of the continuing research and experimentation carried on by electronics manufacturing companies, research which in recent years has given us transistor radios, color television, and satellite communications systems. One index of the importance of equipment manufacturers in the broadcasting industry is the fact that the American people spend as much money each year on new radio and television receiving sets and on parts, tubes, and repairs for existing sets as the nation's advertisers spend for station and network time. During the ten-year period from 1955 to 1964, manufacturers produced an average of 6.82 million new television receiving sets and 16,345,000 new radio sets each year; to buy these sets, the public spent a total of almost $1.8 billion a year.

But radio and television receivers represent only a part of the output of equipment manufacturing companies. Stations and networks buy equipment of almost every type imaginable; how much is spent each year is almost impossible to estimate, but the figure runs into hundreds of millions of dollars. Such companies as Westinghouse, General Electric, and the Radio Corporation of America produce a general line of receiving and transmitting equipment. Others deal in a single type of highly specialized products, such as T.C.A. Radio Tower Company which manufactures all types of antenna towers; Minnesota Mining and Manufacturing Company, which produces most of the magnetic tape used for audio or video tape recording; Ampex Corporation, manufacturer of tape recorders; Eastman Kodak Company, which produces the film used in motion pictures and in filmed television programs; TelePrompTer Corporation, which leases electronic cue-boards to networks and stations; Kliegl Brothers, producers of studio lighting equipment for television and motion pictures; the Zoomar Corporation, manufacturer of self-focusing television camera lenses; or Schaefer Electronics, which specializes in automation systems for radio.

Advertising Agencies

Advertising agencies have already been mentioned in this chapter; they are important in broadcasting because all network and national spot advertising and at least 15 to 20 per cent of all local radio and television advertising is "placed" by agencies. Advertising agencies serve as expert representatives of national manufacturing companies or of local distributors or retailers in the planning of advertising campaigns and the handling of day-to-day details of advertising, whether the medium used is television, radio, newspapers, magazines, billboards, or direct mail. When broadcast advertising is to be used, the agency gives advice on the amount of money to be spent, the stations or the network to be used, and the program or spot vehicle to be selected; it plans the commercial announcements, writes the advertising copy, and often produces the transcribed, filmed, or videotaped commercial spots used in the advertising campaign; it contracts for time on stations or networks, and handles all details connected with the advertising activities of its client. Equivalent functions are performed when advertising is carried in newspapers or magazines, or handled by other methods. For its services, the advertising agency receives a commission of 15 per cent of the total amount the advertiser pays for station or network time, deducted when payment is made to the broadcaster. In addition, the agency collects from the advertiser a commission that in most cases is 15 per cent of the total cost of production of programs sponsored or of commercials used in the advertising campaign. The typical advertising agency may have 15 or 20 different firms as clients, no two of which are engaged in the same type of business.

Most of the more than 7,000 advertising agencies in the United States—the United States Census Bureau reports a total of 7,432 operating in 1963—are small, local concerns with fewer than half a dozen employees each and with only local advertisers as clients. Some national or regional agencies specialize in billboard or in direct-mail advertising. However, most of the major agencies do not specialize, but handle all of the types of advertising required by their clients—the important manufacturing and industrial enterprises, which include the heaviest users of network and national spot advertising. A dozen or more of the largest national advertising agencies spend for their clients collectively from $50 million to $150 million a year each for network and station time. Among the leaders in the agency field in recent years have been such concerns as Young & Rubicam, J. Walter Thompson, Ted Bates & Company, McCann-Erickson, and Batten, Barton, Durstine & Osborn, Inc.

Station Representatives

Extremely important in the handling of national spot advertising on radio and television are station-representative companies, usually referred to in the broadcasting industry as "station reps." Practically every television station or important radio station employs a station-representative concern to act as the station's agent in the sale of time to national and regional advertisers; the "rep" company's salesmen call on time buyers for advertising agencies with clients planning national spot advertising campaigns to attempt to induce the buyers to purchase time on stations the "rep" concern represents. In addition, station representatives assist their clients in determining the rates to be charged for time, in developing sales promotional materials and in planning advertising to be placed in industry trade papers. Some even assist stations in the selection of key employees. In return for these activities, the "rep" concern collects a commission of 15 per cent on amounts paid by national spot advertisers for time on the station or stations it serves. Since 1960 commissions paid representative companies by radio and television stations have totaled more than $100 million a year.

There are more than 150 station-representative concerns in the United States; half these firms represent more than 20 stations each. Practically all "rep" companies specialize in handling the affairs of stations of one particular type. For example, nine companies represent only stations located in foreign countries; others accept as clients only 50,000-watt radio stations or regional 5,000-watt stations with large coverage areas; a few handle only sales for television stations. Naturally, the stations represented by any one concern are located in different cities and are not in direct competition with one another. Among the more important national "reps" in terms of volume of business handled are Peters, Griffin, Woodward; Robert E. Eastman & Co.; the Katz Agency; Edward Petry & Co.; John Blair & Co.; Adam Young, Inc.; the Henry Christal Co.; and the Weed Radio Corporation.

Program Production Companies

In the early days of network radio, practically all network programs were produced by the network companies themselves or by stations affiliated with the network. During the 1930s, a majority of sponsored network programs were produced by advertising agencies. Today, all network news programs and practically all television documentaries are produced by the network companies, as are NBC Television's *Today* and *Tonight* shows, most of the broadcasts of sports events on Saturday and Sunday afternoons, and many of the entertainment programs on daytime schedules. But nearly 90 per cent of all evening entertainment programs in prime time and a considerable number of the daytime entertainment programs come from independent companies known in the industry as "package companies" or "package agencies." These are concerns that develop programs; employ writers, producers, directors, actors, entertainers, and entire production crews; and handle all of the details incidental to preparing a program for broadcast. Most "package" programs are filmed or recorded on videotape; however, most network panel

shows and a few other "live" programs are produced by packagers. The package producer pays all salaries and all costs of
production, and delivers the completed program to the sponsor
or the network company as a "package," for a fixed price agreed
upon in advance; hence the term "package agency" or "package
producer."

Package agencies originated during the 1930s on network
radio; one of the earliest was the company headed by Phillips
Lord, which produced *Gangbusters* and other network thrillers.
Among other independent producers of radio programs were
Frank and Anne Hummert, operating as a subsidiary of the
Blackett-Sample-Hummert advertising agency and responsible
for the "packaging" of a dozen different daytime serials, and
Ralph Edwards, whose *Truth or Consequences* and *This Is Your
Life* programs both appeared first on network radio and were
later transferred to television. These concerns produced live pro-
grams for sponsorship on radio networks; other packagers, notably Frederic W. Ziv, produced transcribed programs for syndication to radio stations.

With the decline of network radio and the heavy use of
recorded music on radio stations, the radio program packagers
have almost completely disappeared, although one or two still
offer taped or transcribed action dramatic programs for radio
syndication. But packaging has reached its real heights in television. A few companies specialize in the production of live or
videotaped programs for network use, notably the Mark Good-
son-Bill Todman combination, which supplies practically all of
the network panel shows. Other companies produce some of
the "game" shows used on daytime television schedules, and several of the important evening variety programs are produced
by companies in which the stars of the program own a controlling interest.

But much more important in packaging for television is
the production of filmed dramatic programs. At one time, nearly
300 small packaging concerns were turning out series of 5-
minute, 15-minute, and 30-minute filmed programs of various
types for syndication to television stations. The Motion Picture
Association of America reports that during a ten-year period
from 1953 to 1962, various packagers produced more than 50,000

filmed episodes in nearly 350 different program series at a total cost over the period of $973 million. In recent years, however, there has been almost no demand from syndication companies or from stations for the types of inexpensive programs that small, independent packagers formerly produced. At least 95 per cent of the filmed television programs now offered in syndication are series previously used on evening network schedules, so the only demand to be filled by packagers is for filmed programs for network presentation. But with production costs of even 13 episodes of a 30-minute filmed evening network program ranging from $750,000 to $900,000, the little concerns have been crowded out of the field, and practically all filmed program packaging since 1960 or 1962 has been carried on by a few major companies, most of them subsidiaries of the big motion picture production concerns in Hollywood. Among the leading television packagers in recent years have been MCA-TV, owned by the Music Corporation of America; Warner Brothers and Twentieth Century-Fox, both major producers of theatrical motion picture features; Four Star and Desilu, companies owned by Hollywood actors-turned-producers; and Screen Gems, a subsidiary of Columbia Pictures.

A number of the smaller concerns once engaged in filmed program packaging are now active in a closely related field—the production of filmed commercial announcements used by network and national spot advertisers. In most cases ideas for such commercials are developed in complete detail by employees of advertising agencies, and the "spot announcement packager" simply handles the technical elements of production and filming. Some companies engaged in production of filmed commercials, however, also provide the ideas to be developed as well as handling production details.

Program Syndication Companies

A syndication company is a concern engaged in the sale— or more accurately, the rental—of recorded, taped, or filmed programs to individual radio or television stations, or in some cases to national spot advertisers. Sometimes the syndication company is also a package producer of programs; more often, however, it merely handles the sale and distribution of programs produced by other companies. Syndication for broadcasting, like package production, was first developed during the 1930s when a number of dramatic or musical program series in transcribed form—recorded on 16-inch disks, to be played at 33⅓ revolutions per minute—were produced for distribution to radio stations. With the almost complete change in the nature of radio station programming since 1950, radio program syndication, like packaging for radio, has largely disappeared.

But in television, syndication is highly important. The typical television station with a network affiliation fills from 30 to 50 hours of its total program schedule each week with syndicated materials; the independent television station makes even greater use of such materials. Four major types of program material are made available to television stations by the various syndication companies. First are "off-network" filmed programs, originally carried on network schedules but available for syndication to stations after their network runs have come to an end. Second are the filmed, or sometimes videotaped, program series that have been produced specifically for syndication and never carried on network schedules. Included in this group are some programs developed by individual stations and offered for use by other stations in videotaped form. The third major type of material consists of motion picture feature films, produced originally for showing in motion picture theaters; the rights to many theatrical feature films have been purchased by syndication companies, which lease prints of the films to television stations. The final type of syndicated material includes cartoons, travelogues, two-reel comedies, and other "short subjects" originally produced for motion picture theater showing. Many of these short films have been made available for syndication to television stations, which frequently use them as segments of programs produced locally for children.

Some syndication companies handle only one type of syndicated material; however, such major syndicators as Screen Gems deal both in filmed-for-television program series and in theatrical motion picture features. Often a single company will hold syndication rights to as many as a dozen or 15 different television program series, each including from 26 to 78 episodes. The same syndication concern may also hold the rights to several hundred theatrical feature films, the latter usually sold to stations in packages including 40 to 50 features each. A station may contract for exclusive first-run rights in a given locality to a television filmed series or to a package of theatrical feature films; rental fees will vary according to the size of market and, of course, the quality of the material involved. Two or three years later, second-run or third-run rights to exactly the same material may be sold to another station in the same community, naturally at a much lower price.

Industry trade publications have emphasized the fact that the supply of theatrical feature films available for first-run showing on television is running low; of all the films produced in Hollywood over the years, only a few hundred remain that have not already been released to television and presumably already had first-run showings on stations in most major markets. In addition, as mentioned in an earlier paragraph, only a very few new "filmed for television" program series have been produced especially for syndication in recent years. However, there are numerous filmed programs still available that were originally carried in series form by television networks, and new programs are appearing on network schedules every year. It might be noted here that one important source of revenue for syndication companies is the leasing of filmed program series, including programs currently being carried on our own national networks, to television stations in other countries. Schedules of national networks and of commercial stations in Great Britain, Japan, Australia, and literally dozens of other countries include many of the same American-produced, made-for-television programs that viewers see in the United States.[5]

Since national television networks frequently are part-owners of syndication rights to program series carried over their facilities, each network company has its own filmed program sales division—ABC Films, CBS Films, and NBC Films, respectively—to handle the sale of some or all of the network-controlled

---

[5] According to *Variety*, American television stations spent approximately $115 million for syndicated materials in 1964; during the same year, American syndication companies received $68 million from overseas sales of their filmed product.

programs to American and foreign television stations. Other important syndicators of filmed television programs include Screen Gems, Seven Arts Associated Corporation, MCA-TV, Four Star Distribution Corporation, Desilu Sales, and the sales or distribution branches of such major theatrical motion picture producers as Warner Brothers, Twentieth Century-Fox, and Metro-Goldwyn-Mayer.

Program Services

Program packagers and program syndication companies deal in finished, complete programs. But both radio and television stations also buy materials for inclusion in their own locally produced programs—news, recorded music, sound effects, and special production effects, among other things. Two companies are the suppliers of most of the national and international news materials included in radio or television news programs: Associated Press and United Press International. Each provides a daily wire news service to broadcasting stations and a still-photo service to television stations. UPI also offers a special newsfilm service for television. Several smaller concerns supply special types of news material to radio stations; these include sports news features, "on-the-spot" taped reports from overseas reporters, and the like. Telenews, associated with the Hearst Metrotone theatrical newsreel service, supplies television newsfilm to subscribing stations, as do all three of the national television networks.

Music suppliers.   While of minor importance in local television, music is the essence of local radio programming. Music in recorded form is available from record companies and music library services. Several concerns, among them Lang-Worth, World, and NBC-Thesaurus, supply stations, for a monthly rental fee, with music "libraries" including from three to five thousand separate selections. Most libraries offer a wide variety of types of music ranging from "standards" to semiclassical, and from familiar hymns to music by military bands. The current popular numbers most heavily used by present-day radio stations, however, are on records or in albums produced by such companies as RCA-Victor, Columbia, Capitol, or Decca. Each of the record companies distributes a limited number of recordings to radio stations without charge for promotion purposes, but the best recordings and most of the albums are usually available only upon the payment of a nominal service fee. For example, a station may subscribe to RCA Victor's Popular Album service for $40 per year, and receive for the money a minimum of 72 albums featuring such performers as Perry Como, Elvis Presley, and Eddie Fisher; in addition, the company often sends out "bonus" albums to subscribers. Since this arrangement allows the broadcaster to buy albums retailing at $5.00 or more for as little as 50 or 60 cents each, most radio stations subscribe to the album and record services of one or more record companies to provide material for their programming in the field of popular music.

The introduction of automation by radio stations—FM stations in particular—makes necessary the supplying of another type of music. The automated station uses music recorded on long-playing tapes, including "cue" devices which automatically switch in, at appropriate intervals, other tapes on which commercial announcements or station identification materials have been prerecorded. Several concerns, among them Heritage and Muzak's Programatic, distribute long-playing tapes to automated stations on a rental basis; music provided consists of "standards" and light semiclassical numbers performed by small orchestras or other instrumental groups.

Suppliers of special materials.   Several companies specialize in providing music in forms other than complete selections—musical bridges, transitional music, theme music for programs. Some supply "singing jingles"—often made to order—for station identifications, weather reports, "lead-ins" for news programs, or commercial announcements for local advertisers. Still other companies offer special sound effects recordings or complete libraries of sound effects. A number of concerns make slides or films for station identification visuals for television stations, or provide art work used in television commercial announcements; some specialize in the production of animated cartoon commercials. A few companies maintain "stock film" libraries, selling stock film footage of places or events or film clips from old newsreels to television stations for use in the production of documentary programs or as filmed "signatures" for local programs of other types. A few concerns sell comedy routines for use by radio disk jockey personalities or by masters of ceremonies of audience participation programs. And two or three companies specialize in providing prizes to be given participants in quiz and audience participation programs, supplying "brand name" goods at prices very much below those that would be paid if the items supplied were purchased separately. Almost any type of material required for the presentation of local radio or television programs is available from some supplier connected with the broadcasting industry.

Subscription Television

During the past several years, a number of experiments have been conducted involving "subscription" or "pay" television, in which programs are delivered to subscribers who pay for the service on a per-program basis. In most cases, programs are delivered over a coaxial cable to receivers in the homes of subscribers—the same method used by community antenna systems. However, for "pay" television a meter-like attachment records the programs used, and subscribers are billed at the end of each month for the amount of service they have received. In 1962 the Federal Communications Commission authorized a "pay" television experiment in Hartford, Connecticut, in which the "pay" company's programs were broadcast by a regular UHF television station; use of a "scrambling" device made reception possible only in those homes having a metered "de-scrambler" attached to the receiving set. Advocates of "pay" television have in most cases promised to provide programs of types not usually available from "free" television stations: concerts, operas, ballet performances, current Broadway plays, outstanding sports events, and the best of the current motion pictures.

Most of the "pay" television experiments have lasted only a few months and were apparently not too successful, although detailed financial information has not been available. The "pay" television companies have had the same problems of high program production costs which have plagued the commercial "free" television networks, with the result that very little of the promised high-quality programming has actually been provided. In fact, the service available to "pay" television subscribers has been limited almost entirely to theatrical motion picture features, which in most cases had already been shown in "first-run" motion picture theaters. As of the autumn of 1965, only one of the "pay" television experiments was still being continued—that in Hartford, Connecticut, using programs broadcast by a UHF television station.

Much more successful than "pay" television has been a somewhat similar enterprise called "theater television." Outstanding sports events, such as heavyweight championship fights, are picked up by regular television cameras and transmitted by A.T.&T. coaxial cables or microwave relay facilities to theaters in major cities throughout the country. Pictures of the events are shown on large screens in these theaters to audiences who have paid as much as $5.00 admission for the privilege of watching the events as they happen. Promoters of recent heavyweight championship fights have usually received many times as much money from sale of theater television rights as from paid admissions to the fight itself. The same closed-circuit television idea is also frequently used for sales meetings of major corporations; programs originated from a "main" meeting in a major city are carried to regional meetings in theaters or hotel ballrooms in a number of other cities.

Industry Groups and Associations

As in any other type of business operating on a national scale, the broadcasting industry has a number of trade associations and other groups representing people who engage in broadcasting. The most important industry trade group is the National Association of Broadcasters which acts as spokesman for the broadcasting industry in national policy matters, in matters related to legislation and government regulation, and in the establishment of acceptable industry practices. The NAB includes as members most of the commercial television stations and approximately half of the commercial radio stations in the nation. State associations of broadcasters have been formed in the various states, not directly a part of NAB but serving as extensions of the national association in matters of common concern. Other management groups operating on a national basis include TvB, the Television Bureau of Advertising; RAB, the Radio Advertising Bureau; and TIO, the Television Information Office. The first two are organizations formed to promote the sale of broadcast advertising time; TIO is a public relations body that attempts, by use of large-scale publicity and promotion, to create a more favorable public image for the television industry.

In addition to organizations representing stations and station management, several professional groups have been formed whose members are station employees working in specialized fields. Among them are such associations as American Women in Radio & Television, the National Association of Television and Radio Farm Directors, the Radio and Television News Directors Association, and the Broadcast Promotion Association whose members are in charge of the promotional activities of their stations. Probably one of the most influential groups is the News Directors Association, which works closely with the NAB and with the newspaper industry in efforts to arrange for greater access to news sources for news broadcasters and reporters.

An organization somewhat unique in the broadcasting field is the National Academy of Television Arts and Sciences, made up of writers, producers, directors, technicians, and featured entertainers involved in the production of television programs. The Academy gives annual awards or "Emmys" for outstanding achievement in writing, acting, directing, music scoring, and technical work in network television programs presented during the year.

Broadcasting Unions

Like other industries, broadcasting has labor unions representing employees of stations, networks, and program production concerns in their relations with employers. In all nearly 50 different unions are involved entirely or in part with broadcasting activities. Most engineers and technicians are members either of IBEW, the International Brotherhood of Electrical Workers, or of NABET, the National Association of Broadcast Employes and Technicians; combined, the two organizations represent some

9,000 network and station employees. Another major broadcasting union, AFTRA, or the American Federation of Television & Radio Artists, has a membership of more than 3,000 announcers, actors, vocalists, dancers and other performers who appear on broadcast programs or in commercial announcements. Many AFTRA members also belong to SAG, or the Screen Actors Guild, a much larger organization made up of actors and other enter-, tainers who appear in motion pictures made for theatrical use or in filmed television programs or commercial announcements. The International Alliance of Theatrical Stage Employees, or IATSE, originally a union of stagehands in theaters and of motion picture projectionists, is also active in television; IATSE represents stagehands and studio floor crews and, in some parts of the country, motion picture cameramen and operators of motion picture projection equipment. Musicians who provide "live" or recorded instrumental music for use on the air are represented by AFM, the American Federation of Musicians. Certain types of industry workers are organized into "guilds," rather than formal unions. Writers of network or syndicated programs are members of the Writers Guild of America; television directors employed by networks or by package production concerns belong to the Directors Guild of America. In addition, numerous smaller unions or in some cases specialized locals of IATSE represent such varied groups as scenic artists, film editors, studio carpenters, wardrobe attendants, makeup artists, hair stylists, and even parking lot attendants.

Unions are an important factor in the broadcasting industry; to a large extent they determine the wages and working conditions of those involved in the production of network and syndicated programs. However, their activities are confined for the most part to the large production centers, and their membership made up of employees of networks, package agencies and large-city stations. Almost all of the engineers employed by radio or television stations in major population centers are members of IBEW or NABET; announcers and other on-the-air personalities employed by the same stations are members of AFTRA. But in smaller communities, few employees of broadcasting stations are union members, aside from musicians and a limited number of station engineers. One industry estimate is that not more than

20 per cent of all station employees throughout the country are members of labor organizations.

Miscellaneous Services

In addition to organizations and business concerns of types already mentioned, there are numerous others providing a variety of services connected with broadcasting. Most of the important network entertainers and writers are represented by *talent agents* who attempt to sell the services of their clients to producing companies, networks or advertising agencies. The largest and best-known concern in this field is the William Morris Agency, which handles contract negotiations for many of the highest-paid entertainers who appear on television. In addition, about 65 smaller agencies handle the business affairs of other broadcasting personalities.

Three organizations are involved in the licensing of copyrighted music: ASCAP, or the American Society of Composers, Authors and Publishers; BMI, or Broadcast Music, Incorporated; and SESAC, or the Society of European Stage Artists and Composers. ASCAP controls copyrights on most standard popular compositions and on almost all music from operettas, Broadway shows, and motion pictures, as well as on much of the music of other types published in the United States before 1940. In addition, of course, the Society's list includes a substantial number of more recent compositions. BMI, organized by broadcasters in 1939 to provide competition to ASCAP, holds copyrights on half or more of all musical numbers written since 1940, especially popular tunes by the less-well-established song-writers and composers. SESAC holds the rights to most music of European or Latin American origin; its catalog also includes some popular numbers written by American composers. The national networks and practically all radio and television stations hold blanket licenses for the performance of music controlled by ASCAP and BMI, and pay license fees totaling between 3 and 3½ per cent of their revenues from sale of time for the right to use copyrighted music. SESAC music is less widely used by radio and television stations.

As in other industries, trade papers serve an important function in broadcasting by providing news and feature articles relating to the industry. Publications such as *Broadcasting, Television, Radio-TV Daily, Variety, Billboard, Television Age, Television Digest,* and *Sponsor* are widely read by broadcasters and others concerned with special aspects of radio and television, and exert a considerable amount of influence in industry affairs.

Many other organizations or individuals offer specialized services to broadcasters. A number of research companies provide national ratings for network programs or detailed information about the buying habits of listeners; activities of research organizations will be discussed at length in a later chapter. Several firms are station brokers, handling the sale of radio and television stations to new owners. Between 1954 and 1962 a total of 3,022 radio stations and 364 television stations changed hands; the amount paid by buyers totaled more than $950 million. There are nearly 250 consulting engineers to assist stations and applicants for stations with their technical problems. More than 600 attorneys are specialists in radio law; they give legal advice to stations, especially on matters relating to federal regulation, and when necessary appear as representatives of their station-clients in hearings on license applications or in presenting oral arguments before the Federal Communications Commission. Some concerns serve as management consultants; others as consultants on station programming. In short, wherever a need for specialized services exists, there are companies available to provide those services.

A final but exceedingly important element in the broadcasting industry is the Federal Communications Commission itself, the federal agency charged with the responsibility of regulating American radio and television. The Commission grants licenses to stations, and also licenses the engineers who put the stations on the air; it determines general policies for broadcasting; it sets technical standards for television; it assigns television and FM radio channels to various communities; it makes recommendations to Congress concerning new legislation relating to broadcasting. More than any other single organization involved in broadcasting activity, the Federal Communications Commission determines the over-all nature of broadcasting service and the patterns which characterize broadcasting in the United States. The Communications Commission will be considered in greater detail in a later chapter.

6

STATIONS AND NETWORKS

Although the broadcasting industry includes companies providing a wide variety of services, the base of the industry pyramid consists of the broadcasting stations, which put radio and television programs on the air. Almost as important, particularly in television, are the national network organizations, which supply informational and entertainment programs that attract audiences of millions of listeners. These two segments of the broadcasting industry and the relationship between them will be considered at length in this chapter.

BROADCASTING STATIONS

All broadcasting stations are alike in one basic respect; they put on the air programs or program materials to be received by the listening public. Commercial stations are alike in another important respect; they are operated by their owners for the purpose of earning a profit. But otherwise, stations are very much different in the types of service they provide, in the areas they cover, in their geographical locations, in the competitive situations in which they operate, and in many other respects. Some are located in large cities, others in rural areas; some operate on a full-time basis, others are licensed only for part-time broadcasting; some are affiliated with networks, others provide programs without network assistance. All of these factors affect the kinds of program service which stations provide, as well as the stations' chances of earning a profit.

Types of Broadcasting Stations

Commercial stations may be classified in several different ways. First, of course, stations are divided into three basic groups: AM or standard-band radio stations, FM radio stations, and television stations. Each group uses a different band of frequencies in the radio spectrum; AM stations are assigned to the "standard band" of frequencies from 540 to 1600 kilocycles, FM radio stations to those between 88 and 108 megacycles—a megacycle is equal to 1,000 kilocycles—and television stations use channels in three separate bands of frequencies, 54 to 88 megacycles, 174 to 216 megacycles, and 470 to 836 megacycles.

AM radio stations.   Probably the most important basis of classification of standard-band radio stations is the amount of power they are authorized to use. First, there are the "high-powered" stations, using power of 50,000 watts—the maximum allowed by the Federal Communications Commission. Most stations in this category are assigned to frequencies designated by the Commission as "clear channels"—that is, channels reserved for their exclusive nighttime use—with only a few stations, widely separated geographically, using the same frequency. With their high power, stations on clear channels may serve listeners in areas that include several states. Next come "regional" stations, operating on 41 frequencies referred to as "regional" channels. Most have power ranging from 500 watts to a maximum of 5,000 watts, and are expected to serve fairly large rural areas, although the stations themselves may be located in large cities. The area covered by a regional station is usually considerably smaller than that served by a high-powered clear-channel station, so a larger number of regional stations may be assigned the same frequency. A third group consists of "local" stations, assigned to one of six "local" channels, and intended to serve a single community and its immediate vicinity. Until a few years ago, local stations were limited to 250 watts power; today, however, a majority of local stations use daytime power of 1,000 watts, although dropping to 250 watts at night to reduce possible interference. A fourth group of stations includes those listed by the Communications Commission as "Class II" stations; these are secondary stations assigned to American clear channels or to channels reserved as "clears" for stations in Canada, Cuba, or Mexico. Power that may be used ranges from 250 watts to as much as 50,000 watts—but to protect the nighttime signals of clear-channel stations using the same frequencies, most Class II stations operate only during daytime hours, although a few are allowed to stay on the air with greatly reduced power at night. Some regional stations are also licensed only for daytime operation or are required to reduce the power they use after sunset. Table 8 shows the number of stations in each major power classification at the beginning of November 1965.

With as many as 40 or 50 stations assigned to each regional channel and from 160 to 180 operating on each local channel, interference between stations has become a serious problem. This is especially true at night, when AM signals can be heard over much larger areas than during the daytime.[1] To deal at least partially with this problem, the Federal Communications Com-

---

[1] During nighttime hours, radio waves tend to "bounce back" from or be reflected back to earth by a layer of ionized atmosphere called the ionosphere or the Heaviside layer, from 30 miles to 250 miles above the surface of the earth, so that the reflected signals can be picked up by receiving sets much farther away from the transmitter than those reached by ground waves paralleling the surface of the earth. During the daytime, when the atmosphere is warmed by the sun's rays, the reflecting power of the ionosphere is much reduced, and radio signals are carried almost entirely by ground waves. The "bounce back" phenomenon is particularly evident with respect to the medium-length radio waves used by AM stations; the degree of nighttime reflection of signals is considerably less for the shorter waves used by FM and television stations.

TABLE 8

POWER CLASSIFICATIONS OF STANDARD-BAND RADIO
STATIONS ON THE AIR, NOVEMBER 1, 1965

With daytime power of	Full-time Stations, Same Power at Night	Full-time Stations, Power Reduced at Night	Daytime Only or Part-time Stations [1]	Total
50,000 watts	73	29	16	118
10,000 watts	23 [2]	39	18	80 [2]
5,000 watts	328	298	276	902
1,000 watts	176	846	986	2008
500 watts	22	18	393	433
250 watts	211	24	243	478
100 watts	6	—	1	7
Totals	839	1254	1933	4026

[1] Includes stations licensed for operation only during specified hours as well as those operating only during daytime hours.

[2] Includes one station operating full time with power of 25,000 watts.

Figures compiled from radio station listings in *Broadcasting Yearbook* for 1966. Commercial stations only.

mission makes use of three types of limitations in the licenses granted certain stations, providing another basis for classification of AM radio stations. First, as shown in Table 8, almost half of the standard stations on the air are licensed for daytime broadcasting only. Next, of those stations that do stay on the air at night, approximately three out of five use less power at night than the amount they are allowed to use during the daytime. And finally, almost all of the regional stations on the air at night are required to use directional antenna systems, which reduce the strength of their signals in certain directions, in order to "protect" other stations on the same frequencies. Many regional stations and Class II stations are also required to use directional antennas during the daytime. Table 8 shows the number of stations in each daytime power category operating on a daytime-only basis or required to reduce power at night

Program schedule of WGY, Schenectady, N.Y., for February 20, 1922

First studio and transmitter of KFI, Los Angeles

Members of the staff that put WEAR (which became WFBR in 1924), the first radio station in Maryland, on the air June 8, 1922.

as of the autumn of 1965. It may be noted, however, that even with the restrictions imposed by the Commission, nighttime interference from other stations assigned to the same frequency remains a serious problem for almost all AM radio stations, except of course for the 50,000-watt facilities licensed as clear-channel stations.

A third possible basis of classification of AM stations is their affiliation or nonaffiliation with national radio networks. In 1965, somewhat more than 1,100 AM stations were listed as network affiliates; nearly three times that number received no network service. However, the distinction between network and non-network radio stations is of relatively minor importance in view of the limited program service the radio networks now provide. More meaningful, perhaps, would be classifications based on the size of communities in which stations are located—big-city stations, medium-city stations, and small-market stations. Or a classification based on the types of program service that individual stations provide—"top 40" stations, "good music" stations, "country and Western music" stations, "talk" stations, Negro-appeal stations, farm-audience stations, and the like. Such classifications are important to advertisers interested in reaching specialized audiences.

FM radio stations.   Since 1962, the Federal Communications Commission has provided for three classes of FM stations, based on the amount of power each is permitted to use. Class A stations may use power of from 100 watts to 3,000 watts; Class B stations, intended to serve larger areas, have power ranging from 5,000 to 50,000 watts; Class C stations are allowed to use power of 100,000 watts or even more, and antennas up to 2,000 feet in height. In 1965, nearly 90 commercial FM stations used power of more than 100,000 watts, and at least 100 others had power of 50,000 watts or more.

FM stations may be classified, too, on the basis of the extent to which they are independently programmed. More than 70 per cent of all commercial FM stations are owned by licensees of AM stations in the same communities; until recently most of these FM stations simply duplicated the program schedules of the AM stations with which they had common ownership. However, a regulation of the Federal Communications Commission effective in October 1965 required all FM stations in cities of 100,000 or more to be programmed independently of their AM affiliates during at least 50 per cent of the broadcasting day; the order affected about 340 of the 551 FM stations operating in major cities at the beginning of 1965. As a result of the Commission's order, by the end of 1965 at least 50 per cent of all FM stations—including of course those not connected with AM operations—were offering their own separate schedules of programs during all or a portion of their time on the air, while the remainder carried the same programs as the jointly-owned AM stations in the same communities.

Some FM stations, especially those in large cities, hold special authorizations from the Federal Communications Commission to engage in "multiplexing," or the simultaneous transmission of two or more signals on different portions of the channel to which they are assigned. One signal must be used for ordinary broadcasting of programs intended for a general audience. Many stations use a second signal to provide stereophonic transmission of music. However, the second signal can be used for nonbroadcasting purposes—in particular, "storecasting," or the providing of background music, uninterrupted by commercials or by station identification announcements, for the use of local stores, offices, and other places of business. Frequently FM stations are also used as relays to carry programs to members of regional AM radio networks; the FM signal of an originating station is picked up and rebroadcast by other FM stations whose signals are in turn picked up and rebroadcast by the AM stations which compose the network.

No mention has been made in the preceding sections of the noncommercial AM or FM radio stations that have been authorized by the Federal Communications Commission. The Commission has set aside no special frequencies for the exclusive use of noncommercial AM stations; however, at the beginning of 1966 about 32 noncommercial AM stations and approximately 269 noncommercial FM stations were on the air, all but 20 of the latter assigned to frequencies reserved by the Commission for the exclusive use of noncommercial stations. Most of the noncommercial radio stations are licensed to universities, colleges, or local school systems and provide educational and cultural programs for listeners. A considerable number, however, are owned by religious organizations and are operated as religious stations.

Television stations. The Federal Communications Commission makes no provision for "classes" of commercial television stations; all are, in effect, local stations, providing service to a single community and the surrounding countryside. In fact, the area over which a television station has effective daytime or nighttime coverage is usually smaller than the area served by a 250-watt AM radio station in the same community. An important difference between commercial television stations, however, lies in the fact that some are assigned to channels in the VHF bands, while others use channels in the much higher UHF bands where signals can be received over a much smaller area. Partly to compensate for this variation in coverage, the Commission allows use of much greater power by television stations on the higher frequencies than by those on channels at the lower end of the band. Television stations assigned to channels 2 to 6 may use maximum visual power of 100 kilowatts, or 100,000 watts; stations using channels 7 to 13 may use maximum power of 316 kilowatts; UHF stations assigned to channels 14 to 83 may be authorized to use power up to 5,000 kilowatts—power a hundred times as great as clear-channel AM radio stations are allowed to use. In actual practice, few UHF stations broadcast with more than a fraction of the maximum power permitted; most VHF television stations, on the other hand, operate at the top power levels permitted by the Commission.

A second basis of television station classification relates to affiliation with national networks. Most station operators *want* network affiliation; networks provide programs of types and of degrees of popularity not otherwise available to individual stations. But in markets with four or more stations, there are not enough network services to go around. In addition, a few stations are located in communities so small and so far distant from existing network lines that network companies would not find it profitable to have them as affiliates. In any case, at the end of 1965 about 50 commercial television stations were operating as "independents" with no regular access to network programs. Of necessity, these non-network stations have to be programmed in a manner considerably different from that of stations with network affiliations.

The Market Situation

A factor greatly affecting both the programming and the business success of broadcasting stations is the size of the market in which a station is located. Markets, or the home communities and surrounding trade areas served by stations, can be divided into three basic groups from the standpoint of their relation to broadcasting. First are the "major" markets—the 100 or so largest cities in the country, in most cases with three or more commercial television outlets each and from five or six to as many as 20 radio stations, or even more. Almost all of the powerful 50,000-watt radio stations are located in these major markets. An important subdivision of the major market category would include the 25 or so largest cities in the nation, since stations in these cities get a disproportionate share of all expenditures for radio and television advertising time. The second group includes what are known as secondary markets, usually cities with populations ranging from 50,000 to roughly 125,000, and their surrounding trade areas. Most of the secondary markets have service from one or two home-community television stations and from three or four local radio outlets. Finally we have a third group of still smaller markets with urban populations of less than 50,000, not large enough to support commercial television stations but with from one to as many as three or four local radio stations each. About 300 of these minor markets are served by two or more local radio outlets, but there are also about 1,700 small communities which are "one-radio-station" markets—some of them small towns with populations of hardly more than a thousand inhabitants.

As shown in Table 9, market size is extremely important in broadcasting. National advertisers buy time on stations in major markets and largely ignore those stations located in smaller communities. As the table indicates, approximately 44 per cent of all national spot advertising on radio and television in 1964 went to stations in the nation's ten largest cities, and another 17.7 per cent went to outlets in the 15 cities next in size.[2] Similarly, more than 42 per cent of all money paid by networks to their affiliates went to television stations serving the 25 largest cities. The effects on average station revenues are obvious; the larger the city, the greater the average station revenues of stations in that city.

Naturally, size of the market is not the only factor influencing the economic success of broadcasting stations. In the case of television stations, network affiliation is also highly important. In most large cities with four or more television outlets, nonnetwork or independent stations are able to charge only about one-half as much for advertising time as are the television stations in the same cities which have network connections. Average revenues of independent stations, as a result, are much lower than those of affiliates. However, in the case of radio, station power rather than network affiliation is the highly important factor—aside, of course, from market size. In selecting stations on which to place national spot advertising, a time buyer in New York tends to judge relative values of stations in the same market by the amount of power used; it is reasonable for him to expect that the station with greater power can cover a larger area and consequently attract a larger total number of listeners than can a station whose power is limited. No separate revenue figures are provided, however, by the Federal Communications Commission.

Ownership of Stations

As noted in an earlier chapter, ownership of American radio and television stations is scattered among nearly 4,000 different

---

[2] The list of the nation's 25 largest cities used to compile the figures used in Table 9 omitted Newark, New Jersey, and the Paterson-Clifton-Passaic complex in the same state, as being included for broadcasting purposes in the New York City metropolitan area. San Diego was similarly omitted from the list used to provide figures for television, since the Federal Communications Commission did not provide financial data in 1964 for the two American television stations serving that market. To bring the number of cities used in each case to 25, additional cities next in size were added, based on population figures for metropolitan areas reported in the 1960 Census.

TABLE 9

SOURCES OF REVENUES OF TELEVISION AND RADIO STATIONS DURING 1964 IN MARKETS OF VARIOUS SIZES

	Number of stations	Total revenues, in thousands of dollars, from		
		Network payments	National spot adv'g [1]	Local adv'g [1]
Television stations in				
10 largest cities	46	56,183	316,418	98,576
15 next largest cities	52	33,709	126,031	52,018
77 other 3 st'n markets [2]	247	77,572	173,755	92,232
173 smaller markets	230	47,027	73,303	54,161
All stations	575	214,491	689,507	296,987
Radio stations in				
10 largest cities	219	2,507	88,430	96,507
15 next largest cities	218	1,869	36,843	55,345
195 other metrop'n areas [3]	1,127	4,066	75,568	161,867
Nonmetropolitan areas	2,292	1,926	28,246	168,173
All stations	3,856	10,368	229,087	481,892

[1] Figures for advertising revenues are gross billings before deduction of agency and station representatives' commissions.

[2] Includes some markets with more than three commercial television stations each.

[3] Metropolitan areas as defined by the United States Census Bureau.

Figures compiled from annual reports for 1964 of the Economics Division of the Federal Communications Commission, based on financial reports filed by stations operating during the calendar year 1964.

individuals or corporate groups. The Federal Communications Commission prohibits ownership by the same company of two stations of the same type located in the same community, or in adjacent communities where station signals would cover much the same general area. However, the same licensee may own an AM radio station and an FM station in the same city, or an AM station and a television station, or all three. Common ownership of this kind is frequent; more than 70 per cent of all FM stations and nearly 65 per cent of all commercial television stations are owned by licensees of AM radio stations operating in the same community.

In addition, a number of corporations operate a number of radio stations or television stations located in different cities. In 1965, approximately 250 companies were "group owners," or owners of several radio or television stations located in different communities. Some owning groups operate small radio stations in several different cities in the same general area; others are large corporations with both television and radio interests in major cities from coast to coast.[3] All three of the national television networks are group owners of both radio and television stations; each of the three companies operates VHF television stations in five of the nation's ten or twelve largest cities, and the three concerns combined are owners of 19 AM radio stations. Other important group owners include Westinghouse, Storer, Metromedia, Cox, Hearst, Taft, and RKO General, each of which owns television outlets in three or more of the nation's 25 largest cities as well as operating large-city AM radio stations. Other concerns, such as Gene Autry, Plough, United, and Todd Storz, are important as group owners of radio stations. At the beginning of 1965, various owning groups were licensees of no less than 76 of the 96 television stations located in the 25 largest metropolitan areas, along with 46 high-powered 50,000-watt AM radio stations and some 70 other stations with lower power operating in those same 25 largest cities. In all, the approximately 250 group-ownership companies owned or had interests in 390 of the nation's commercial television stations and in more than 850 AM radio stations.

An interesting feature of broadcasting station ownership is the extent to which stations have been licensed to newspapers and publishing concerns. During the 1920s, a considerable number of the nation's more important radio stations were newspaper-owned. As broadcasting became more important as a dis-

---

[3] Regulations of the Federal Communications Commission limit the number of stations which may be licensed to one owner or one corporate group to not more than seven AM radio stations, seven FM stations, and seven television stations; of the seven television stations, not more than five may operate on VHF channels.

Television formally inaugurated
the space era with two historic
broadcasts in 1962. Top: the start
of America's first manned orbital
flight; bottom: the picture transmitted across the Atlantic via
Telstar, the first communications
satellite.

seminator of news and information, the interests of publishers in the ownership of broadcasting stations have increased. By the beginning of 1965, newspaper or magazine publishers owned or held substantial interests in 391 AM radio stations, including 20 with 50,000 watts power, in 158 FM stations, and in 176 television stations, of which 34 operated in the country's 25 largest cities.

Station Organization

Like other business enterprises, broadcasting stations vary in size, in number of employees, and in total annual revenues and net profits. Some small-market radio stations get along with no more than five or six full-time employees. At the other extreme, some radio stations have staffs of more than a hundred people, and some large-city television stations have as many as 150 to 200 employees. In the circumstances, it is impossible to provide an employee organization chart that would fit all stations. However, in every station, certain functions must be performed, and these functions at least can be outlined.

First, there is a managerial function; every station is under the supervision of a station manager. While he exercises general oversight over activities of other station departments, he and his immediate subordinates are responsible for financial operations, handling "billings" and collections, and paying station expenses. In addition, the station manager prepares reports, which must be filed with the Federal Communications Commission, and applications for license renewal; he handles all dealings with national networks, negotiates contracts with employee unions, selects the men who serve as managers of the station's various departments, handles payments of music royalties and of charges for news services, and in a broad sense determines general station policies.

Next comes the engineering function, in the hands of a chief engineer and a staff of assistants. The engineering department selects, buys and maintains all technical equipment, operates the transmitter and handles control room activities. In television stations, engineering department personnel operate television cameras and film and slide projectors and also serve as members of studio floor crews. In most stations, the chief engineer has supervisory control over building maintenance and janitorial services.

The sales function is performed by a sales department headed by the station's commercial manager. The department handles local sales and cooperates with the station representative concern in sale of time to national advertisers. In most stations, the sales promotion department and traffic department are also under the control of the commercial manager—the traffic department maintaining an up-to-date "log" or schedule showing when each program and each commercial spot announcement is to go on the air and what spot positions are available for sale.

The programming function involves specialized activities on the part of a number of employees under supervision of the station's program director. Included are staff announcers, news broadcasters and news editors, radio station disk-jockeys, station "personalities" such as masters of ceremonies, conductors of women's programs, farm directors and children's program specialists, and continuity writers who provide program scripts or continuity and also write much of the commercial copy used by local advertisers. Program departments of television stations also include producer-directors of programs, film editors, members of art departments, and, in larger stations, motion picture photographers, and processors of locally made film. Staff musicians and music librarians are also members of the program department.

Illustrating the variation in staff requirements are breakdowns of employees of two or three typical stations. One radio station in one of the nation's ten largest cities has a staff of 134 persons in seven operating departments. Seven are engaged in executive duties—the station manager and his immediate assistants; 15 others are involved in accounting and purchasing, or act as receptionists; 17 are engaged in sales, sales service, or handling traffic; the news department has seven employees; 49 persons are required for programming, announcing, and writing continuity; 20 others make up the music department including musicians and music librarians; and 19 employees are engaged in engineering and maintenance. The station in question still makes some use of "live" musical programs and employs 13 full-time staff musicians, as well as five or six others on a part-time basis. In contrast, one small independent "good music" radio station operates with only eleven employees; a station manager who also acts as sales manager, two salesmen, four announcers includin one who serves as program director, a girl who handles both continuity and traffic, a chief engineer and one other technician, and a secretary-receptionist. This second station is far more typical than the first; *Broadcasting Yearbook* for 1966 reports that 56 per cent of all AM radio stations have no more than ten full-time employees each.

Television stations require the services of a much greater number of types of employees and usually have regular staffs considerably larger than those of average radio stations. Listed below are the 119 employees of one fairly typical television station serving a community of something over half a million population:

1 general manager	1 program director
1 assistant manager	1 public service director
10 clerical employees	1 music director
4 maintenance men	1 news director
1 commercial manager	4 news editors
5 salesmen	5 producer-directors
3 promotion workers	6 production assistants
2 traffic supervisors	5 continuity writers
1 chief engineer	5 announcers
4 transmitter engineers	3 art department employees
12 control room engineers	2 film editors
2 audio engineers	4 photography department
3 camera operators	employees
5 projection room engineers	17 classified as "talent"—
10 floor men	not all full time

Stations in smaller communities, of course, get along with decidedly fewer employees. A survey of television station employees made in 1964 indicates that somewhat more than half of all stations have no more than 50 full-time employees each, and that only one television outlet in seven employs more than a hundred people on a full-time basis.

Economics of Station Operation

Broadcasting stations differ in size and in physical character; they also differ widely in earning potential. Station owners hope, of course, to operate at a profit. A station earning substantial profits can afford to pay high wages, employ competent personnel, and provide programs of high quality for listeners. But when revenues barely meet expenses or when a station operates at a loss, efforts to reduce costs result in lower pay for employees, the hiring of less-well-qualified personnel, and deterioration in the quality of program service. Of course, if losses continue, the station must sooner or later be forced off the air.

Every station's revenues depend on the amount of time the station sells and on the prices charged for time. Since the total time available for sale is substantially the same for every station, revenues depend largely on the rates the station is able to charge. Naturally, the station operator charges as much as he thinks advertisers will pay. The advertiser, in turn, wants to reach as many listeners as possible for each dollar he spends. Consequently, a station's charges for time must be roughly in proportion to the size of the audience the station can deliver. More specifically, the base rate a radio or television station is able to charge for its time is determined by the size of the community, by the amount of power the station uses—a measure of its "coverage" and its ability to reach listeners in the "outside" trade area—and the attractiveness and popularity of the station's programs. Large-city stations can charge more for time than can stations in rural communities; high-power stations can fix rates at a higher level than those with less power, even in the same community; very popular stations are more attractive to advertisers than are those with small audiences. And since less total time is devoted to radio listening than to watching television programs, and since the television audience is divided among fewer stations than is the radio audience in any community, a television station can fix its rates at a much higher level than can a radio station with which it competes in the sale of time to advertisers.

Rate structure. The factor of audience size also determines the rate structure used by each station. The number of available listeners varies considerably at different hours of the day, so time charges made by any given station are varied to reflect these differences. More people are at home and available for television viewing in the evening than during the daytime; as a result, television stations make their highest charges for so-called "prime" evening hours, or "Class A time," usually between 7:00 and 10:30 or 11:00 at night. With fewer listeners available during the daytime, rates charged for daytime advertising on television stations are lower in proportion—usually about half as much as the "prime time" rate. Charges for time on Sunday afternoons, or between 6:00 and 7:00 in the evening, are usually set somewhere between the "prime time" rate and the lower, daytime rate. The same pattern of varying charges was used by radio stations until evening listening was so largely taken over by television; then radio stations changed their rate structures. Many radio stations now charge less for advertising time during evening hours than for that used during the daytime; others use a single rate applying to both daylight and evening time. Some stations in large metropolitan areas, capitalizing on radio's ability to reach motorists during peak traffic hours, have established their highest rates during "drive" time, the hours when large numbers of people are driving to or from work. On the rate card of one large city station, "Class A" prime time is the period between six o'clock and nine o'clock in the morning, with spot announcements costing $50 each; the lowest-priced spots available are in "Class C" time, between 7:00 and 11:15 P.M.; during those hours, one-minute announcements are carried at a rate of $18.50 each.

In television, the "prime time" program hour is the basis of all time charges, with charges for shorter periods computed as percentages of the hour rate. A half-hour program period is usually priced at 60 per cent of the amount charged for a full hour; a 15-minute period costs 40 per cent of the base hour rate. The highest charge for a one-minute spot announcement is usually between one-sixth and one-fourth of the hour rate, but spot rates vary tremendously from station to station. Many stations charge a premium spot rate for "adjacencies" in the chain-break period preceding or following an unusually popular network program. In radio, the sale of program time in units longer than five minutes or 15 minutes has become so infrequent that station rate comparisons are made on the basis of the charge for a one-minute spot announcement in the station's prime time period.

Discounts. To induce advertisers to buy greater amounts of time, stations offer discounts, based upon the frequency of use or the volume of advertising bought on the station. A television station will sell a 15-minute period, five times a week, on a 52-week contract, at a price substantially lower than the 15-minute, one-time rate. Discounts ordinarily range from 5 per cent to 25 per cent, although some stations give discounts of as much as 40 or 50 per cent for unusually large time purchases. In radio, with the transfer of emphasis from the sale of program time to the sale of spot announcements, conventional discount patterns have been largely replaced by various "package" plans offering unusually heavy discounts to advertisers who buy large numbers of spots each week over a period of from four to eight weeks.

Station Revenues and Profits

Radio and television station revenues come mostly from sale of time to local and national spot advertisers; television stations also receive considerable amounts from network payments for the use of station time to carry commercial network programs. Stations also have some revenues from other sources: sale of station-produced programs to advertisers, fees paid by advertisers for services of station announcers and other talent, payments for production of filmed or taped commercial announcements, and the like.

As shown in Table 10, total revenues of the average television station are nearly ten times as great as those of the average AM radio station. From the gross revenues from sale of time, of course, commissions to advertising agencies and to station representatives must be deducted, and from what is left, station operating expenses must be paid. Because functions performed by staff members of most small radio outlets overlap, it is difficult to make breakdowns of the various types of expenses that must be met by radio stations. However, of the total broadcasting expenses of the average television station in 1964, about 12 per cent represented costs of making sales of time; another 16 per cent went to cover technical expenses, including equipment, power, maintenance, and salaries of engineering personnel. Program expenses made up 41.2 per cent of total station costs,

TABLE 10

AVERAGE PER-STATION REVENUES AND NET PROFITS OF NON-NETWORK-OWNED RADIO AND TELEVISION STATIONS FOR THE YEAR 1964

	Average of 3877 AM radio stations	Average of 560 television stations
Revenues from		
Payments from national networks	$ 2,040	$ 316,428
Payments from regional networks	564	1,072
Sales of time to		
National or regional advertisers	54,364	940,536
Local advertisers	121,631	445,357
Total gross revenues from time sales	$ 178,599	$1,703,393
Less commissions to agencies and representatives	17,694	250,714
Net revenues from sale of time	$ 160,905	$1,452,679
Other revenues		
From sale of programs, talent	2,694	17,322
Other miscellaneous revenues	3,551	73,928
Total broadcasting revenues	$ 167,150	$1,543,929
Total broadcasting expenses	149,226	1,081,251
Net profit before federal taxes	$ 17,924	$ 462,678

Averages computed from figures for all stations as reported by the Federal Communications Commission.

and the remaining 30.8 per cent covered general and administrative expense. Radio stations in 1964 had net profits before federal taxes averaging a little less than $18,000, as compared with average profits of nearly $463,000 for television stations.

Variations in station revenues. But average figures for station revenues and profits do not tell the entire story. As already noted, revenues of AM radio stations, and profits as well, are strongly affected by two factors: the power the station is authorized to use, and the size of the market in which it operates. As shown in Table 9, more than half of all the money spent for national spot radio advertising goes to stations located in the nation's 25 largest cities, as well as about 30 per cent of the amount spent for local advertising. Actually, in 1964, revenues from sale of time to advertisers averaged more than $600,000 for the 408 radio outlets operating in those 25 largest cities, as compared with only $78,000 for the nearly 2,400 stations located in nonmetropolitan areas. No separate figures are provided by the Federal Communications Commission concerning revenues of high-powered stations and those operating with power of 1,000 watts or less, but it is a recognized fact in broadcasting that advertisers show strong preferences for the 50,000-watt and 5,000-watt stations—usually the "prestige" stations in each market—and that advertising revenues of such stations are always much higher than those of their low-powered competitors.

Revenues of FM radio stations are much lower than those of AM outlets. The 1,175 FM stations operating during 1964 had combined revenues of only $19 million or an average of less than $17,000 per station. Of course, nearly 70 per cent of all FM outlets were operated in conjunction with AM stations under common ownership, and in most cases time on the FM stations was not sold separately. The 306 FM stations operated independently during 1964 showed average total revenues of a little more than $41,000, and in 1963 of about $38,000 per station.

The average television station, as shown in Table 10, has revenues far in excess of those of radio stations. Station revenues are affected strongly by three factors: the size of the market in which the station is located, its status as a network affiliate or as an independent station, and whether it is assigned to a VHF or to a UHF channel. No separate figures are provided by the Federal Communications Commission for stations affiliated with networks and those without such affiliations; however, some indication of relative revenues is given by the fact that in markets with four or more commercial television stations, the rates charged for time by independent stations are as a rule only about half as high as those of network-affiliated stations. Effects of market size are clearly indicated by the figures given in Table 9; in 1964, more than 60 per cent of all money spent for national spot and local television advertising went to the 98 stations operating in the nation's 25 largest cities. The situation is reflected even more strongly by the average total revenues

Delegates take a back seat to give television cameras better vantage points to report a political convention.

of stations in those large cities. In 1964, the 46 television stations in the ten largest cities had total revenues from all sources averaging nearly $9 million each; the 52 stations in the 15 cities next in size had average total revenues of about $3.7 million. At the other extreme, stations in cities not included among the nation's 100 largest markets had total revenues averaging only about $710,000 each. Not quite so striking but still impressive are the differences in the revenue figures reported for VHF and UHF television stations. In 1964, average total broadcasting revenues of 468 VHF television stations were nearly $1,753,000 each; revenues of the 92 UHF stations operating during the year, however, averaged only $481,000 per station, although a considerable number of the UHF outlets were located in the 25 largest markets in the United States.

Profits earned by stations.   But the amount of revenues received is not the final test of successful station operation. Radio and television stations are operated for the purpose of earning profits for their owners. Most broadcasting stations do return a profit on their operations, as indicated in the average figures shown in Table 10. But amounts earned vary with different types of stations and with different market situations—and a considerable number of stations each year operate at a loss. In 1964, AM radio stations showed average net earnings of a little more than $17,900 before federal taxes. But this net income was not equally distributed; some stations had decidedly larger earnings, especially those located in large cities. But 1,108 of the 3,789 stations reporting income figures to the Federal Communications Commission—29.3 per cent of the total—lost money on their broadcasting operations averaging a little more than $22,500 per station. This showing was better than that in 1963, when nearly 33 per cent of all AM stations failed to show a profit, or in 1962, when 34 per cent operated at a loss. In addition, according to members of the Federal Communications Commission, another 30 per cent of all AM stations operate on a marginal basis each year, earning less than $5,000 each.

As might be expected, stations located in major cities have largest total revenues and report the largest net earnings. In 1964, radio stations operating in cities of more than a million population reported average profits of nearly $110,000 per station before federal taxes. At the other end of the scale, the nearly 1,200 AM stations in cities with populations of less than 10,000 had average net profits of only a little more than $5,700 each.

FM radio stations find themselves in a difficult competitive position. Throughout the country, probably no more than 20 or 30 per cent of all homes have receiving sets that will bring in FM signals; FM stations, as a result, have difficulty in selling time to advertisers, as is indicated by their limited advertising revenues. It is hardly surprising that of the 306 FM stations operating independently in 1964, only 93 reported operating profits to the Federal Communications Commission; 213, or nearly 70 per cent, failed to earn expenses. The 306 stations combined reported operating deficits totaling more than $3 million, or an average of about $10,000 for each station. Although some FM stations show moderately good earnings, FM stations collectively have never operated at a profit since commercial FM operation was authorized a quarter of a century ago.

The profit position of television stations is considerably better than that of radio outlets. Average earnings of all non-network-owned stations was more than $462,000 in 1964—more than $100,000 more per station than during the previous year. As in the case of radio, some stations lost money on their broadcasting operations: about 14 per cent of all VHF stations, and 32 per cent of the UHF stations filing financial reports with the Federal Communications Commission. The 15 network-owned stations, all located in large cities, had combined net earnings of $96.3 million—more than one-fourth of the total profits of all television stations combined—or an average of more than $6.4 million per station. Other stations operating in the nation's 25 largest cities showed profits averaging about $1.74 million each. At the other extreme, stations in markets with only one or two television outlets each showed what were still very impressive net profits averaging nearly $175,000 per station, even when the tabulation includes those television facilities that operated at a loss.

Of course, the situation was not as bright for UHF stations as for those using the more desirable VHF channels. While profits earned in 1964 by VHF stations—network-owned stations included—averaged about $730,000 for each outlet, the 92 UHF outlets on the air at the end of the year had combined net earnings of only $2.7 million, or a per-station average of only $29,300. Even this was an improvement over 1963, however, when the 86 UHF stations reporting showed average revenues exceeding costs of operation by only $2,500 per station. In only four of the twelve years from 1953 to 1964 have UHF stations collectively had revenues great enough to cover costs of doing business; during the other eight years of the period, they reported average operating losses ranging from $6,000 to as much as $80,000 per year for each station.

One problem faced by UHF stations is that in most areas only a small proportion of television-equipped homes had sets which could bring in the signals of stations on UHF channels. In August 1965 a survey made by the United States Census Bureau indicated that only 12 million of the nation's 53.7 million television homes had sets providing UHF reception. That problem will be less serious in future years, as a result of an act of Congress requiring all-channel tuning on all sets put on the market after April 1964. Estimates are that by 1970 or 1972 television sets in at least three-quarters of all homes will be able to receive UHF signals, with the result that stations on UHF channels will be able to show revenues and profits more nearly in line with those of VHF stations.

NATIONAL NETWORKS

National radio and television networks occupy an important place in American broadcasting. They perform special services with no direct counterpart in the operations of stations. For the national advertiser, they provide a nationwide interconnected system of stations, which enables him to deliver his advertising message simultaneously to all parts of the country. For the affiliated station, they provide a program service that could not be duplicated locally. Television networks provide their affiliates with programs that are more expensive and of higher quality than would otherwise be available, and television and radio networks offer excellent national news service and coverage of important special events, which no station could even attempt individually.

Network Operations

Each of the national television networks maintains studios for the origination of programs in New York and Hollywood; in addition, many of the networks' news programs come directly from Washington. The same cities serve as origination points for radio networks; some radio network programs are also produced in Chicago. Each national network serves four basic functions. First, it provides a schedule of programs ranging from an hour or two a day for radio networks to as much as nine to twelve hours a day for each of the television networks. Some of these programs are produced by the network itself; others, especially evening-hour programs on television, are secured from outside package production companies on a contract basis. Second, the network sells these programs—most of them at least—or advertising spots within the programs, to national advertisers. Third, the network distributes its programs over A.T.&T. facilities to affiliated stations throughout the country and pays the affiliates for carrying the programs having commercial messages. And finally, in an effort to attract larger audiences for its programs, the network carries on a continuous promotion campaign to bring its offerings to the attention of the public.

Each of the network companies is organized in a somewhat different manner, and the organizational structure of even the same network is changed from time to time, especially when changes are made in top administrative personnel. However, on the basis of functions performed, the approximately 2,500 employees of a national television network company, other than top management, might be grouped into about ten major departments, as follows:

> *Financial department.* Prepares and approves budget, handles accounting, billings and collections.
> *Legal department.* Clears literary and music rights, handles contracts with talent and with program package producers,

negotiates contracts with unions, and handles other miscellaneous legal business.

Sales department. Sells programs, talent, program time, and spot announcement time to advertisers and handles all of the network's contacts with advertisers and advertising agencies. Usually includes or works closely with a *sales promotion department* and a *research department,* both of which prepare materials to be used by sales personnel.

Program department. Responsible for the network's weekly schedule of programs. Selects programs to be produced by packagers and develops and produces some programs for the network. Employees include producers, directors, writers, announcers, entertainers, casting experts, musicians, and others involved with presentation of programs.

News and public-affairs department. Responsible for the planning, production and presentation of all news programs, public-affairs programs, and special-events broadcasts. Usually includes a separate *sports department,* which handles all broadcasts of sports events.

Continuity acceptance or program practices department. The network's "censoring" agency; checks all scripts and all copy for commercials and screens all filmed materials to see that nothing is broadcast that is contrary to law or to network policy standards.

Operations department. Concerned with actually presenting programs and putting them on the network line. Includes engineers, camera men, sound technicians, lighting experts, sound effects specialists, floor men, ushers, maintenance men, and the like.

Information department. Provides program logs and program information to newspapers, handles on-the-air promotion for programs, etc.

Station relations or affiliate relations department. Selects stations to be affiliated with the network and also handles all contacts with affiliated stations, secures clearances for commercial programs, and keeps affiliates informed about programs to be presented. Includes a *traffic department,* which orders A.T.&T. circuits to connect affiliates with the network and procures the special circuits used for special-events broadcasts.

Owned-and-operated stations department. Supervises general activities of the stations owned and operated by the network company itself.

By far the largest department is Operations; in 1962 nearly 1,300 employees of the CBS Television Network were included in the Operations Department, as compared with approximately one-third that number in the network's Program Department. Smallest of the operating departments is usually Continuity Acceptance; about 40 or 45 people are needed to screen programs and commercial materials prior to broadcast. The department in charge of network-owned-and-operated stations will also have a relatively small number of employees in headquarters of the network company itself, although, combined, the 15 television stations owned by the three national networks required the services of at least 2,500 people—not classed technically as network employees.

Radio networks require a relatively small number of employees, since they provide only a limited program service to their affiliated stations. However, the same basic functions performed for television networks also apply in the case of radio network concerns, and organizational patterns are roughly the same for radio as for television.

Network Program Service

The success of any national network organization depends on the quality and popularity of the programs it provides. Although radio networks offer a limited program service made up primarily of news reports and short features, each of the national television networks provides its affiliates with from 60 to 80 hours of programs a week, at least 95 per cent of which consists of commercial programs. This volume of programming must be maintained whether the network is able to sell all of its programs or not; affiliates depend on the television network to fill a large proportion of their broadcasting time. A major part of each television network's evening programming is provided by outside package suppliers and usually is in filmed form. Network program offerings will be considered in a later chapter; however, one or two aspects of network service should be mentioned at this point.

Television networks are in vigorous competition with one

another both for audiences and for advertising. In part, a network's success depends on the popularity of the programs included in its schedule, which of course reflects the ability of the network's program executives to select those entertainment programs that will best satisfy the public's tastes, and to schedule them at hours when they have the best chance of reaching audiences. But also important in its competition with other networks is the "prestige" each network enjoys—its "image" in the minds of listeners and of advertisers. Consequently, each network spends millions of dollars each year to enhance its corporate "image." NBC's experiments with color programming over the years were encouraged, certainly, by the interest of its parent company, the Radio Corporation of America, in selling color television sets; but NBC's adoption of a virtually "all-color" evening schedule in the autumn of 1965 also added to that network's prestige with the general public—and forced its rivals to offer substantial amounts of color programming as well. But network prestige, the network "image," depends also on the "special" programs it provides. Some are entertainment features of unusually high quality or special audience appeal. Others are programs important for their cultural values—broadcasts of operas, or programs featuring symphony orchestras or ballet companies.

But a majority of each network's prestige offerings are in the fields of information and special events. The regularly scheduled news programs provided by each network cost far more to produce than can be recovered by the sale of such programs to advertisers. The same is usually true of the many documentary programs each network presents at frequent intervals. Coverage of special events—national elections, national political conventions, the various Gemini space flights, and the like—entails production costs in each case of millions of dollars, in addition to loss of network revenues resulting from the cancellation of regular commercial programs. Also a factor in network prestige is the broadcasting of various sports events; *Sponsor* magazine estimates that national television networks spent more than $99 million during the 1965–66 season for broadcasting rights to such sports features as football, basketball, and baseball games; golf matches; and similar events—and the *Sponsor* figure does not include costs of production. Networks spend literally millions of dollars each year in an effort to outdo their competitors in the programs they offer for listeners.

Network-Affiliated Stations

With the exception of the Mutual Broadcasting System, each of the national network companies is the owner of a number of television and radio stations—a combined total for all three networks of 15 VHF television stations and 19 AM radio stations. In addition, each network provides program service to other stations in which the network companies have no financial interest whatever, stations known as "affiliates," linked to the network operating companies by "affiliation" contracts in which the station agrees to broadcast certain commercial programs provided by the network. To enable national advertisers to reach the largest possible number of listeners, every network company attempts to secure affiliates in all or practically all of the nation's major markets.

But there are three television networks, and not all major cities have as many as three commercial television stations. A number have only two stations; a few fairly important markets have only one. As a result, a television network is not always able to secure a "primary" affiliate in every major city—a station obligated by contract to give first preference to programs offered by that network. So in markets with only one or two commercial television stations, a television outlet not only has a "primary" affiliation arrangement with one network, but may also have a "secondary" affiliation with another. The station gives preference to programs offered by the first network; however, it also carries programs provided by the second network when these can be worked into its weekly schedule. In many cases programs of the second network are supplied on film or video tape and carried on a delayed basis at hours convenient to the station. Table 11 shows the number of cities in which each national television network had primary affiliates during the latter part of 1965; in addition, CBS had secondary affiliation contracts with stations in 19 cities and NBC with stations in 38 cities. The American Broadcasting Company with fewer primary affiliates than either

TABLE 11

TELEVISION STATIONS LISTED AS PRIMARY AFFILIATES OF NATIONAL TELEVISION NETWORKS, AUTUMN 1965

Cities with	Number of Cities	Stations affiliated with						Nonaffiliated Stations	
		ABC		CBS		NBC			
		VHF	UHF	VHF	UHF	VHF	UHF	VHF	UHF
4 or more stations	23	22 [1]	1	22	1	21	2	21 [1]	17
3 stations	69	56	12	58	10	60	9	—	2
2 stations	50	11	6	35	7	35	4	2	—
1 station	177	26	6	69	5	47	16	8	—
Totals	319	115 [1]	25	184	23	163	31	31 [1]	19

[1] Figures include one VHF Mexican station serving as the ABC affiliate in San Diego, and one VHF Canadian station, unaffiliated with any American network, serving the Detroit area.

Figures based on information given in station listings in the 1966 *Broadcasting Yearbook*.

of its competitors had secondary arrangements with stations in 110 different cities.

Network affiliation is much less important to radio stations than to television outlets, in view of the limited program service that radio networks provide and the very small amounts that stations receive for carrying network programs. During 1965, only about one AM radio station in four was affiliated with a national radio network. In the 50 largest cities throughout the country, the NBC and CBS radio networks had fewer than 45 affiliated stations each, including network-owned stations. ABC had 36 affiliates and Mutual a slightly smaller number, according to information given in the *Broadcasting Yearbook* for 1966.

Network payments to affiliates. Affiliation contracts usually provide that the station is paid by the network for the time used to carry commercial network programs. Since the four national radio networks have combined revenues totaling only $35–40 million a year, not much money remains after payment of rental on network lines and other network operating costs, so that most of the radio affiliates receive only nominal payments for carrying network programs. Many of the smaller stations receive no cash payments at all; they are simply allowed to carry the network's programs without charge and, if possible, to sell to local advertisers certain unsponsored programs the network makes available. High-powered stations, especially those in major markets, fare somewhat better; in 1964 the network-affiliated radio stations in the 25 largest metropolitan areas—network-owned stations not included—received an average of approximately $45,000 each from the network companies with which they had contracts. However, network payments to the more than 1,000 affiliates in smaller communities averaged not more than $4,500 to $5,000, and at least a part of this amount represents revenues from programs provided by regional rather than national networks.

Television stations receive much more substantial payments for the time used to carry network programs; in 1964, national television networks paid more than $177 million to their approximately 500 affiliated stations—the 15 network-owned stations not included—or an average of more than $350,000 for each affiliate. The amount received by each station naturally varies, according to the number of hours of commercial network programs the station carries and the rates charged for station time. Compensation for primary affiliates is determined on the basis of a rather complicated formula, varying in details from one network to another. Usually the standard affiliation contract requires the station to broadcast about 24 hours of network commercial programs each month without payment. For each additional hour of commercial programming carried the station receives one-third of the highest one-time hourly rate on the station's own rate card. The "hours" referred to are not actual clock hours, however; the station is given full credit for programs scheduled in "Class A" time, but in other time periods two "clock hours" of network programming are counted as equaling one "contract hour" for purposes of affiliate compensation. In some cases, network affiliation contracts omit the "free hours" provision; in others, payment for station time may be somewhat higher than the standard one-third of the station's base rate. Or at the other extreme, some stations in very small markets receive no payment whatever from the networks with which they are affiliated; they are simply allowed to carry the network's programs—commercials included—and to derive what revenues they can from the sale of spot announcements in chain-break periods between programs. Stations with secondary affiliation contracts are usually paid from 25 to 30 per cent of their one-time rates for the time in which network programs are carried, but with no deductions made for "free" hours.

Other contract provisions.   In almost all cases, network contracts call for the network companies to pay the costs of delivering the network programs to the affiliated station—in other words, the rental on A.T.&T. lines connecting the station with network originating points. Affiliates, of course, have the privilege of carrying network sustaining programs without payment. In addition, several provisions are standard in all contracts as a result of regulations laid down by the Federal Communications Commission. Affiliation contracts may not provide that any station is the "exclusive" outlet for any one network in its community; the network retains the right to allow other stations in the area to broadcast its programs, although in practice only those programs the affiliate does not wish to carry are offered to other stations.

The affiliated station on its part may accept programs offered by competing networks, and does in fact accept large numbers of such programs—at least if it is a station in a one- or two-station market with a primary affiliation contract with one network and a secondary arrangement with another. Every affiliate has the right, by contract, to reject any program the network offers, whether because the station's manager considers it unsuitable or a program of low quality, or because he prefers to use the time period to present a locally produced or syndicated program or even a program provided by a different network. The network company may not determine the rates the affiliated station charges for advertising time, other than the rates charged for network programs. Prior to 1963, standard affiliation contracts gave the network an option on certain hours of the station's time each day; this practice is now prohibited by a regulation of the Federal Communications Commission. Finally, by Commission regulation, network-affiliation contracts cover periods of not more than two years; at the end of any contract period either the network or the station is free to make other arrangements.

Networks and Advertisers

National advertisers buy time on networks partly because of the convenience of being able to have a single sponsored program or commercial message broadcast by stations throughout the country, and also, in the case of television, because network programs fill the most desirable hours of station time and attract larger audiences than the advertiser could reach by national spot advertising. Whether the advertiser buys time to present his own sponsored program or buys time for spot announcements, his dealings with the network company will be handled through his advertising agency. Program time is ordinarily bought on a 13-week, 26-week or 52-week basis; the contract covering the purchase gives the advertiser an option on renewal for an additional period, or allows him to cancel the program at the end of any 13-week cycle. In most cases, spot announcements to be included in a network participating program are bought on the same basis, although other spot purchase arrangements are also common. Occasionally an advertiser may purchase time for a "special" one-time program, usually an hour or more in length; to make room for such programs, the network cancels or "pre-empts" for that date the regular programs normally broadcast during the time period the "special" is to use.

Costs of network time.   Network salesmen always attempt to sell an advertiser a "full network" of stations—all of the stations with which the network has affiliation contracts. After all, most costs of presenting the program—administrative, selling, technical, and costs of the program itself—remain the same whether the program is broadcast by 50 stations or over the facilities of 200 stations. But the advertiser is not required to buy the full network, at least if he sponsors his own program or shares sponsorship with another concern. He can "order" stations in some markets, and omit affiliates in other markets less important in his advertising campaign, provided he buys enough stations to bring his total expenditure for network time up to a network-stipulated minimum figure. If the advertiser buys a "spot" in a participating program, however, he takes whatever lineup of stations the network has already secured to carry that program. In either case, however, the amount he pays for time will be based on the rates charged for the specific stations carrying his sponsored program or the program in which his participating spot announcement appears.

As noted in an earlier chapter, the one-time rate for a 60-minute program in prime time in 1965 or 1966 was a little more than $140,000 for a full network of television stations. The actual rate charged by CBS during the 1965–66 season was $153,725 for the full network of 213 CBS stations; the NBC rate for a 201-station network was slightly less, and the ABC basic hourly rate for a network including all of its 124 primary affiliates was only a little less than $114,000—but higher, of course, if some of ABC's secondary affiliates also carried the program. In each case, cost of time for a 30-minute program would be 60 per cent of the base hourly rate, in line with industry practice. Even on a one-time basis the actual charge for program time would be somewhat less than the figures given. The advertiser may not order all of the stations affiliated with the network, or some affiliates may decide not to carry the advertiser's program; in either case, the network rate upon which charges for time are based would be somewhat reduced.

Discounts on charges for time.   Other factors also operate to reduce the amounts actually paid for program time. Figures in the preceding paragraph relate to Class A time—periods between 6:00 or 7:00 P.M. and 11:00 P.M. For programs broadcast in other than Class A time, the rate charged for time is reduced by 50 per cent in some cases, and by as much as 66 per cent in others. In addition, networks follow the practice of giving quantity discounts for the purchase of time. An advertiser is given a discount if he contracts for his program to be carried for 13 weeks and a decidedly greater discount if he commits his firm to use the time period for a full 52 weeks. The amount of the discounts given is difficult to estimate; it is influenced in each case by the total amount of money the advertiser spends with the network involved, as well as by the number of weeks the sponsored program stays on the air. Perhaps an average figure would be in the area of 20 to 25 per cent, but it has been reported that in certain special cases, discounts have been allowed of as much as 40 per cent of the base one-time rate charged for time.[4]

It is difficult to provide specific information concerning charges made by television networks for spot announcements inserted in participating programs. Amounts paid by advertisers for each "commercial minute" vary widely, according to the time of day, the popularity of the network, the size of the audience reached, and the "prestige" value of the program. As noted in an earlier chapter, the average amount charged—of course before discounts—for one-minute participating announcements in prime time during the latter part of 1965 was a little more than $40,000. However, during the 1965–66 season, charges for one-minute announcements in a number of nighttime shows have run as high as $50,000—and in one popular situation comedy, as high as $62,000. And indications are that average charges for commercial participating spots will go even higher; the trade magazine *Sponsor* estimates that by the middle of the 1966–67 broadcasting season, the amounts paid for one-minute spots in evening network programs would average at least $50,-000. This is of course before discounts; television networks give discounts for quantity purchases of spot announcements just as they do for purchases of program time.

There is little likelihood, however, that rates charged for commercial announcements carried by radio networks will experience any similar increase. In comparison with the charges for television network time, the amounts charged for one-minute

---

[4] Early in 1966, CBS-TV released new rate cards which virtually eliminated quantity discounts for purchase of either program time or spot announcements. Under the CBS plan, an advertiser spending $50 million a year for sponsorship of CBS television programs would pay the same rates per program or per announcement as one spending less than one-tenth that amount. Although no discount was provided for purchase of time on a 52-week basis, the new card set rates for summer months at levels appreciably lower than those charged during the regular winter season from mid-September through March.

announcements on radio networks are extremely low—from $800 to $1,600, depending on the network and the program used. Even costs of time and talent for a 5-minute radio network program, including a little more than a minute of commercial material, were in 1965–66 no more than $1,300 to $1,530 for a full radio network.

Network Revenues and Expenses

Network revenues, of course, come primarily from the sale of time to national advertisers. Television networks also have substantial revenues from other sources: sale of programs or of talent to sponsors of programs, for example, and the syndication of filmed programs to American and foreign stations. In 1964, the three national television networks had combined revenues of $562.8 million from sale of network time and announcements, according to the financial report issued by the Federal Communications Commission. In addition, the three companies had revenues totaling $409.2 million from sale of programs and talent, and $37.9 million from various other activities. These figures are for the three companies' network operations as such, not including revenues accruing from the operation of network-owned stations. But from the total of more than a billion dollars the network companies received, expenses had to be paid. Something more than $83 million went to advertising agencies as commissions on sale of network time. Another $214 million was paid to network-owned and affiliated stations for the use of station time to broadcast network commercial programs. Payments totaling between $36 million and $40 million were made to the American Telephone & Telegraph Company for rental of cable and relay facilities used to transmit the networks' programs to affiliated stations. More than $540 million was spent for programs—a part of the total representing production costs of network-produced programs and a larger amount representing amounts paid for programs supplied by outside package-agencies. Other expenses—salaries, administrative costs, purchases of equipment, costs of selling, promotion, and the like—reduced net profits of the three national networks before federal taxes to a combined total of $60.2 million or about 6 per cent of total revenues for the year. In comparison, the 15 network-owned television stations reported combined net profits for the same year totaling $96.3 million, before federal taxes.

The four radio networks find themselves in a much less desirable financial position. During 1964, the four national network companies had total revenues of only a little over $37 million, of which $31 million came from sale of network time after payment of agency commissions. But operating expenses, including payments to affiliated stations, totaled more than $36.3 million, so that for the year 1964 the four companies showed a combined net profit before federal taxes of only $671,000 on their network activities. Fortunately, the 19 radio stations owned by three of the network companies had combined earnings of $3,631,000 in 1964. The radio network companies made their best recent financial showing in 1963, when they reported a combined operating profit of about $900,000. But during the preceding year, the radio network companies combined had a net loss of $2,000; in 1961, a loss of $3.01 million; and in 1960, a loss of more than $6.9 million.

The operation of a television network, involving tremendous risks and the expenditure each year of hundreds of millions of dollars, has proved to be a highly profitable undertaking. But at least in recent years, the same is hardly true of the operation of radio networks.

7

BROADCASTING AND GOVERNMENT

The system of broadcasting used in the United States is based on private ownership and operation of radio and television stations and on the licensing and regulation of such stations by an agency of the federal government. The first radio law, enacted by Congress in 1910, required American passenger ships to install wireless equipment as a safety measure; both transmitters and the operators who used them were licensed by the Department of Commerce. A 1912 amendment to the original Radio Act extended the licensing provisions to cover wireless installations on land. Both laws of course dealt with radio as a device used for point-to-point wireless communication; "broadcasting," or the dissemination of radio signals to be picked up by the public at large, had not yet come into being.

When more or less formal broadcasting

operations did begin about 1920, the early stations were licensed by the Department of Commerce; as the number of broadcasting stations increased, the Department specified the wavelength on which each station could operate and the hours during which it would be allowed to broadcast. But in 1926, as already noted in Chapter 3, a ruling by a federal court held that the Department of Commerce had no legal right to impose such restrictions on radio stations. The result was a state of chaotic interference between signals of various stations—and the enactment by Congress of the Radio Act of 1927.

The Federal Radio Commission

The Act of 1927 created a five-member Federal Radio Commission; it gave the Commission power to "classify stations" —partly at least to differentiate between broadcasting stations and those engaging in point-to-point communication—and to issue and renew licenses if the granting of such authorizations would serve "the public interest, convenience, or necessity." Specific authority was given to assign each broadcasting station to a particular frequency, to designate the power it might use, and to specify the hours during which it could operate. Through regulations it issued and through policies it applied in the relicensing of stations, the new Commission was able to put broadcasting on a much more orderly basis and to deal with the problem of interference, eliminating in the process a number of stations which failed to meet the regulatory body's minimum engineering requirements.

When the Federal Radio Commission was created, most broadcasters believed that its authority was to extend only to technical matters so that problems of interference between stations could be dealt with effectively. Apparently many members of Congress had the same understanding, since the Act of 1927 included a provision stating specifically that the Commission was to have no power of censorship over programs. But members of the new Commission took a broader view of their responsibilities. They were instructed by the Radio Act to issue licenses in "the public interest, convenience, or necessity"; this at least implied that they were to take into account the *kind of material* a licensee put on the air, no less than his technical engineering record, before granting license renewal to his station. In ruling on conflicting applications for the same radio facilities in the *Great Lakes* case in 1929, the regulatory body laid down what it considered standards for desirable programming by stations. Even more to the point, at least with respect to the "no censorship" provision of the Radio Act of 1927, the Commission during the first two or three years of its existence, refused to grant license renewals to several radio stations whose owners had persistently broadcast materials that Commission members felt were contrary to "the public interest." One licensee had used his station to advertise a cancer cure; another gave wide publicity over his station to a "goat gland" rejuvenation operation performed regularly in the hospital he owned; two others had broadcast what the Commission held to be vicious attacks on religious and civic groups. When the stations involved were denied license renewals and their owners appealed to federal courts, the courts held that the Commission was required by law to determine the elements involved in broadcasting "in the public interest." Consequently, in the courts' opinion, the Commission had not exceeded its legal authority by refusing license renewal to stations which broadcast materials which, in the judgment of members of the regulatory agency, were not in that "public interest." With the Commission's authority so upheld by the courts, the offending stations were taken off the air.

The reasoning used by the Commission in justifying its actions in spite of the "no censorship" provision of the Act of 1927 is at least interesting. Censorship, argued the Commission, refers only to the use of *prior restraint*. For example, if the federal regulatory body would refuse to allow a station to broadcast some specific program, that would constitute censorship as prohibited in the Act. However, consideration of a station's *past* programming operations, taken as a whole, to determine whether or not the station has operated "in the public interest" during the period of its license, is not censorship. No *prior restraint* is involved, even when the Commission considers the applicant's past record as indicating the type of programming he will likely provide in future years. This very narrow interpretation of the "no censorship" provision of the law has been upheld consistently by federal courts whenever the issue has been raised. As a result, for all practical purposes, "censorship" by the Commission—the Federal Radio Commission or its successor, the Federal Communications Commission—refers only to restrictive action taken *prior to* the broadcast of a specific program, and the Commission is in no way prevented, in its actions on license renewal, from punishing a licensee for past programming offenses or shortcomings.

The Federal Communications Commission

In 1934, Congress passed a new radio law, the Communications Act of 1934, and placed the responsibility of regulating broadcasting in the hands of a new agency, the Federal Communications Commission. The Communications Commission has seven members, appointed for seven-year terms by the President of the United States with the consent of the Senate; the President also designates the member who is to act as Chairman of the Commission. Those appointed to the regulatory agency may have no financial interest in any broadcasting operation, including the manufacture of equipment; not more than four Commissioners serving at any one time may be members of the same political party. The Act of 1934 gives the Communications Commission jurisdiction both over broadcasting stations and over those engaging in point-to-point wireless communication—amateur stations, airplane, ship, taxicab and other industrial radio installations, police radio, and the like. The Commission also regulates interstate telephone and telegraph communications, whether by wire or by microwave relay systems. However, the Act of 1934 gives the agency no authority to regulate network operations, at least directly, or to deal with telephone or telegraph wire systems entirely within the borders of a single state. Similarly, the Federal Communications Commission has no jurisdiction over closed-circuit television installations, since such installations do not engage in broadcasting or wireless transmission of signals, and being intrastate in character are not covered by the Congressional authority to "regulate interstate commerce."

The Communications Act of 1934 includes practically all

of the provisions of the earlier Radio Act; licensing stations in "the public interest, convenience, or necessity" is continued as the basis of regulation. Also included in Section 326 of the Act of 1934 is the no-censorship provision of the earlier law: "Nothing in this Act shall be understood or construed to give the Commission the power of censorship over the radio communications or signals transmitted by any radio station." But in view of court decisions which limit the interpretation of censorship to some form of prior restraint, any question as to the power of the Federal Communications Commission to consider the past or proposed programming of a station in passing on applications for licenses has become almost entirely academic, although the situation is one that many broadcasters resent.

THE LICENSING OF STATIONS

The Communications Act of 1934 states that its purpose is to "make available ... (an) efficient, nationwide ... radio communication service," and by implication, to maintain competition in broadcasting, since "all laws of the United States relating to ... monopolies and to combinations in restraint of trade are declared to be applicable to ... radio communications." The Act offers no further guides to the Commission's activities in regulating radio, or regulating television, since television is considered technically as a form of radio broadcasting. The Act gives the Commission authority to make such rules and regulations and to require such reports and other information from licensees or applicants "as may be necessary in the execution of its functions." However, it leaves to the Commission the decision on what constitutes "the public interest" in broadcasting and what principles should be applied to achieve its basic objectives.

As interpreted by the Federal Communications Commission, the responsibility of serving "the public interest" in the licensing of radio and television stations has two principal aspects. First, the Commission is concerned with the formulation and execution of policies that will provide an efficient broadcasting service throughout the nation, that will place the operation of stations in the hands of well-qualified men, and that will maintain a high degree of competition in broadcasting. And second, the Communications Commission, like the Federal Radio Commission before it, is interested in the type of programming provided for listeners.

Efficient Broadcasting Service

The Commission's first objective, of course, is to insure the creation of a nationwide, efficient broadcasting service. In this area, the regulatory body has been guided by four basic principles. First, as far as possible, service should be made available to listeners in all sections of the United States—in remote rural areas as well as in areas of dense population. Second, listeners in each area or each community should have access to signals of as many different stations as possible to permit a wide choice in the selection of programs. Third, a *local* broadcasting service should be available in as many different communities as possible, to serve distinctly local needs. And finally, interference between stations should be held to a minimum; the Communications Act specifically enjoins the Commission to adopt regulations "to prevent interference between stations."

No one, certainly, would question the desirability of any of these objectives. In putting the principles into practice, however, the Commission has encountered serious problems. All too frequently steps taken to attain one objective have resulted in serious injury to others.

The clear-channel problem. Take, for example, the matter of clear-channel stations. In 1934, the Communications Commission set aside as "clear" channels 40 of the 86 channels or frequencies then available for use by standard radio stations in the United States. Each such channel or frequency was to be used by a single, high-powered AM station; no other station was to be permitted to use the same frequency at night, and daytime operation of a secondary, low-powered station on that frequency was to be authorized only in rare instances. The purpose obviously was to insure a dependable, interference-free service, day and night, to listeners in every part of the United States. But the exclusive use of these frequencies by a few high-powered stations conflicted with other basic Commission objectives: the availability of service from as many different AM stations as possible for listeners in each area and the providing of local station service in large numbers of individual communities. So although the Commission still supports the clear-channel idea in theory, in practice the concept has been greatly weakened by the authorization of a constantly increasing number of secondary stations operating on the theoretically "clear" channels. By the end of 1965, a total of 88 high-powered, 50,000-watt AM stations had been assigned to the 43 channels then designated as "clear," as well as nearly 300 secondary stations, some using power of as much as 5,000 or 10,000 watts. Approximately one-third of these secondary stations also remained on the air at night as well as in the daytime.[1] As a result, the areas over which the 50,000-watt clear-channel stations are able to provide interference-free service have been greatly reduced.

The increasing number of stations.   The Federal Communications Commission's objectives of providing local service in as many communities as possible and of giving listeners a choice of signals of a large number of different stations have also resulted in serious interference between radio stations assigned to local and regional channels. During the 1930s, the Commission's rules required that there be a substantial mileage separation between any two stations operating on the same frequency—the distance of course was greater when the stations involved used power of more than 250 watts. But by the end of World War II these standards had been so much relaxed that four or five times as many stations are now assigned to each frequency as the number which could have been allowed to use that frequency

---

[1] In addition, by 1965 a total of 30 high-powered 50,000-watt American stations and more than 430 stations with lower power had been assigned by the Federal Communications Commission to twelve channels reserved by treaty for primary use by high-powered stations in Canada, Mexico, and Cuba.

in 1940 and earlier years. Each of the 41 "regional" channels in
the standard band of frequencies now accommodates from 35
to 40 stations with power of from 1,000 to 5,000 watts, two-fifths
of them broadcasting at night as well as during the daytime.
In addition, each of the six "local" channels is used by an average
of at least 160 full-time stations, all using no more than 250
watts power at night, but in most cases allowed to increase
power to 1,000 watts during the daytime. The result is that
even though nearly all of the full-time regional stations are
required to use directional antennas, interference between stations on the same frequencies has become an extremely serious
problem. In fact, the situation was so serious that, as noted in
Chapter 4, the Federal Communications Commission ordered a
partial "freeze" in 1962 on the grants of authorizations for new
AM stations to give members of the agency an opportunity
to find means to deal with the problem. The freeze lasted only
two years, however, and since 1964, the number of stations and
the power stations are permitted to use have both steadily increased.

It might be noted in passing, too, that station overpopulation has probably been one factor contributing to the economic
problems faced by many of the stations in the AM band, referred to in an earlier chapter.

Television authorizations.   In the case of television, interference
between stations using the same channel has not become a
problem, largely because the Commission made plans for assignment of stations before issuing authorizations for any considerable number of television facilities. At the end of the television
"freeze" in 1952, as noted in Chapter 4, the Federal Communications Commission issued a "table of allocations" specifying
the exact channels which might be used in each of about 1,300
large and small cities; mileage separations between stations using
the same channel were made great enough to prevent possible
serious interference. Of the nearly 2,000 commercial television
stations provided for in the table, only about 550 were to be
VHF stations; the remainder would be assigned to UHF channels. In 1965 the Commission made a major revision of its
allocations table which reduced the possible number of UHF

stations which might be constructed; no major change was made, however, in allocations for VHF stations.[2]

Although the Commission's original allocations table made provision for a possible total of nearly 2,000 commercial television stations, many of the cities to which assignments were made were far too small to support a television operation—communities in some cases with no more than four or five thousand inhabitants. In addition, nearly three-fourths of the stations provided for in the original table were to be assigned to UHF channels and, collectively at least, the UHF stations which have come on the air since 1952 have not been financially successful. Adding to the problem, the allocations table created nearly 250 "mixed markets" in which any UHF stations constructed would be forced to compete with stations on VHF channels in the same community. Partially to deal with this problem, the Commission has since "de-intermixed" a few cities, shifting channel assignments to require all stations in some markets to operate on UHF channels, and in other communities on VHF channels. But this sort of action has been feasible only in a small number of cases; in most of the "mixed markets" created by the allocations table, the problem still remains. Of course, difficulties of UHF stations have been somewhat lessened by the requirement of all-channel tuning equipment on television sets. But with few unused VHF channels still remaining, except in extremely small markets, it is doubtful whether the number of commercial television stations will increase beyond the 700 or at most the 750 mark in the predictable future; even with all-channel tuning, UHF stations are still at a competitive disadvantage in markets also served by VHF television outlets.

Qualifications of Licensees

A second aspect of "public interest" in the granting of licenses relates to the type of individuals to whom the Commission grants the privilege of operating broadcasting stations.

---

[2] In 1963 the Federal Communications Commission issued a table of allocations for FM radio stations, to minimize the possibility of interference between stations in the FM band.

The Communications Act of 1934 provides only that applicants for licenses must be citizens of the United States and that an authorization for a station may not be granted to a person who has had a previous license revoked for violation of federal anti-trust laws. Beyond this, standards are left to the discretion of the Federal Communications Commission; the Act merely provides that written applications for licenses must set forth "such facts as the Commission may prescribe" as to the citizenship, character, and "financial and other qualifications" of the applicant.

Legal, technical, and financial qualifications. The Commission's requirements with respect to the personal qualifications of an applicant are reasonably clear. As provided in the Communications Act, an individual licensed as the owner of a station must be an American citizen. If the applicant is a corporation, it must be incorporated under the laws of one of the states of the Union; no officer or director of the company may be an alien; and not more than one-fifth of the capital stock of the corporation may be owned by aliens or their representatives. The charter of the corporation must also authorize it to engage in broadcasting activities, either specifically or in general terms.

A licensee must also be "technically" qualified. As interpreted by the Commission, "technical" qualifications relate to the special technical knowledge and skills required to construct and operate a broadcasting station. Either the applicant must himself possess these technical skills or he must show that he has or will engage a staff of employees with the competence to carry on the actual operations of the station, including engineers with the necessary technical qualifications. The Commission also considers the applicant's plans for construction of studios and for the equipment to be used, as set forth in the written application, to determine whether they are such as to make possible an effective operation.

For an applicant to be "financially qualified" means simply that he has enough money in hand—or assurances of its availability from loans or from sale of stock in a corporation—to cover costs of construction of the station and to pay for its initial costs of operation. Although requirements vary from case to case, the Commission usually expects the applicant to have the financial resources needed to operate the station for at least two or three months without having to depend during that period on revenues derived from the sale of advertising time.

Character qualifications. In addition, the Commission considers the "character" qualifications of the applicant, whether the application is for the construction of a new station or for renewal of license of an existing station. Licenses for broadcasting facilities have consistently been denied to individuals who have been convicted of violations of federal laws, especially of laws relating to monopolistic practices. However, license renewals have in a few cases been granted to corporations wholly owned by larger nonbroadcasting concerns, after officers of the parent corporation have been found guilty in federal courts of violating antitrust laws. Licenses and license renewals have also been denied in a number of cases to individuals found to have made false statements in applications or in reports to the Commission; the Commission holds that the making of such false statements is *prima facie* evidence that the applicant "lacks the character qualifications necessary for the licensee of a broadcasting station." In several instances the Commission has refused to grant licenses or license renewals to applicants who have broadcast misleading medical advertising or have used station facilities to launch attacks on racial or religious groups. In one or two instances, license renewals have been refused to stations whose owners conducted fraudulent promotional contests; in at least one case in recent years a station was ordered off the air because an employee was allowed, over a period of several months, to make frequent use of "smutty" or suggestive language in programs of recorded music. In all of these situations, the Commission held that the objectionable activities reflected on the character of the applicant or licensee and made him unfit to be the licensee of a broadcasting station.

Preventing Monopoly in Broadcasting

The Federal Communications Act of 1934 provides that all federal laws relating to illegal monopolies are to apply to broadcasting. The Federal Communications Commission interprets the Act as requiring it to take such steps as may be necessary to preserve competition in broadcasting, and in some degree at least, competition in the control of the various media of communication in any given community. Many of the Commission's policies in this are are set forth in formal rules and regulations. One set of regulations is intended to prevent a network from exercising too great a degree of control over the programming or other activities of affiliated stations. Since the Communications Act gives the Federal Communications Commission no direct authority over network companies, the regulations in each case relate to stations; usually the regulation starts with the language, "No license shall be granted to any station which has a contract with a network organization which," followed by the type of network activity at which the regulation is aimed. As noted in an earlier chapter, a station may not enter into an "exclusive" contract with a network prohibiting it from carrying programs offered by another network or preventing the network company from offering programs to other stations in the same community. A station may not give a network company an option on the use of any specified hours of its broadcasting time; it must retain for itself the right to reject any program offered by the network with which it is affiliated. One Commission regulation, prohibiting affiliation of any station with a network company operating more than one national network system, forced the National Broadcasting Company in 1943 to dispose of one of its two national radio networks. When NBC challenged the legality of this regulation in federal courts, the Commission's action was upheld by the Supreme Court of the United States.

Concentration of control over media of communications.   Both by regulations it has adopted and by its actions in the licensing of stations, the Federal Communications Commission has indicated its concern over the possibility of any one individual or corporation exercising too great a degree of control over agencies of mass communication. Regulations referred to in an earlier chapter limit the number of stations that may be licensed to any one owner or owning group; in 1965, the Commission took steps to limit still further the number of television stations that could be acquired in major cities by any one licensee corporation.

In addition, the Federal Communications Commission refused to allow one licensee to operate two stations of the same type in the same community, or two stations of the same type in different communities when the primary service area of one "substantially overlaps" the primary service area of the second. In one case, an applicant for a new television station was refused the grant at least partly on the grounds that the applicant company owned several other television stations in the same general part of the country; the Commission's position was that while no overlapping of station service areas would be created, the addition of the proposed new station would result in an "undue concentration of ownership of the agencies of mass communication" in the area. In four or five cases in which several applicants were competing for the same facility, the Commission has rejected the application of a local newspaper publisher to prevent a "concentration of control over media of communications" in the community. In a number of other cases, station authorizations have been refused because applicants were charged with "unfair competition" in nonbroadcasting business activities related to mass communications.

Maintaining competition in broadcasting business interests.   Probably the Federal Communications Commission's desire to prevent monopoly control and to maintain competition in broadcasting was a major cause of the regulatory agency's proposal in 1965 that national television network companies be barred from holding part-ownership interests in more than a fixed proportion of package-produced television programs included in evening network schedules. It was also proposed that the network companies be prohibited from acting as syndication companies in the distribution of off-network filmed television shows to stations in the United States, although syndication of the same programs to foreign stations would not be affected. The proposal was directly in line with a number of earlier actions taken by the Commission to restrict the activities of network companies in areas not related directly to network operation. Objections from the Commission as early as 1941 forced the national network companies to dispose of their company-owned talent agencies, which represented—and collected talent-management fees from —the announcers, actors, vocalists, and other entertainers who appeared on network programs. The Commission has also expressed its strong disapproval of network-owned spot sales agencies—NBC Spot Sales, CBS Radio Spot Sales, and the like— acting as station representatives for radio and television stations not owned by the networks themselves. Members of the regulatory body have been consistent in their belief that network companies should not be allowed to exert too great a power over the business activities of other facets of the broadcasting industry.

Few Americans would disagree with the Commission's basic purpose of maintaining competition and preventing monopoly control in broadcasting. Nor would many question the fact that at least partly as a result of the Commission's activities in this field, a high degree of competition actually does exist in the broadcasting industry in the United States.

THE COMMISSION AND PROGRAMS

Obviously, "public interest" in broadcasting does not relate solely to the distribution of station facilities among the several states, to qualifications of licensees, and to questions of monopoly control. It is affected also by the kinds of programs that stations provide for their listeners. As stated earlier in this chapter, both the Federal Radio Commission and the Federal Communications Commission have shown a continuing interest in station programming and in the types of material included in programs; program considerations have often been the basis upon which licenses or license renewals have been granted or have been refused. Furthermore, federal courts have held repeatedly that the "no censorship" provisions of the Acts of 1927 and 1934 do not prohibit the consideration of past programming records of licensees, or even their future program plans, when regulatory bodies created by the two Acts are passing on license applications. In fact, in some decisions courts have held that the Federal Communications Commission would be remiss in its duties if in making its decisions it failed to give due weight to questions relating to programming. In its decision in the *National Broadcasting Company* case in 1943, the Supreme Court of the United States said,[3]

... we are asked to regard the Commission as a kind of traffic officer, policing the wave lengths to prevent stations from interfering with each other. But the Act does not restrict the Commission merely to supervision of the traffic. It puts upon the Commission the burden of determining the composition of that traffic.

Program Regulation before 1946

Almost immediately after its creation, the Federal Radio Commission outlined its ideas on the requirements of providing programs in "the public interest." In the *Great Lakes* opinion in 1929, it held that broadcasters were expected to provide a balanced or "well-rounded" program structure, including programs of such types as agricultural information, religion, education, and discussions of public issues. In addition, the Radio Commission held that the broadcasting of programs or materials that tended to injure the listening public—attacks on civic or religious groups, for example, or fraudulent medical advertising—raised serious questions as to the desirability of granting license renewals to owners of offending stations. As has already been noted, several stations were taken off the air by the Federal Radio Commission because of the objectionable character of materials they broadcast.

Following its creation in 1934, the Federal Communications Commission gave relatively little attention to the requirement of balanced or well-rounded program service, possibly because at that time practically all radio stations *did* offer programs of a wide variety of types, including the kinds of program offerings that had been recommended in the *Great Lakes* opinion in 1929. But the Communications Commission did, in the years before the war, follow the policies of the Radio Commission with respect to the broadcasting of objectionable or harmful materials. Stations were taken to task for carrying questionable

---

[3] *National Broadcasting Company v. United States*, 319 U.S. 190, p. 215 (May 10, 1943).

medical advertising; hearings were ordered on license renewals of stations that had broadcast astrology programs or other materials tending to "create superstition." Similar action was taken against stations advertising lottery schemes, and in one or two cases the Commission threatened punitive action against any stations carrying network programs that included profanity or "materials bordering on obscenity." In 1939, the Commission released an informal memorandum warning stations against practices that "would be taken into consideration when licenses came up for renewal"—among them "hard liquor" advertising, overcommercialization, the broadcasting of programs creating excessive suspense, the overuse of phonograph records, and failure to provide "balance" in discussions of controversial public issues. In the years immediately preceding and during our nation's participation in World War II, the Commission seemed most concerned with problems relating to controversy and with the need to make time available for the views of minority groups. In any case, no actions were taken against stations for program shortcomings of other types until after the release in 1946 of a Commission memorandum popularly known as the *Blue Book*.

The Blue Book of 1946

The official title of the Commission's 1946 memorandum was *The Public Service Responsibility of Broadcast Licensees;* it has been more widely known as the *Blue Book* because of the color of its paper cover. In it, the Commission laid down two major criteria for determining whether or not a radio station was "serving the public interest" in its programming. The first criterion was an elaboration of the standards outlined in the Federal Radio Commission's *Great Lakes* opinion. To meet its responsibilities, a broadcasting station was expected to provide "balance" in programming. This involved the carrying of "a sufficient number" of "local, live" programs—as opposed to recorded materials or programs provided by networks. In addition, to insure that it provided "balance" in the programs it offered, a station was expected to include in its weekly schedule a "reasonable number" of educational programs, news programs, programs providing agricultural information, programs devoted to the discussion of important public issues, programs serving the interests of local nonprofit civic and religious groups and labor organizations, and programs intended to appeal to minority interests and tastes, such as broadcasts of classical music.

The second *Blue Book* criterion of "public interest" in programming related to the number of commercially sponsored programs and the number of spot announcements included in the station's weekly schedule. For the first time, the regulatory body took a strong stand against "the evils" of overcommercialization. And although intentionally vague as to the amount of advertising a station might properly carry, the *Blue Book* made it very clear that stations were expected to schedule a "sufficiently large" number of sustaining programs each week to insure balance in its over-all program structure. Also branded as objectionable was the carrying of an excessive number of commercial spot announcements—the memorandum noted that in some instances, stations had scheduled as many as 1,000 "spots" each week—and the "piling up" of commercials, or presenting two or more announcements in succession, without intervening entertainment materials.

To give effect to its new programming requirements, the Federal Communications Commission adopted new forms to be used in applications for new station authorizations and for renewal of licenses of stations already on the air. The new forms required applicants to indicate the proportions of time to be devoted each week to programs of each of the types called for in the *Blue Book* and the maximum number of spot announcements that would be carried. In addition, applicants for license renewal were asked to state the number of hours and minutes actually devoted to each of the types of programs and the number of commercial announcements broadcast during a week chosen by the Commission. Applicants were warned that promises made in applications would be compared with actual performance when applications for license renewal came up for consideration.

Broadcasters were understandably concerned over the *Blue Book's* assertion of the Commission's right to *require* stations to provide certain specific types of programming—even though such programs were already included in the schedules of nearly all stations. They were equally disturbed at the imposition of even vague limits on the amount of station time which could be sponsored, and on the number of commercial announcements broadcast each week. However, in several cases in which applicants appealed Commission decisions to federal courts, the courts ruled that consideration of future program plans was not "censorship," as prohibited by the Communications Act of 1934, and that the Commission was not exceeding the powers given it by Congress in laying down its *Blue Book* standards of programming.

Application of Blue Book Standards

For several years following the release of the 1946 memorandum, the programming and commercial standards laid down in the *Blue Book* were rigidly applied by the Commission in acting on license renewals and applications for new facilities. In a number of instances, stations already on the air were allowed to operate for months on a temporary license basis, until the program plans outlined in renewal applications were changed to meet Commission requirements. In other cases, stations were called to account by the Commission's staff for carrying an excessive number of commercial announcements. But the rapidly increasing number of radio stations, combined with economic problems created by the growing importance of television, forced the Commission after 1950 or 1952 to make some modifications in its requirements. In a number of major markets, the regulatory agency allowed certain stations to develop highly specialized types of programming aimed at limited segments of the total audience; for such stations, the *Blue Book* requirement of a "balanced" program structure was waived on the ground that other stations in the community were providing other kinds of programs. Radio stations using a "news and music" formula are now generally allowed to offer noncommercial spot announcements in support of community undertakings in place of presenting complete programs serving the interests of local groups. Stations in large cities are not required to provide programs of farm information, and only a small proportion of radio stations schedule programs that could technically be called "educational," or offer broadcasts of classical music or other programs of types described in the *Blue Book* as serving "minority interests and tastes."

Presumably, the Commission still holds to the ideal of a "balanced" and "well-rounded" program structure, but in recent years it has permitted a tremendous number of exceptions to be made to the general rule. Early in 1961, the regulatory agency issued a public notice that made it easier for stations to ask that such exceptions be made in the type of programs provided. The report imposed on every licensee or applicant for a license the obligation of surveying the needs and interests of listeners in his community and of developing a pattern of programming that would satisfy those needs and interests, especially those not already being met in programs offered by other stations. In addition, revised radio application forms adopted by the FCC in 1965 reduced the number of categories of more or less required programs, although the forms still required applicants to indicate the types of program service they expected to provide.

Changing conditions in broadcasting have also resulted in a relaxing of the Commission's standards with respect to commercial schedules. The *Blue Book* called for broadcasting stations to carry "a sufficient number" of programs on a sustaining basis; it also implied, at least, that a station broadcasting as many as a thousand commercial spot announcements in any one week was guilty of "commercial excesses." But with sponsorship of programs largely replaced by spot announcement advertising, the Commission's views have been materially modified. Since the middle 1950s, few radio or television stations have devoted more than three or four hours a week to sustaining programs; at the same time, the number of spot announcements has increased steadily, with no formal objection from the Commission. To be sure, members of the regulatory body still evidence a concern over "commercial excesses," but their ideas as to the number of announcements that may be carried have changed considerably—perhaps as a result of the fact that so many radio and television stations are operating at a loss. In any case, when in 1963 the Commission proposed the adoption of rules to limit the total time a station might devote to advertising announcements, the limits proposed were so lenient that a station would be allowed to schedule as many as 18 one-minute announcements in a single hour of broadcasting time, and a weekly total of more than 1,400 commercial spot announcements.[4] Changing conditions have forced the Federal Communications Commission to make substantial modifications both in the programming and in the commercial standards laid down in its 1946 memorandum.

Controversy and Political Broadcasts

An area in which the Communications Commission has shown a continuing interest is the handling of controversial issues by radio and television stations. During the late 1930s, several Commission rulings dealt with the need for "balance" and "two-sidedness" in presentations of a controversial nature. In 1938, an application of a religious organization for a proposed new station was denied, solely on the grounds that operation of a "propaganda" station would be contrary to the public interest. Three years later, the Commission released its famous *Mayflower* decision, flatly prohibiting the broadcasting of editorial opinions by owners of radio stations; "the licensee," said the Commission, "may not be an advocate." However, in 1949 the regulatory body modified its stand; in a revision of its *Mayflower* opinion, it held that a licensee might editorialize, provided that he followed the general "requirement of fairness" in making time available to spokesmen for opposing points of view. Of course, just what is involved in "fairness" is not entirely clear; broadcasters have never been certain just how far they are required to go in providing time, or to *which* individuals with opposing views time must be provided. Nor has it ever been made clear whether a charge may be made for time used to reply to a station editorial, though it seems likely that whatever time is granted should be provided without charge. At any rate, in one 1963 opinion, the Federal Communications

---

[4] Even these proposed limitations were later withdrawn by the Commission as the result of a vote in the House of Representatives indicating that members of that body opposed any attempt by the regulatory agency to assume formal jurisdiction over commercial practices of stations collectively.

Commission held that to meet the requirements of "reasonable fairness" a station that sells time for a *sponsored* propaganda program is expected to provide *free* time, if necessary, to present the views of those who disagree. Similar rulings have been made in a number of more recent cases.

Broadcasters also have difficulties when the facilities of radio or television stations are used by candidates for public office. Section 315 of the Communications Act of 1934 provides that if station time is made available to one candidate, it must also be made available on the same terms to any or all other candidates for that same office, in the same election. The section also prohibits censorship by the station of materials broadcast by any qualified candidate, and the charging of higher rates for time used by candidates than the rates applying to ordinary commercial programs. A 1959 amendment to the section excludes appearances of candidates on *bona fide* news programs from the area covered by this portion of the Communications Act.

Although the provisions of Section 315 seem definite and clear, broadcasters have often had difficulty in applying the requirements to specific local situations. Even the networks have had their problems in living up to the letter of this section of the Act. Variations in the laws of individual states make it difficult to know which candidates are "qualified" and which are not and at exactly what point in time an office seeker becomes a "qualified candidate." Problems are created by "splinter party" candidates and others who have no practical chances of election. There is also the question of whether a candidate's appearance in a dramatic or an interview program relieves all portions of that program from possible station censorship, and the equally serious question of whether a candidate who appears on a station in a filmed or taped program is actually "using" the station in the manner that Congress intended in adopting this portion of the Act. These and similar problems have forced the Commission to issue literally dozens of interpretations in an attempt to clarify the meaning of Section 315, so that what originally seemed to be a simple, straightforward requirement of freedom of opportunity for candidates for public office has evolved into a complicated structure of rules and interpretations that broadcasters find highly confusing.

Problems of the equal time provision were dramatically revealed in 1960 when the FCC required NBC to permit a splinter party candidate to appear on the *Jack Paar* show, since Senator John F. Kennedy had previously appeared on the program.

The Great Debates of 1960, credited by political experts as decisive factors in Kennedy's victory over Nixon.

Computers ended the all-night vigil on election night in 1964. Predictions based on early returns allowed network anchor men and commentators to pack up and go home by midnight.

But appearances of candidates for office, like broadcast discussions of vital public issues, are highly important in our system of democratic government. Both must be provided by stations whose owners are honestly attempting to "serve the public interest" regardless of the difficulties involved. But both areas have created problems for broadcasters, and equally serious problems for the Commission in its attempts to insure equality of opportunity and fairness in the handling of broadcasts in these important fields.

COMMISSION PROCEDURES

The Federal Communications Act authorizes the Communications Commission to grant applications for station licenses if "public interest, convenience, or necessity will be served by such grants." It may also revoke licenses, in certain situations. But it gives the Commission no other powers with respect to the operation of broadcasting stations, aside from requiring licensees to file such reports as the regulatory agency finds necessary. Consequently, the Commission's only direct means of requiring stations to operate "in the public interest" is that provided by the agency's power to grant or to refuse applications for station authorizations—or perhaps even more important, applications for renewal of station licenses.

When a would-be owner wishes to construct a new radio or television station, he files with the Federal Communications Commission a detailed written application, indicating the community in which the proposed station will be located, the frequency or channel on which the station will operate, the power to be used by the station transmitter, and the proposed hours of operation. The application also includes information about the applicant's legal, technical and financial qualifications, a detailed description of the type of technical equipment to be used, and information with respect to the type of programming to be provided by the station and general program policies to be followed. If an examination by the Commission's staff shows that the proposed station can operate without creating harmful interference with signals of other stations, that the equipment proposed conforms to Commission requirements, and that the applicant is fully "qualified"—and if no other applicant has filed for the same facility—a construction permit is usually issued without further formality. Later, after the station has been built and the equipment tested, its owner may apply for and receive a regular license to broadcast.

The licensee of an operating station is required to make certain reports to the Communications Commission—an annual financial report and special reports, including copies of contracts with network organizations and any other agreements that might in any way affect ownership or control of the station or supervision over the station's financial or programming operations. In addition, licensees are required to keep operating logs and other records, which are open to inspection from time to time by Commission representatives. But the most important element in Commission regulation of broadcasting stations is the requirement that at the expiration of each three-year license period, the owner of every broadcasting station must file an application for renewal of the station's license. Applications for license renewal call for substantially the same information as that required from applicants for new station facilities, but with one major addition. The applicant for license renewal must describe the type of programming his station has provided during the period the existing license has been in effect, as well as outlining plans for future programming operations. This gives the Commission staff an opportunity to compare actual programming performance with the promises made in earlier applications—and to evaluate the reasons the licensee offers in some cases for failing to live up to those earlier promises. In most actions on license renewal, of course, the Commission's staff finds no serious ground for objection to the licensee's programming or other activities or to the program proposals outlined in the application, and license renewal is granted without question. But when the application shows serious discrepancies between "promise" and "performance" in programming, or when the Commission's staff is not satisfied with proposals for future programming, or when questions have arisen concerning the licensee's character qualifications, or when serious complaints have been made by listeners about the operation of his station, the application may be held up to give the licensee an opportunity to explain the apparent shortcomings. In extreme cases, the application is set for a public hearing.

Hearings

When two or more applicants contest for the same new broadcasting facility, a public hearing is held to determine which applicant is to receive the grant. Sometimes a hearing is ordered when only one applicant is involved, if questions are raised with respect to his financial or character qualifications or if the owner of an existing station protests on grounds that operation of the new station would create serious interference. And as already noted, hearings are occasionally held on applications for license renewal; a license for a broadcasting station is never revoked or license renewal permanently refused without a hearing to determine whether the licensee's conduct warrants such an action.

Whether on applications for new facilities or for license renewal by existing stations, hearings are always open to the public. Each hearing is presided over by a hearing examiner from the Federal Communications Commission's staff; procedures followed are generally similar to those in a court of law, with witnesses appearing and with applicants represented by attorneys. Following the hearing—in most cases, several months later —the hearing examiner issues his decision, either granting or refusing the application for license renewal, or in situations involving a number of applicants for a new station facility, indicating the applicant to whom the facility is to be granted. The examiner's opinion summarizes the evidence presented, and states the basis for the decision rendered. An adverse decision may be appealed to a staff Review Board or in some instances to the Federal Communications Commission itself; occasionally without an appeal the Commission may itself elect to review and possibly overturn the examiner's decision. If no appeal is filed or if no review is ordered, however, the examiner's decision automatically becomes final—at least as far as the Commission is concerned. The Communications Act provides, however, that any Commission or examiner's decision on the grant of a station license may be appealed to the United States Court of Appeals for the District of Columbia, and the court may order the Commission to reconsider its original action. Appeals from Commission decisions are fairly frequent, but only in a small proportion of cases are such appeals successful.

Issues in Hearings

In every hearing, the decision of the hearing examiner is based on evidence presented on a number of "issues," announced before the hearing begins. In a hearing on license renewal, issues may concern the question of whether control over the station has been transferred illegally to a person other than the licensee, or whether the licensee has made false statements in reports filed with the Commission, or whether the licensee has been guilty of serious shortcomings in programs put on the air. In hearings on grants of new facilities, issues may range from the financial qualifications of applicants to the types of programming the various applicants expect to provide. Sometimes a dozen or more such issues will be considered in a hearing. However, the examiner's decision will usually be based on two or three key issues, and the emphasis laid upon each of the issues raised may vary greatly from one hearing to the next. In one case, the facility may be awarded primarily because the successful applicant lives in the community to be served and has been active in local community affairs, while his competitors are nonresidents. In another, the examiner may give strong preference to an applicant with a record of successful station operation in another community, or to one who plans to devote his full time to the management of the station rather than leaving executive functions in the hands of paid employees. In still another case, the decision may be based on the thoroughness with which one applicant has surveyed the needs of the community, or on a comparison of program plans of the various applicants. As a rule, competing applicants for new facilities are likely to be almost equally well qualified in most respects; as a result, decisions are made on the basis of the applicants' respective qualifications in those areas in which one shows an outstanding superiority over others competing for the facility at stake.

It might be noted that the Commission is represented at all hearings by one or more attorneys from its own legal staff; in hearings on license renewal, attorneys for the Commission serve, in effect, as prosecuting attorneys, presenting evidence compiled by Commission staff members concerning the alleged misdeeds of those licensees whose right to license renewal has been questioned.

Sale of Broadcasting Stations

Securing an authorization for the construction of a new station is often a difficult matter, especially if a number of competing applicants are involved. In comparison, purchase of a station already on the air offers few problems, at least as far as the Commission is concerned. As a rule, no hearing is required on an application to transfer the ownership of station facilities. The only questions considered by the Commission are whether the person seeking to buy the station is "legally, technically, and financially qualified," whether he meets the necessary character requirements, and whether he is not already the owner of the maximum number of stations allowed by the Commission. If the applicant is found to be qualified in all these respects, he is allowed to purchase the station. There is, however, one exception; if the buyer is already the owner of one or more television stations, and the facility involved is a television station located in one of the nation's 50 largest television markets, a hearing on the proposed transfer is mandatory on the basis of a 1965 Commission order.

Enforcement of Commission Requirements

As already stated, the Federal Communications Commission exerts its regulatory control over broadcasting primarily by the granting or the withholding of station licenses. A regular license is issued for a three-year period; at the end of that time, an application must be made for license renewal, and the station's past record is taken into account in actions on license renewal. Prior to 1952, the only method provided in the Communications Act for punishment of licensees who failed to live up to Commission requirements was the outright revocation of the station's license or refusal to grant license renewal. However, a 1952 amendment to the Act gives the Commission the right to issue "cease and desist" orders, requiring a station or another offender to discontinue an objectionable practice, and another amendment passed eight years later allows the Commission to impose fines ranging from $1,000 to $10,000 for noncompliance with regulations.

Only a relatively small number of stations have been actually taken off the air by the Commission since the regulatory agency was created in 1934. Most of those that have failed to receive license renewal were guilty either of making false statements in applications or reports to the Commission or of transferring control over station facilities to unauthorized persons. A few stations have lost their licenses to broadcast for other offenses, as noted in earlier paragraphs in this chapter. The Commission's power to issue cease and desist orders has been used almost as infrequently—sometimes against owners of diathermy equipment or other electronic devices which interfered with reception of signals of radio or television stations. The power to assess fines on station operators has been used much more often; a number of stations have been forced to pay penalties for using more power than the amount specified in the license, or for failure to have a licensed engineer on duty, or for similar violations of regulations.

But in addition to the methods provided specifically in the Communications Act, the Federal Communications Commission has developed a number of informal but highly effective devices for applying "pressure" on station licensees who fail to conform to its standards of operation, particularly in the area of programming. One such method, of course, is the issuing of "public notices" outlining the Commission's ideas of the obligations of station operators—sometimes in formal publications like the *Blue Book*, sometimes in informal press releases, sometimes in speeches delivered by members of the regulatory body. These notices outline the Commission's views on program requirements, on practices to be taken into account in consideration of license renewal, on use of advertising, or on other subjects concerning which no formal regulations have been adopted.

Another and more direct form of pressure consists merely of sending a letter to the owner of a station, inquiring about some alleged failure to live up to the station's obligations. In a number of cases, the Commission has simply failed to take any action whatever on renewal of a station's license—often with no reason given—so that the station automatically is placed on a temporary license basis. In still other cases, a letter may be sent to a station licensee asking him to "show cause" why a hearing should not be ordered on the renewal of his license; if the licensee could not report that the alleged shortcoming had been corrected, an actual hearing might be ordered. All of these devices, of course, are either indirect or very direct *threats* of Commission action—not actual punishment for offenses. But the requiring of a hearing on license renewal is a much different matter; even if the outcome is favorable to the station and a license renewal is granted, station prestige with advertisers and listeners is seriously damaged by the fact that a hearing is held, and in addition, the station is subjected to the not inconsiderable expense of defending its record in the hearing. One 1950 hearing on renewal of the license of a high-powered Los Angeles radio station is estimated to have cost the licensee nearly $2 million; in this case, hearings were continued at intervals over a period of more than a year. Less protracted hearings have frequently cost the licensees involved from $75,000 to as much as $200,000 for attorneys' fees, the photostating of records, and the preparation of exhibits. And of course, although actual refusals of license renewals are rather infrequent, a hearing *can* result in the imposition of the "death penalty" on the station involved.

By use of fines for violations of regulations, by use of its variety of "pressures" and threats, by its ordering of hearings on license renewal, the Federal Communications Commission has been generally successful in inducing broadcasters to "go along," willingly or otherwise, with the policies and standards the Commission has adopted for the regulation of broadcasting stations.

REGULATION BY THE COMMISSION

The whole matter of regulation of broadcasting by a government agency raises questions of considerable importance.

Especially is this true when the regulation extends into the field of programming. Few people would question the need for regulation which involves assignment of stations to frequencies, limiting the amount of power to be used, or when necessary, limiting hours of operation. Nor has there been any appreciable opposition to actions that have been taken against station operators for the broadcasting of objectionable materials. But differences do exist concerning the legal or moral right of a government agency to regulate programming in general or to exercise control over the business activities of broadcasting stations, either directly or indirectly.

The Justification of Regulation

Some national leaders, including most of the members of the Federal Communications Commission in recent years, take the position that the regulatory body should determine in some detail the type of programming that should be offered by broadcasting stations. The Commission itself has specified, through its *Blue Book* standards and its license application forms, that certain types of programs must be included in station schedules if a station is to operate "in the public interest." It has also sought—with little success, to be sure—to limit the amount of time devoted to commercial announcements in station programs, and it has taken steps to exercise control over the sources from which programs are secured by television networks and stations. What broadcasters find disturbing is the fact that the extent of actual Commission control over both programming and business practices is steadily increasing; almost every year the government agency finds some new area over which to extend its regulatory jurisdiction.

Advocates of strong government control over programming often support their position with the rather vague argument that "the airwaves belong to the people." Perhaps a stronger argument might be found in the fact that every licensee of a broadcasting station has been given a government-created and government-supported legal monopoly—he has the exclusive right, at least in his own community, to use a specified channel or frequency. And the terms under which his monopoly is held may well include specifications concerning types of programs that must be presented to justify his monopoly position. But at the same time, opponents of Commission control over programming can point to the provision in the First Amendment to the Constitution of the United States, which guarantees "freedom of speech and of the press"—a provision that has been held by the United States Supreme Court to apply also to broadcasting. This would seem to limit the right of Congress, of the Commission, or of any other agency of government to determine the nature of programs offered by broadcasting stations, just as it prohibits government control over the content of newspapers and magazines. At present, there seems to be little chance of resolving the conflict in philosophies over the extent to which government may properly regulate station or network programming.

The Commission's Problems

Many of the policies of the Federal Communications Commission have been vigorously opposed by broadcasters. No one really wants to be regulated—and men in the broadcasting industry are no exception. Most broadcasters feel that the Commission's exercise of control over programming operations, over commercial practices, over relations between networks and stations has gone far beyond the kind of regulation of broadcasting that members of Congress had in mind when they created the regulatory body. Although, as intelligent citizens, they may deplore the existence of conditions that have led to Commission action, most broadcasters feel that any corrective measures should be left to the industry itself, at least in fields of programming and business affairs.

At the same time, broadcasters recognize the fact that there are numerous problems involved in broadcasting that can be dealt with only by the Commission, and that many of those problems are not of a type easily solved. What, for example, should be the Commission's policies with respect to the number of radio stations? What methods can be found to deal with the financial problems encountered by UHF television stations and to allow listeners to receive television service from a greater number of stations? What about fraudulent or deceptive advertising practices, or about unfair competition between stations in the same community, or about unauthorized use of television programs by community antenna systems? These are problems with which the broadcasting industry itself cannot deal—and problems typical of those with which the Commission *must* deal if a more effective broadcasting service is to be provided for American listeners. In many fields, the formulation of intelligent policies concerning broadcasting becomes a very complex and difficult matter.

The problems of the Federal Communications Commission are made all the more acute by the very volume of the licensing and regulatory activities in which the Commission and its staff are engaged. Not only does the government agency regulate broadcasting and determine policies affecting broadcasting, as well as handling the day-to-day activities of licensing radio and television stations, but the Commission is required by the Federal Communications Act to regulate and to pass on rates charged by interstate telephone and telegraph systems. In addition it issues licenses for radio transmitters used in point-to-point communications—those on fishing and pleasure boats, passenger vessels, airplanes, and taxicabs, and those used by railroads, police authorities, large industrial companies, and even private individuals who have radio telephones in their automobiles. A Commission report indicates that as of March 1964, no fewer than 1,382,000 licenses were outstanding for broadcasting facilities or for transmitting facilities used in point-to-point communications. And in addition, nearly three million licenses issued by the Commission were held by commercial or by amateur radio operators. Each of these licenses must be periodically renewed, of course, as well as the licenses for broadcasting stations. In view of the work load involved, it is surprising that even with the assistance of a large staff of employees the Federal Communications Commission ever finds time to deal with the vital problems of the American broadcasting industry.

The Commission's difficulties become even more obvious when it is remembered that, with very few exceptions, the men appointed as members of the Federal Communications Commission have had, at the time when they were appointed, no previous contact with broadcasting or the broadcasting industry and almost no knowledge of the complex problems with which they are expected to deal. Commissioners are usually political appointees, very often selected because of outstanding services rendered to the party in power rather than because of any technical training or experience relating to broadcasting. Even after their appointment, they have little opportunity to become acquainted with the day-to-day problems of operating a radio or television station; their regulatory activities necessarily have something of an "ivory tower" limitation. The situation naturally is disturbing to station operators who are subject to regulation. However, nearly all broadcasters would concede that the individuals appointed to the Commission have conscientiously tried to "serve the public interest" in their efforts to regulate broadcasting and have made every effort to be fair and impartial in their decisions. Despite the fact that Commission members are frequently political appointees, charges of partisanship or political bias in decisions have been exceedingly rare. Mistakes undoubtedly have been made; policies adopted by the Commission have sometimes failed to work out in practice in the way they were intended. But most leaders of the broadcasting industry feel that the mistakes made have been honest ones, resulting in most cases from the complexity of the problems to be solved and the difficulties of finding solutions that are equally applicable in every situation.

Criticisms by Broadcasters

However, no matter how great may be their respect for the integrity and good intentions of the individual members of the Commission, broadcasters generally have two serious complaints with respect to the Commission's regulatory activities— complaints other than those related to specific Commission policies or to the regulatory agency's apparent desire to extend its jurisdiction into new areas. First, they complain, and with a good deal of justice, that in making its decisions the Commission is often much too slow. The television "freeze," which lasted for three and a half years while the Commission's members pondered the problems of station allocations, of television color systems, and of providing for educational television, illustrates the extremely deliberate nature of many Commission actions. More recently, consideration of proposed revision of application forms for new and renewed licenses dragged on for more than four years before new forms were finally approved. An even more striking example has been the agency's inability to arrive at any final decisions concerning the future status of high-powered "clear-channel" radio stations—a problem which has been before the regulatory body for nearly 20 years. These, of course, are matters involving major policy decisions; perhaps deliberate action is justified. But even in the licensing of individual stations, the Commission has at times been almost painfully slow; in some cases, applicants for new station facilities have waited for as long as three or four years before final action was taken, and occasionally license renewal applications have been held up for as long as 15 or 18 months, with the stations involved not even told the reason for delay.

A second complaint of broadcasters is that Commission policies are constantly changing. Things accepted a week ago by the Commission as right and proper may today be held to be objectionable; practices frowned upon a year ago are now permitted—and in some cases even approved. Take for example the Commission's varying rulings about station editorializing, or "fairness" in the discussion of controversial issues, or the requirement of "balanced" programming. Regulatory policies do change; often the changes are of major importance. In part, modified policies of the Commission are a result of changing conditions in the broadcasting industry. But probably to a greater degree the changes in major policies reflect the constantly changing membership of the Commission. New members often have different ideas from those of their predecessors about the obligations of station licensees or the extent of regulation desirable. Similarly, appointees of any administration tend to reflect administration attitudes as to the desirability of regulation in general. Many of the Commissioners appointed by President Kennedy, for example, were much more "regulation minded" than those who served during the Eisenhower administration, and Commission attitudes changed correspondingly.

Whether or not this is the *major* cause of changes in

policies applied by the Federal Communications Commission, it is an unquestionable fact that policy changes have been frequent from the time the Commission was first organized in 1934. The result is that broadcasters find themselves threatened by a sort of regulatory "sword of Damocles," not knowing from one year to the next or sometimes even from one day to the next just what is required of them as licensees of stations. The frequent changes in Commission policies have created serious problems for station operators and undoubtedly have been one cause behind the opposition of many broadcasters to regulation of any type.

8

PROGRAMS

According to reports of a leading audience-research concern, the average American family can receive the signals of at least three different television stations and of six or eight different radio stations. At almost any hour of the day or night, the listener may choose what he finds most attractive from a number of radio or television programs, all different, but all designed to capture his attention. Probably the average listener or viewer gives little thought to the way these programs get on the air; he is concerned only with whether or not he likes the programs he hears. But programs don't "just happen" by accident. They have to be created, produced. Someone has to develop the ideas on which the programs are based and shape those ideas into the product that finally goes on the air.

THE DEMAND FOR PROGRAMS

Networks face one set of programming problems, their affiliates another set, and independent stations still another. Radio stations have different needs in program development than do television stations. But in one respect at least, the situation is the same for all. Every network and every station must constantly be looking for new program ideas and new concepts of programming if they wish to capture and hold the attention of listeners.

Local Station Programming

As contrasted with nonaffiliated outlets, television stations with national network affiliations have relatively simple requirements in the area of planning and developing programs. Since an affiliated station can count on 60 to 80 hours of network programs each week and have access in addition to a wealth of syndicated filmed program material, it needs to produce no more than two or three hours of locally originated programs a day to complete its weekly schedule. Most of these local presentations are standard "service" shows—news, weather, sports, religious broadcasts, public affairs discussion programs, children's shows, or in some cases daily or weekly women's programs. Of course, some stations in larger markets go considerably further with their local programming, scheduling locally originated variety shows, interview or audience participation programs, or broadcasts of local sports events. A considerable number of major stations throughout the country produce occasional documentary programs on a "special program" basis; a few offer local dramatic shows. But most affiliated television stations fill the bulk of their non-network hours with syndicated filmed materials—theatrical feature films, and produced-for-television syndicated programs. In any case, development of new and original program ideas is not a critical problem, since the affiliated station can depend on network programs to carry much of the load of attracting listeners to the station.

Figure 2 shows the extent to which affiliated stations depend on national networks to fill their weekly schedules. The station used as an illustration is a CBS primary affiliate located

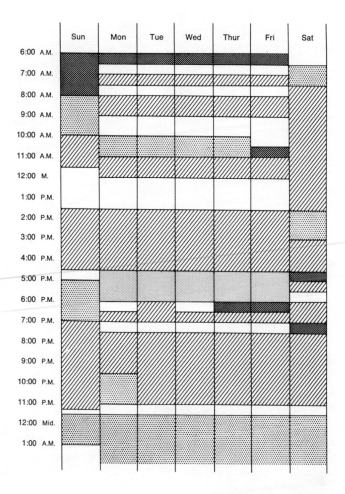

Figure 2. Sources of programs carried on the schedule of a CBS-affiliated station.

A 1923 production of the WGY players, the first radio group to broadcast drama on a regular and continuing basis. Note the ingenious "live" sound effects devices.

Divorce Court, originated by KTTV, Los Angeles, is one of the oldest and most successful syndicated series in American television.

Since the earliest days of radio, local stations have made substantial program contributions, often creating program series that later became network attractions.

in a relatively important three-station market. During the week analyzed, the station was on the air for nearly 133 hours between the hours of 6:00 A.M. and 1:00 A.M. The weekly schedule included a little less than 67 hours of network programs and 30 hours of syndicated program materials, primarily motion picture feature films. The remaining time was used to present local programs, including about seven hours representing a mixture of "live" children's programming and motion picture films. To make room for its unusually heavy schedule of local programs, the station did not carry ten or eleven hours of program materials available from the network; in addition, seven hours of network programs were videotaped from the network line and broadcast at more convenient times.

The independent television station, lacking programs provided by a national network, has a much more difficult problem than that of the network affiliate. Not only must it fill its entire schedule with either locally produced programs or syndicated materials, but it must find or develop programs attractive enough to compete with the network programs offered by other stations in the community. A few independent stations have been quite successful in developing effective local programs; some such programs, first presented "live" by independent stations, have been made available in videotaped form for syndication to other stations—among them *Divorce Court, I Search for Adventure, Roller Derby,* a number of wrestling shows, and the New York-originated *Play of the Week.* In addition, a substantial number of programs originally carried on network schedules are now in syndication and consequently are available for use by independent television stations.

Local radio stations also need programs and program ideas; even those with network affiliations are forced to depend primarily on local offerings to attract the listening public. At a time when listeners have access to the signals of perhaps eight or ten different stations, each station must look for effective ways to make its own programming distinctive and different. In part, the typical radio station attempts to meet this need by developing distinctive and attractive program personalities and news announcers. But successful stations also try to provide unique and different features in the programs they present, or new approaches to programming, and to find such "different" elements calls for the use of imagination and creative ingenuity. As a rule, coming up with an elaborate production is less important than finding a novel way to present the conventional, or inserting striking and unusual materials in programs to intrigue the listeners. One radio disk jockey, for example, to break the monotony of his regular four-hour shift of platter spinning, placed a long-distance telephone call a few years ago to the Kremlin in Moscow, in an effort to speak to Premier Khrushchev. He didn't reach the Premier—understandably—but his listeners had the novel experience of hearing every word that was spoken, including the comments of the Moscow long-distance operator and of a Kremlin official. For a relatively minor cost, the disk jockey had offered his listeners something completely new, and phone calls to famous personages became a regular part of his daily program. Obviously, as an idea it soon lost its novelty, and other methods of intriguing the listeners had to be found. But the telephone-call device illustrates the importance in radio of the use of fresh, new ideas, and the extent to which success in radio programming depends not merely on use of personalities but on the availability of a variety of program ideas.

Program Needs of Networks

Television networks in the United States operate under highly competitive conditions. To hold its affiliated stations, to make its services attractive to advertisers, and to capture the attention of listeners, each network must provide a reasonably well-rounded program service with a wide variety of programs of different types. To compete effectively, a network must offer some programs at least that are unique and distinctive and that in some way are more attractive than are most of the programs of rival companies. And of course, the network must strive to keep abreast, and if possible even a little ahead, of the public's constantly changing program tastes—to anticipate the kinds of programs that will be most attractive to listeners a year or two in the future. To provide the needed quality of uniqueness in programs and to offer enough change to keep ahead of the competition, network program executives are constantly looking for new talent, new personalities, new program ideas, new types of programs, new approaches to programs of familiar types, and new plot situations for dramatic shows.

Regular program series. During a typical week each national television network carries from 60 to 65 different program series presented on a regularly scheduled basis. During the 1964–65 season, the three networks combined offered a total of more than a hundred different evening programs each week, from 35 to 40 different daytime program series on weekdays, and nearly 40 other programs during daytime hours on Saturdays and Sundays. But although nearly every major program type was represented on each network, the "balance" of programs of different types varied in considerable degree from one network to the next. As shown in Table 12, CBS was laying greater stress than the other network companies on evening comedy and vaudeville-type variety programs; however, Columbia had no evening musical programs whatever and no late-night "talk-variety" programs like the NBC *Tonight* series. The NBC network scheduled fewer situation comedy programs than either of its rivals, but devoted four hours each week to presentations of theatrical feature films. Similar variations from network to network are found in the numbers of hours devoted to other types of programs. However, the table represents programs carried during a typical week of the 1964–65 season; a year or two earlier or a year or two later it might be NBC that was most active in the field of comedy variety or ABC that offered the heaviest schedule of evening panel or "game" shows.

Almost all evening programs are presented in regular series form, with one episode or broadcast presented each week. Daytime programs, aside from those on weekends, are scheduled "across the board," five days a week, Monday through Friday. The typical nighttime series runs for 39 weeks, the customary network "season," starting in the fall and continuing until early in June. During the summer months a variety or musical show is usually replaced by a less expensive program, while nearly every filmed dramatic series will fill the summer months with reruns of episodes presented during the regular season. Since daytime programs are usually of less-expensive types, most day-

TABLE 12

HOURS PER WEEK DEVOTED TO VARIOUS TYPES OF NET- WORK TELEVISION PROGRAMS, JANUARY 1965

	Hours per Week on			3-Network
	ABC	CBS	NBC	Total
Evening program types				
Variety, comedy variety	1.0	6.0	3.5	10.5
Musical variety	4.0	—	3.0	7.0
Talk variety	8.5	—	10.0	18.5
General or anthology drama	2.0	5.5	4.5	12.0
Adventure, crime, suspense	5.0	—	4.0	9.0
Western drama	1.0	2.0	3.0	6.0
Situation comedy	7.0	7.5	2.0	16.5
Animated cartoon comedy	1.0	—	.5	1.5
Theatrical feature films	2.0	—	4.0	6.0
Panel, game, human interest	—	2.5	—	2.5
News broadcasts [1]	2.0	2.5	2.5	7.0
Documentaries, public affairs	1.0	1.0	1.5	3.5
Total evening hours	34.5	27.0	38.5	100.0
Daytime program types				
Amateur variety, music	1.0	.5	—	1.5
Talk variety	—	—	10.0	10.0
Daytime serial drama	10.0	12.5	5.0	27.5
Adventure, action, Western	5.5	1.0	.5	7.0
Situation comedy	5.0	8.0	3.0	16.0
Panel, game, human interest	5.0	8.0	20.5	33.5
Children's programs, cartoons	3.0	9.0	2.0	14.0
News broadcasts [1]	.5	1.5	2.0	4.0
Public affairs, documentaries	.5	1.0	.5	2.0
Information, religion	1.5	4.5	2.5	8.5
Sports broadcasts	5.5	4.0	2.0	11.5
Total daytime hours	37.5	50.0	48.0	135.5

[1] Figures given to nearest half hour.

Compiled from program listings for selected week in January 1965. One-time "specials" not included; programs ordinarily broadcast at same hours at which specials were presented have been counted instead.

time series run for a full 52 weeks without interruption and without the use of taped reruns.

New program requirements. But as already noted, network programming is highly competitive. Each network tries to build a weekly schedule that will be stronger and more attractive to listeners, program period by program period, than that of either of its rivals. As a result, each new season brings a considerable number of changes in the program lineup of each network, as the network's program executives try to find programs that will be tuned in by greater numbers of listeners. Usually from 35 to 40 completely new evening program series are added to network schedules during September and October each year. During the next few weeks, network executives review the ratings of their various shows and study popularity trends and the comparative standings of the three networks. If major weaknesses appear, some schedule changes may be made; strong programs may be shifted to bolster weaker time periods, weak programs may undergo changes in format or in some cases be canceled outright and replaced by other new programs that network officials hope will be more attractive to listeners.

As the season continues, other changes are planned, to become effective in January, April, or more often the following year. A surprisingly high proportion of the new evening program series introduced with high hopes each year are canceled before the next season gets under way. Over the five-year period from September 1960 to the spring of 1965, a total of 240 new evening program series made their debuts on the three national television networks. Of this number, 194 were September or October entries; the remaining 46 series were midseason replacements. Of the total of 240 new programs, 46 failed to last out even the season in which they were introduced, and 111 others were not renewed for a second year. In other words, nearly two-thirds of all of the new evening programs added to network schedules during that five-year period fell short of expectations and were not kept on the air for longer than a single season. Network program executives are kept busy practically twelve months of the year, trying to discover or to develop new programs or program ideas that will meet the test of competition.

Plans for "specials." Of course, in addition to regular program series, each network presents a considerable number of entertainment or informative "special" programs during the course of each season. As early as August, 1965, the three networks had already made definite plans for more than 180 such special programs to be presented during the 1965–66 broadcasting season —about 40 entertainment specials, nearly 50 broadcasts of a cultural nature, at least 70 public-affairs special programs in addition to documentaries presented on regularly scheduled series, and more than 20 special broadcasts of important sports events from the World Series to the Kentucky Derby. These, of course, are in addition to on-the-spot coverage of important news events, presented as the occasion demands. The planning of special broadcasts places an additional burden on network program executives in their search for new ideas for programs to be offered for the approval of listeners.

Radio networks have a much less serious problem than do the national television network companies, since most of their program offerings are in the form of news, short talks, or music. But even the radio networks must discover new talent and new ways of presenting familiar materials. And there is still a demand for new program ideas, especially for programs that can be produced at low cost but which can attract substantial audiences in the face of competition from television.

HOW PROGRAM NEEDS ARE MET

Radio and television programs come from three possible sources: local stations, networks, and outside package agencies. Since each source functions in a different manner, each represents a different situation in the production of programs. Similarly, there are differences between the requirements of radio and of television; in addition, the production of television programs on film involves a different set of problems from those encountered when "live" programs are presented on television networks. Because of the differences that exist, each production will be considered separately.

The Local Radio Program Situation

Radio networks provide only a limited amount of pro-gramming; in recent years, syndicated programs have been little used in radio. Consequently, 80 to 90 per cent of all radio program time consists of "local live" programs, produced by individual stations. Because of their limitations with respect to talent, facilities, staffs, and budgets, radio stations concentrate on the production of simple, low-cost shows. The simplest and least expensive type of program obviously is the "one-man" show, presented by a staff employee—a disk-jockey musical pro-gram, or a short news broadcast with news items taken directly from the wire of a news service. For public service programs, the most widely used format calls for the use of a staff an-nouncer acting as master-of-ceremonies or moderator who inter-views one or more "guests" on subjects of local interest. Costs of such programs are nominal; they are usually completely un-scripted and require no rehearsal. As a result, stations can operate with relatively small program staffs and with very limited pro-gram budgets.

There are, of course, some program expenses in addition to salaries of staff announcers, even for stations that adhere rigidly to a news-and-music programming formula. Stations must secure the recorded music to be used on their disk-jockey pro-grams, and they must subscribe to a wire news service provided by one of the national news-gathering agencies. But these costs may be held to a very low figure. Often recordings are provided without charge by music distributors or local music stores; in most cases, albums can be purchased by stations at a fraction of their retail cost. News-gathering organizations will provide a limited news service to a small-market station at a cost no higher than the amount the station pays as a salary to an in-experienced new announcer.

On the other hand, some stations in large cities spend substantial amounts of money for their news programs, with expenditures for other types of programs in proportion. They may employ a staff of news writers and editors; they may have a number of special roving reporters in mobile units; they may arrange for correspondents who cover the news in outlying areas or in other cities in the state; they may develop three or four highly paid "news personalities" who devote full time to presenting the news. But these elaborate provisions for news coverage or for the presentation of expensive programs of other types are found only on large stations operating in major markets. The standard pattern of programming in hundreds of small radio stations throughout the country is the so-called "combo" operation in which the announcer on duty acts as his own control engineer, plans and handles all of his own programming, and in effect serves as a one-man programming, production, and engineering staff.

Radio Network Programs

The national radio networks are in much better position than are local stations with respect to the availability of talent and facilities. However, network program budgets are limited; commercial offerings consist almost entirely of news broadcasts and short features—the same sort of one-man shows provided by local stations. The networks of course do have much better facilities at their command for handling such programs—nationally known entertainment or news personalities to put materials on the air, news correspondents in all parts of the world, much larger budgets for programming than are available to local stations. But even with these resources, the radio network companies concentrate on low-cost programs; their limited revenues in recent years have made elaborate programs impossible.

Local Television Programming

The programming situation in television is decidedly different from that in radio. If the local television station is a network affiliate—and all but 40 or 50 do have network connections—it depends primarily on network programs to fill its weekly schedules. In addition, television stations have access to a tremendous supply of syndicated materials—theatrical feature films, motion picture short subjects, and filmed or videotaped programs produced especially for television. The result, as previously mentioned, is that most television stations devote only two or three hours a day to the broadcasting of locally produced programs. A programming survey conducted by *Broadcasting* magazine and referred to in an earlier chapter indicates that during the spring of 1965, commercial television stations, including non-network stations as well as affiliates, carried an average of 70 hours of network programs each week, and 29 hours of syndicated programs. Local "live" or local videotaped programs accounted for an average of a little more than 16 hours a week on station schedules. Stations with no network affiliations broadcast for an average of only 68 hours a week, but 28 of those hours were used to present local programs.

Production cost considerations. To fill these local hours, the aim is of course the same as in radio—to develop simple, low-cost programs. But even for these programs, costs in television are tremendously greater than are the costs of similar programs on radio, largely because of television's much greater technical requirements. Take the case of the television local news program, as compared with its counterpart on radio. In radio, the news broadcaster can come to the station, check the late news wire reports, make a few telephone calls to secure up-to-date information on local happenings, select and organize the materials he wishes to present, and then go on the air, requiring at most the services of one control-room engineer and possibly of an announcer to introduce the program and read the commercials. But if the program is to be presented on television, a special "set" is needed, news photographs must be provided, as well as short motion picture sequences of local or national news events. Consequently, one or more news photographers must be employed to cover local news stories; their filmed materials must be developed, edited, and cut to appropriate lengths; the services of an art department are required to prepare visual headlines and captions for pictures as well as special production effects. When the newsman goes on the air with his copy, he still needs the announcer who introduces the program and handles any "live" commercials; but in addition to the audio engineer in the control room his program requires the services of one and usually two cameramen, a floor director, and sometimes an audio engineer in the studio, as well as a director, a video engineer and switcher in the control room, and another technician in the projection room to handle films, slides and other visual materials. Even a one-man show on television represents the work of a dozen or more individuals whose combined efforts may involve as many as 20 man-hours in preparing and presenting an ordinary 15-minute program.

To keep their total programming costs at a reasonable level, practically all local television stations depend heavily on "one-man" programs—news, weather reports, sports news summaries, and the like, in which a single staff "personality" appears before the camera. Frequently interview shows or children's programs are included in the daily schedule; even these are essentially "one-man" shows, since each program is built around a staff "personality" who works with unpaid "guests"—local adults or children. When more elaborate programs are attempted, every effort is made to hold production costs to minimum levels. Local programs are scheduled adjacent to other local shows, so that the same studio and control-room crews are available; only "ad libbed" shows are used, presented without the use of written scripts. Entertainers are expected to follow a predetermined "format" for each broadcast, but to provide their own dialogue; rehearsals are held to a minimum, with "on-camera" rehearsals almost never arranged. Permanent sets are designed and used over and over again to save the costs of new set construction.

Typical local production costs.   But even "ad libbed" shows presented with little or no rehearsal have relatively high production costs. For example, one television station in a medium-sized market presents a weekly half-hour Western-style "jamboree" program, talent for which includes seven or eight instrumentalists, three or four regular vocalists, eight square dancers, a square dance caller, and a master-of-ceremonies. Total costs of talent alone for this program comes to approximately $350 a week—a fairly high figure for a 30-minute live show on local television. Another station in a somewhat larger city presents a weekly "courtroom" drama, unscripted, of course, and with limited time for rehearsal. Talent costs for the program average from $225 to $250 for each 30-minute broadcast; an additional $100 goes to court officials and a researcher-writer who provide accounts of the "true" courtroom cases presented. In both cases, figures given represent talent costs only; they do not include the other important production expenses—services of announcers, directors, engineers, cameramen, and floor crews, or costs of construction of sets and preparation of special filmed materials used.

Program Development at a Television Network

Networks are in a much more favorable situation than are local television stations in program development, since they have plenty of money to spend and almost unlimited access to new program ideas, to outstanding talent, and to production resources. However, the network problem is extremely complex. Individual programs are less important to the network than the development of a strong over-all program schedule. While a local station can depend on its network for its most popular program offerings, the network must develop a new schedule of programs every season, with sometimes as many as 15 or 20 entirely new series included. And of course, the program lineup for each season must surpass that of the preceding year.

The planning of the network schedule and the selection of programs for each new season begins from a year and a half to two years before the time the new programs are to go on the air. The network's program executives meet, discuss suggested new ideas, review program weaknesses of past seasons, evaluate the offerings of competing networks, and consider possible changes in programming philosophies or program objectives for the seasons ahead. These strategy sessions continue at frequent intervals, with special attention given to changes in the popularity of programs currently being broadcast and to indications of trends in listener acceptance of programs of various types. Current schedules are examined to determine which programs are strong enough to be continued and which ones must be replaced. And of course ideas for new programs are considered, evaluated, and weighed in an effort to find replacements to strengthen the network's schedule.

Probably several hundred possible new program ideas are examined by the network's program staff each year. Most have little merit, and are dropped without further consideration. But perhaps 70 or 80 of the ideas presented to the network's program executives seem to justify further examination and investigation—most of them ideas submitted by outside package production agencies, others possible programs suggested by employees of the network itself.[1] By the autumn preceding the start of the season for which plans are being made the number of ideas under consideration will have been cut to perhaps 40 or 50, selected on the basis of the variety, freshness, and novelty offered, the success of programs of similar type in attracting audiences, the proven creative ability of the producer who will develop the program, and the stature of the featured entertainers involved.

Contracts with program packagers.   Once an idea submitted by an outside production company has been given tentative approval, a preliminary contract is drafted, calling for the preparation of a detailed treatment or outline of the series and the submission of one or more sample scripts. The contract of course gives the network first rights to the use of the program; usually it also provides for the package company to produce a "pilot" film or tape of a complete episode of the proposed series, if one is requested by the network, with the network paying costs of production. The "treatment" and sample scripts are carefully scrutinized by the network's legal department to make sure that there is no infringement on copyright or other property rights in format or materials used; both this preliminary material and the pilot film are weighed by program executives in a final determination of the program's suitability for network use.

If the program in this preliminary form is approved, a

---

[1] In March 1965, Robert W. Sarnoff, chairman of the board of directors of the National Broadcasting Company, reported to a meeting of NBC affiliates that, in preparing for the 1965–66 television season, network program specialists had considered nearly 450 different program ideas submitted by outside program package concerns. Of this total, more than 200 ideas were made the subject of follow-up discussion between the independent packagers and the network's program executives, and half of this number were carried to the point where sample scripts were written. The 26 ideas that seemed most promising were developed as pilot films, largely at the network's expense; of this number, 15 were chosen to become new programs on NBC's 1965–66 schedule.

second contract is signed with the production agency, not committing the network to use the program, but covering in detail the financial arrangements to be made if the program is scheduled, including the allocation of profits, the extent of the network's participation in revenues from syndication or overseas sales, and terms under which the contract may be canceled or renewed by the network.[2] If the program idea is one proposed by a network employee, no contracts are required; the program would be network-owned and network-produced with no outside agency involved.

After this second contract has been signed, the producer begins work on the selection of stories, on arranging for writers, on choosing talent, on placing at least the principal performers under contract, and on preparation of his production budget and production schedule. In the meantime, the network's promotion department gets into action with preliminary publicity for the series and the development of sales presentations. Pilots for the proposed series are turned over to the network sales staff, which in turn arranges for them to be seen by interested sponsors. If the series can be sold, or if several sponsors can be found who are willing to share the costs on a participating basis, final arrangements are completed with the producer, writers, and talent and the series is set for production. In the case of filmed programs, actual production will usually get under way late in the spring, so that six or eight episodes will be ready before September when the new season officially begins.

Sources of new program ideas.   Ideas for new television network programs come from a variety of sources. While programs on local stations are usually developed within the station itself, a majority of network shows are the product of outside professionals. Sometimes an idea for a series may grow out of the

---

[2] In recent years members of the Federal Communications Commission have expressed concern over the extent of network control over programs produced by outside package agencies. Early in 1965, the Network Study Staff of the Commission urged the adoption of rules to prohibit any network company from having an ownership or part-ownership interest in more than half of the programs carried on its evening schedules, and to prohibit networks from engaging in the syndication of programs to stations within the United States.

program-planning sessions of the network staff, or occasionally even from a suggestion made by a sponsor or by an advertising agency. But as a rule the new series owes its existence to ideas developed by individual writers, producers, or agents, working with program packagers or independent production companies. If an idea generates any interest within the staff of the production company or advertising agency or network, a tentative format for the series is developed, possible entertainers considered, and a "treatment," or detailed description of the program, is prepared to serve as the basis of discussions with network executives.

While most network series are developed in the routine manner described, some programs are created in an entirely different way—developed to fit the requirements of a particular situation, to utilize the services of an available "name" entertainer, to meet the demands of a sponsor who wants to present some special type of program, or to balance out the network's over-all program schedule. For example, the *DuPont Show of the Week* a few years ago was the result of a combination of several factors: the interest of NBC executives in the possible values of "actuality" or "true-to-life" dramas, the network's need to strengthen its program lineup for a particular night during the week, and the desire of the DuPont executives to present a series strikingly different in concept from the programs offered by other advertisers. In the case of many variety programs built around such established entertainers as Danny Kaye, Judy Garland, or Jerry Lewis, the network first contracted for the services of the "star" entertainer, and worked out details concerning the format used in the program sometimes weeks or even months after the "star" had signed the contract.

Financial risks in network programming. The development of new programs calls for a heavy expenditure of money each season by each of the network companies—millions of dollars certainly, and possibly tens of millions of dollars. Much of this early expense represents payments for the production of pilot films for new series under consideration. Each pilot represents an investment of from $75,000 to $100,000 for a half-hour series and of up to $200,000 for an hour-long program, with additional expenditures required for scripts, story outlines, screen tests, and demonstration films. If the series can't be sold, the money so spent is a complete loss. An even greater financial risk comes from the fact that a network must contract for a certain number of episodes of filmed series—usually 13 or 26—long before the series actually goes on the air, with the amount committed for each new series often running to as much as two million dollars. Walter D. Scott, then executive vice president in charge of the NBC television network, in testimony before the Federal Communications Commission in January 1962, stated that his network's advance commitments for programs produced by various packagers ran to more than $100 million a year. As to the risks involved in such contracts with a supplier for a given new series, Mr. Scott made the following comment:

If the series proves to be an out-and-out failure and sponsorship lapses, we have to absorb the committed costs for the unsponsored programs. Or if the series is even below the mid-range of audience succcess, we may have to reduce the price to advertisers below our cost to maintain sales, or continue the program with partial sponsorship, or both. In such cases our program revenue falls to a fraction of the program cost.

The total costs of providing prime-time evening programs alone average about $3.5 million a week for each network. Additional costs are involved in providing daytime programs—and more money must be spent for program research and development. Running a television network can be a very profitable business undertaking, but the amount of money involved is enormous, and the risks are great in proportion.

Requirements in new programs.   The network companies naturally attempt to hold these risks to a minimum. One commonly used device is to work out some kind of cooperative arrangement with the outside program packager under which both expenses and profits are shared, reducing the amount of possible financial loss to either party. But even more important is the selecting of programs that offer the greatest promise of success. As a rule, the network deals only with outside producers with established reputations, on the assumption that a company with an established record of success is much less likely to produce a weak program than would be a less experienced concern. But regardless of source, each proposed program series must satisfy network executives on a number of major counts before that program is finally scheduled for network presentation. It must have audience appeal—the ability to attract large numbers of listeners. It must show originality and novelty value. It must not offer any unusually great production problems—in other words, it must be feasible from the standpoint of production. There must be certainty that the entertainers needed for the program are available. There must be agreement between the network and the producing company on program costs and budgetary arrangements. The program must offer features that give it good publicity and promotion potentials. And finally, it must be the type of program that, on the basis of past experience, is likely to attract sponsors.

Failure to meet network requirements in any one of these areas is usually enough to result in the abandonment of any program idea, even though its prospects otherwise seem excellent. A program with limited audience appeal is not likely to justify its cost of production or its place in the network's schedule; one too much like other programs already on the air may fail to attract a large enough following of listeners, and is also likely to injure the network's reputation through its very lack of originality. Some program ideas call for extensive production in remote locations, likely to create major technical problems and possibly causing unexpected production delays and expense. Competent writers who fit the program's requirements may not be available; perhaps the series may call for the use of particular "stars" who are already committed to other programs, or who demand an excessive price for their services.

Or there may be circumstances which make the proposed series difficult to sell. Few sponsors are greatly interested in documentary programs, in "arty" drama or in programs of classical music; the scandals connected with network quiz shows completely destroyed for years to come any chance of selling an idea for a new "big-money" quiz or give-away program; oversaturation of network time with Western programs a few years ago has greatly reduced the salability of any new Western series. Unless the network is reasonably confident of the success of any new program in terms both of attracting listeners and of satisfying the requirements of sponsors, that program is not likely to find its way into the network's tentative schedules; even if it has been scheduled, it may be dropped as late as a week or two before its announced starting date. Every year at least five or six evening programs scheduled to start in September are canceled just before the new season begins and replaced by other programs which seem to have a better chance of success.

Production of "Live" Network Shows

Television networks depend heavily on outside production agencies for evening-hour programs; in recent years, practically all of the evening entertainment programs on each network have been "package agency" produced. But unless these programs are prepared on film, they are produced in network studios, sometimes presented "live," sometimes by use of videotape, as are the great majority of each network's daytime offerings. Consequently, every network has an enormous investment in studios, staff, and equipment to make possible the production of its schedule of diversified programs. CBS, for example, had 16 television studios in 1963, twelve in New York and four in Hollywood. To serve these studios and to provide remote coverage of sports and news events, the network's equipment that year included 116 television cameras, 33 videotape recorders, 14 film recorders and 32 camera chains, in addition to a vast array of miscellaneous electronic equipment: thousands of special lights, more than 800 microphones, other hundreds of video amplifiers, picture monitors, sound monitors and projectors, and miles of cable. This physical plant initially cost in the neighborhood of $40 million, and another $6–7 million a year to maintain. The network's New York plant was considerably expanded in 1965 with the completion of a new CBS building in the Rockefeller Center area and the construction of a second building a mile or more away to provide facilities for the company's news operation. Both ABC and NBC also have major production studios in New

York and Los Angeles; all three of the networks have leased additional facilities—theaters, warehouses, film studios, space in office buildings—to supplement the studios they own.

There are heavy demands upon these studio facilities since the production of a single one-hour "live" or taped dramatic program or musical variety show usually requires at least three full days of studio time. Ten or twelve hours are needed on the first day to erect the sets, previously built and painted in a construction shop and transported to the studio, and to put lighting equipment in place and adjust it to produce the desired mood and effect. During the next two days the schedule calls for at least eight or nine hours of intensive camera rehearsal, first of separate sections of the program, followed by a run-through and a dress rehearsal; and finally, the show is either put on the air or recorded on videotape for broadcast a few hours or a few days later. In addition to the work in studios before the broadcast, a great amount of advance preparation is required. Usually two weeks are required to plan, make, and fit the costumes used in the show; an equal amount of time must be allowed for the designing, fabrication, and painting of scenery and sets. The actors who take part in the ordinary one-hour dramatic program spend several days in rehearsal, without cameras, in a rehearsal hall before they move into the studios; daytime serials, interview programs, and the like usually require no more than from two to eight hours of rehearsal time. News broadcasts and daytime "game" shows are of course presented without advance rehearsal.

After each major program has gone on the air or has been recorded on videotape, as many as six or seven hours may be required to remove sets and clear the studio for its use by another program. Often network studios are in use 24 hours a day, and seven days a week.

Production requirements of a specific program. The *Garry Moore Show*, a one-hour variety program formerly carried on CBS, offers an excellent illustration of the amount of time and effort required in a major network production. The show was produced for CBS by Bob Banner Associates, an independent program packager. According to information given by the pro-

duction agency in 1963, the program operated on a weekly
budget of $134,000, allocated as follows:

Above-the-line costs: These include talent, orchestra, production staff, office expenditures, travel expenses, television
rights, and other creative elements in the show $94,000

Below-the-line costs: The physical production portion of the
budget including costumes, scenery, props, theater rental,
camera and audio equipment, rental of video tape machines and film facilities, employment of technicians and
stagehands $40,000

TABLE 13

**PERSONNEL REQUIREMENTS FOR
THE GARRY MOORE SHOW**

	Number of individuals	Average total man-hours
Principal performers and guests	6	210
Singers	13	450
Dancers	7	240
Production staff	29	1300
Secretaries	6	270
Studio technical crew	18	315
Stagehands	35	615
Wardrobe personnel	10	90
Make-up	3	25
Special effects	1	20
Tele-Promp-Ter	3	30
Orchestra	30	270
Studio manager	1	20
Ushers	20	160
Carpenters and painters	30	1000
Properties shop	8	200
Plastics shop	2	25
Total	222	5240

Figures provided by Bob Banner Associates.

As shown in Table 13, each program required the services of nearly 230 different people working for a total of approximately 5,000 man-hours. Programs were recorded on videotape several weeks ahead of the date of their actual use on the network, with rehearsals taking up an average of three days for each program. The permanent cast and the production staff devoted their full time to the presentation of the show, with technical men and stage crews joining rehearsals on Wednesday, the orchestra on Thursday, and the ushers on Friday, the day on which the actual taping was done. The preproduction people —carpenters, painters, costumers, prop staff, and so on—went to work as soon as the scenic designer had completed his plans, sometimes as early as two weeks prior to the actual taping of the show on which they were working.

The production staff of the *Garry Moore Show* consisted of 29 people, working under the supervision of executive producer Bob Banner. Included were a producer, a director, six writers, a choreographer, a musical conductor, a choral director, a scenic designer, a technical director, a lighting director, an audio director, a set decorator, a production supervisor, two stage managers, and ten other persons who served in various minor capacities.

Even a relatively inexpensive network show involves far more elaborate preparation and many more man-hours of work than the most elaborate programs presented on local stations. For example, the *Nat 'King' Cole Show,* a half-hour musical program on ABC several years ago, was a fairly simple affair, presented "live," and produced in a single day. Preparations for the program commenced at 8:00 in the morning; the entire day's schedule was approximately as follows:

8:00 A.M.–10:00 A.M.	Carpenters and property men erect sets
10:00 A.M.– 1:00 P.M.	Audio engineers check equipment; electricians set up lights and plot lighting changes for show
12:00 M.– 2:00 P.M.	Orchestra rehearsal; audio engineers check music balance of each number

1:00 P.M.– 2:00 P.M.	Video engineers, boom men set up cameras and other equipment
2:00 P.M.– 5:00 P.M.	General rehearsal with cameras, lights, audio, etc.
5:15 P.M.– 5:45 P.M.	Complete run-through of program
6:00 P.M.– 6:30 P.M.	Dress rehearsal with orchestra
7:00 P.M.– 7:30 P.M.	Actual broadcast of program
7:30 P.M.– 8:30 P.M.	Crew strikes sets, cleans up studio, returns properties and equipment to proper departments

Increasing costs of network programs.   During the middle or late 1950s, a program like the *Nat 'King' Cole Show* could be produced for perhaps $35,000 to $40,000 a week; by 1965 or 1966 the same program would cost considerably more. Illustrating the increase in costs of production, the *Ed Sullivan Show* in 1951–52 had a weekly budget of $29,500; five years later, the figure was $79,500; for the 1965–66 season, *Broadcasting* magazine estimated the program's cost at $148,000 a week. For 1965–66, the average production cost of all evening programs on television networks was a little more than $136,600 for each program hour— roughly $64,700 each for 30-minute programs, and $141,000 each for programs an hour in length. Entertainment "specials" and other programs featuring top entertainers frequently cost as much as $200,000 or $250,000 for a single hour-long show. In part, increased costs are a result of more elaborate production and use of a much larger technical crew than formerly was required. Such costs have increased considerably in recent years as a result of the greatly increased use of color; production costs of a color program run anywhere from 10 to 20 per cent higher than those of the same program presented in black and white. But program costs are also increased by the intense competition among the three national television networks and among package program suppliers in attempting to secure the best possible talent for their programs. Writers, actors, and producers command much higher salaries than was the case a few years ago. Prices of dramatic scripts for ordinary 30-minute programs range from $2,000 to $4,000 each; to write the scripts for some situation comedy programs or for major comedy variety shows the services of from two or three to as many as six writers are required. Actors in principal roles in dramatic series receive $4,000 or more for each program. Veteran movie actor Lee J. Cobb earned $10,000 a week for his services in the 90-minute Western series, *The Virginian*, which made its debut in the autumn of 1962, while screen writer Sam Fuller received an equal amount for the scripting assignment plus another $4,000 to direct the series. The big variety stars and "name" comedians—the Danny Kayes, Bob Hopes, and Judy Garlands—command fantastically high salaries for their appearances in programs. Comedian Jerry Lewis reportedly received a salary of $50,000 a week out of the total production budget of $191,000 for the two-hour-long *Jerry Lewis Show* which had a brief run on the ABC network in the autumn of 1963.

Rising production costs have been a factor in the changeover to film production of dramatic shows on the networks, since filming offers the possibility of added revenue from the syndication of a program series after its network run has come to an end. But filming itself has helped increase production costs; performers who appear in filmed dramatic shows have demanded greater protection of their earning capacities through higher initial salaries and guarantees of "residuals," or additional payments for each rerun of the series in which they appear. Nevertheless the trend since the middle 1950s has been toward film production, wherever program content has made filming possible.

The Television Film Series

In the early years of network television, all programming was "live," with practically all programs produced in New York. Today a majority of all evening network shows are produced on film in Hollywood, generally by one of the major motion picture production companies. During the 1965–66 season, 77 of the 95 nighttime network entertainment shows were Hollywood film productions, including four motion picture feature presentations. For a time, the television film industry operated independently of the networks; program series were developed by film packagers and marketed through syndication companies to whatever buyers could be found—networks, sponsors, or individual stations. In recent years, however, practically all of the important programs in syndication were originally carried on network schedules, and filmed production is largely limited to series developed for network use by independent packagers under contract to network companies.

Production on film. The production of a film series differs in several important respects from that of the conventional "live" television program. In "live" television, the director is in complete charge of all elements of production: camera work, switching, audio control, lighting, and staging, as well as direction of entertainers. In film production, the director's role is more limited; he has responsibility for cast direction, but a "first cameraman" is in charge of all camera work, selection of camera angles, and the like, and other technical matters are in the hands of expert technicians. A filmed program consists of a series of short scenes; since there is no reason why scenes must be "shot" in the same sequence in which they will appear in the final program, those scenes involving the same set or location are usually "shot" in groups, to reduce costs. Each scene is rehearsed and shot as a separate unit; actors run through the scene in rehearsal until the action is clearly established, then do the same scene again with cameras running. If the director isn't satisfied with the result, he can order a "retake" of the scene; several retakes are usually made of each scene. Several hours of "shooting" are ordinarily required to produce enough film footage to provide ten or fifteen minutes of viewing time.

But the shooting is only one stage in the production process. At the end of each day's filming, exposed film is developed; during the evening, the film footage produced during the day is reviewed by the director and chief cameraman, who select the "take" of each scene to be used. Then the film goes to the film editor who cuts out unwanted footage and splices the remaining scenes together in proper sequence. When all of the scenes for the program have been shot and edited, the finished product is timed and cut to required length; titles and credits are added; and the complete program is reviewed again by the director and producer of the series to determine whether last-minute changes are needed. After this, the filmed episode goes to the film editorial department, which "dubs" sound effects and musical backgrounds into the sound track. And finally, the film in its completed form is sent to the laboratory where prints are made of the complete program, ready for use in the projection room of the network or of individual stations.

Production costs. Production costs of a filmed program are higher than those of a similar program with "live" production; the filming itself adds from 10 to 15 per cent to the direct costs. But the use of film offers many advantages, beyond the obvious fact that a filmed program can be shown again and again, or offered in syndication, or sold to television companies abroad. More individual scenes can be included in each program, thus giving the production more variety and a greater effect of pace. Weak elements in the program can be shortened, or eliminated entirely. Filming makes it possible to shoot some scenes "on location" in places where television cameras could hardly be used. And of course, the practice of making several "retakes" of each scene allows the film editor to choose the "take" best suited for inclusion in the final program.

A conventional half-hour filmed episode, requiring three days of photography in the studio and two or three days of rehearsal, usually costs from $50,000 to $65,000 to produce. The various cost factors—most of them at least—are listed in Table 14, based on cost levels prevailing in 1963 or 1964. One factor, however, is not included in the table. Actors, directors, musicians, writers, and others involved in the production of a filmed program work for stipulated fees set forth in their contracts with the producing company; these fees, however, cover only one network showing of the program in question. Contracts provide that actors and others have "residual rights" in the filmed series, and are entitled to additional payments each time the series is rerun—payments equal to a stipulated percentage of the original fee for the first rerun, a somewhat smaller percentage for the second rerun, and so on. Union contracts require the producer

TABLE 14

PRODUCTION COSTS OF A TYPICAL HALF-HOUR FILMED TELEVISION PROGRAM

	Costs per episode	
Above-the-Line Costs		
Script and rights	$ 3,500	
Supervision (producer, director, and staff)	3,750	
Cast (principals and extras)	11,000	
Music (original theme composed for series)	500	
Miscellaneous (insurance, contingency allowances, legal fees, etc.)	3,500	
Total above-the line costs		$22,250
Below-the-Line Costs		
Production staff	$ 1,400	
Camera operators	1,200	
Sound recording	1,165	
Set design and construction	2,100	
Film and laboratory expense, film editing	5,400	
Set dressing, drapery, props	1,950	
Grip and standby (labor used in handling scenery, painters, police, firemen, gardeners, etc.)	1,020	
Electrical	1,600	
Wardrobe, makeup, hairdressing	1,135	
Scoring and dubbing (adding music and sound effects)	1,100	
Location expense (transportation, lodgings, etc., for out-of-studio shooting)	1,200	
Transportation (trucking, car rentals, etc.)	700	
Stage space rentals and studio charges	2,200	
Miscellaneous (office overhead, taxes, publicity, pension and welfare fund contributions, screening, special effects, stock shots, etc.)	6,200	
Total below-the-line costs		$28,370
Total estimated costs for episode		$50,620

Figures provided by the editors of *Telefilm* magazine.

to set up a reserve sufficient to cover such "residual" payments; since when a series is filmed, it is impossible to know whether any programs in the series will be rerun, or whether the program will go into syndication following its run on the network, it is difficult to estimate the actual total cost of a series produced on film, including both initial costs and residuals, until long after the filming has been completed.

Use of reruns. The high production costs of evening network programs are responsible for the practice in recent years of making extensive use, in every filmed dramatic series, of reruns of programs broadcast earlier in the season. Since the early 1960s, reruns have filled the entire 13-week summer schedule of nearly every evening dramatic program series; in addition, reruns have been inserted on from three to five dates during the regular 39-week winter season. The reason for the practice is a matter of simple economics. A one-hour evening dramatic program would involve, in 1965, a cost for each new episode averaging around $140,000; value of the time used to carry the program would add another $110,000 to $120,000, after discounts. So to get its hoped-for return for the presentation of the series, the network would need to receive revenues of approximately $250,000 a week, and to get this amount of revenue, the network would have to sell the six commercial positions within each broadcast of the program for at least $42,000 each.

But networks usually have difficulty in selling spot advertising positions for that amount during summer months, when total evening listening to television drops by as much as 25 per cent—a situation which, incidentally, existed long before the use of program reruns was introduced on television networks. With smaller audiences, advertisers demand corresponding reductions in the amounts paid for advertising time. Consequently, networks use reruns during the summer months—available at a cost of from 25 to 35 per cent of the original cost of production of the filmed program presented. By use of the rerun device, the network companies are able to sell commercial positions in their programs at appreciably lower prices, and still receive revenues large enough to cover both program costs and the value of network time. The system has proved so successful that reruns are inserted three or four times in most series during the regular season—usually with no reduction in charges for commercial time, since research organizations report that ratings of rerun programs during the regular season are practically as high as when the programs so used were originally presented in the series.

THE SHORT LIFE OF A PROGRAM

One factor that causes headaches for network executives is the exceptionally short life span of the average television program series. A few network programs seem to go on forever— *Ed Sullivan, Ozzie and Harriet,* the *Red Skelton Show,* and *What's My Line*—but these are the exceptions. Relatively few television programs last for more than three or four seasons; one can be reasonably sure that two out of every five evening programs carried on network schedules during any year will be replaced before the start of the next season.

The Survival Pattern

As has already been noted, a television network originates from 18 to 20 new programs each season, of which perhaps 15 or 16 will be new nighttime programs. On these new programs rest the network's hopes for increasing its share of the viewing audience, its prestige as a developer of new program ideas, and most important of all, its economic future. In network programming, nothing succeeds like success, for if a network's new program offerings fail to win the approval of listeners, both sponsors and affiliated stations are injured, and the network will find it difficult to sell next season's shows.

What happens to the new programs added each year to the network's evening schedules? According to performance records over the period from 1960 to 1965, some of the new programs will be canceled before the end of the season, after network runs of not more than 13 or 26 weeks. Others will be dropped at the start of the following season; in all, at least nine or ten of each year's new evening program offerings will not be carried into a second year. These, with six or eight "old" programs dropped, make it necessary for the network to develop another 15 or 16 new programs for the start of the following program year.

Why this tremendously large number of programs dropped each year—from 35 to 40 per cent of the network's entire evening schedule, and nearly two-thirds of the new programs the network develops each year? Does it mean that all of the programs dropped were hopelessly bad, incapable of holding the interest of listeners? Or that network executives lack knowledge and understanding of audience tastes and are unable to develop successful shows? Not necessarily, by any means. Many factors contribute to a program's success, or to its failure.

Why Programs Fail

Some new programs, certainly, fail to measure up to expectations, and to the demands of listeners and of network advertisers. They attract too limited audiences, and consequently must be dropped. Producers may have shown poor judgment in gauging the responses and interests of the listening public. Or a program which held forth excellent promise as a pilot film may have failed to show the strength expected as a continuing once-a-week series. Or a program idea may have built-in limitations which make long runs impossible. The *Union Pacific* series, carried by one of the networks several years ago, illustrates this problem. A series built around an important method of transportation would seem to have excellent dramatic possibilities. But after the series was on the air, it was found that there is a limit to the number of dramatic situations in which a train crew may reasonably be involved; after those situations had been exploited, there was nowhere for the series to go but off the air. Built-in limitations rarely are responsible for the dropping of a new series, but they do quite often limit the network run of a program to one or two seasons. A situation comedy built around a small child loses its appeal rapidly as the child grows out of the "cute" age; a series like *Hennessey*, in which the continuing plot was based on a romance between a Navy doctor and a nurse, lost its attractiveness when the two leading characters were married.

Sometimes a change in the production situation is responsible for the failure of a program series. The illness or death of a leading character creates serious problems for the producer, to say the least; the same result takes place when a popular entertainer leaves a series because of contract difficulties, or simply because he wants a change of scene. When the actress who played the part of the wife and mother in *The Real McCoys* left the series to appear in the cast of another show, her characterization was too firmly established for the part to be taken over by another actress, and the basic appeal of the program was greatly weakened when her husband was presented as a widower. Then, of course, we have had other types of changes in conditions; when some years ago, accusations were made that two of the popular quiz shows on network evening schedules were "rigged," every other quiz show was automatically "dead," as far as audiences were concerned; within two months, all of the six or eight "big-money" shows, which previously had attracted large numbers of listeners, had been dropped from network schedules.

The problem of "saturation."   One factor accounting for the failure of many network programs is the scheduling of too great a number of programs of similar type, during a given season. Programming runs in cycles; a new or relatively new form is introduced; it becomes successful; a few months or at most a year or two later, half a dozen programs using a similar basic idea are on the air. We have had, on network television, cycles of variety programs, of quiz programs, of musical shows. We have had "private eye" detective programs, "real life" police detective shows, "costume-type" adventure programs, and in recent years, courtroom dramas, medical dramas, and, of course, dozens of "family" situation comedies. The television "adult" Western provides an excellent illustration of this tendency in network programming. The success of *Gunsmoke* and *Wyatt Earp* during the 1955–56 season found other producers anxious to develop programs with a Western setting that could achieve the same high levels of popularity. Five years later, no less than 29 Western series were being presented by the networks each week. Unfortunately, the number of possible plot situations and the number of possible "hero" characters, were not unlimited—so every series began to resemble every other Western series on the air. Producers resorted to "gimmicks" in an effort to make their own programs different; *Bat Masterson* wore a derby hat and carried a cane; *The Rebel's* leading character wore a Confederate uniform; *The Rifleman* used a rifle instead of a pistol; *Shotgun Slade* carried a shotgun, and had only one arm. But these devices could not change the fact that each story was largely the same as the stories used on other series—and most of the Western programs introduced on the networks were dropped at the end of a single season. Overuse of any idea for a series destroys listener interest.

The problem of scheduling.   Another important factor in the success or failure of a program is the place given the new series on the network's schedule. If it follows a very popular program on the same network and has only weak competition from programs on the other two networks, a program of only average attractiveness may be quite successful. But the same program may be a complete failure if forced to compete with a highly popular program broadcast during the same period. *Empire State* in the autumn of 1962 was placed opposite the popular *Red Skelton Show;* it had little chance of survival. The same situation existed in the case of the *Gallant Men* series, competing for listeners with *Rawhide* on CBS and *International Showtime on* NBC's network. *Jamie McPheeters* in 1963 had to compete with both the *Ed Sullivan Show* and Walt Disney's *Wonderful World of Color;* it would take a decidedly strong show to cope with that competition, and the *McPheeters* series did not merit that characterization. On the other hand, some programs have been helped by the time at which they have been scheduled—the *Dick Van Dyke Show,* new in the autumn of 1962, had the tremendous advantage of following the highly successful *Beverly Hillbillies* on Wednesday nights, with weak competition from *Going My Way* and only moderate opposition from NBC's *Perry Como* series. And *Petticoat Junction,* scheduled in 1963 between the *Red Skelton Show* and *Jack Benny,* certainly profited from its position. But lead-in and following programs are not enough to carry a show alone, especially when competition is strong, as evidenced by the CBS venture in 1963 with the *Judy Garland Show*, following *Ed Sullivan* and followed in turn by the high-rated *Candid Camera* series—but with *Bonanza* and *Arrest and Trial* competing for listeners on other networks.

The time at which a program is scheduled, the attractiveness of the program it follows, and the strength or weakness of competing programs, all have much to do with the success or the failure of every new program series.

The penalty of success.   A factor often contributing to the demise of a well-established and still-popular program series is the spiraling cost of production, created by the program's very success. Most new dramatic programs make use of relatively unknown actors. Frequently "regulars" in a series may be paid as little as $300 a week during the program's first season on the air, with leading characters receiving a little more. But if the series proves successful the $300-a-week actor demands and can get more money for his services each year the program continues on network schedules. Actors and writers are almost always represented by business agents whose major function is to negotiate salary contracts, and to secure as much compensation as possible for their clients. Thanks to the success of the program, by the time the series goes into its fourth season on the air, the once unknown actor may be receiving $2,000 or more each week. Or in some cases, he may quit the show entirely to accept a part in a Broadway play or in a motion picture—or in another television series.

One great fear in the life of every television actor is that of being "typed" to the point where he cannot find other employment for his talents. Unfortunately, the stars of nearly every television series are closely identified with the roles they take on the air, with the result that later they usually have difficulty in finding other types of roles to play. Fear of being unable to break away from a "type" was considered as being at least one reason for Kathy Nolan's leaving *The Real McCoys,* for Richard Boone's giving up his leading role in *Have Gun, Will Travel,* for George Maharis dropping out of *Route 66,* and for numerous other actors leaving established programs at the height of the program's success.

So the success of a dramatic program—its continuing on the air for more than a single season—creates serious problems for the producers of that series. Production costs go up, almost in proportion to the show's success. And actors and writers, established by their participation in a successful series, may leave the program for more lucrative work in other fields. And of course, what is true of dramatic programs applies equally in the case of variety shows, of musical programs, of audience participation—of every type of entertainment show on network television.

Not all of the programs that leave the air may properly be classed as failures. Even some of the programs that fail to attract a sufficient number of listeners may possess a considerable amount of merit. But at the same time, it must be added that few really strong programs, with sound ideas, good writing, excellent production, go off the air at the end of a single season. Some of those canceled should never have been presented in the first place. Some rest upon the abilities of an entertainer with too little personality to "carry" his own show. Some fail because of poor production, poor writing, poor acting; an even larger number fail because of poor basic program ideas.

Whatever the reason, only a very few programs possess the ingredients necessary to keep them on the air more than three or four seasons. There are, of course, exceptions—programs that seem to live forever as permanent fixtures on network program schedules—programs of the type of the *Ed Sullivan Show*, or *Walt Disney*, or the *Red Skelton Show*, or the perennial *What's My Line* panel show. But the fact that so few do survive emphasizes the need for new programs, new ideas, new talent, and the search for successful programs continues unabated with little change from year to year.

9

AUDIENCE
MEASUREMENT

In broadcasting, as in other media that carry advertising, numbers are important. When an advertiser pays $25,000 or $30,000 for a full-page advertisement in a national magazine, he knows pretty well what he is getting for his money. The magazine has a guaranteed circulation of, say, two million copies each week; consequently, his advertisement will go into two million homes, and has at least a chance of being seen and possibly read by people living in that number of homes. Similarly, the advertiser who buys space in a local newspaper knows the number of homes in the community in which the newspaper is received, and in which the advertisement may perhaps be read. The printed media provide the advertiser with definite figures on circulation.

In the case of broadcasting, "circulation" is not as easily measured. But the advertiser who uses radio or television, no less than the newspaper advertiser, is very much interested in the number of homes into which his advertising message is delivered. So the broadcasting industry is forced to provide some system of measurement that will give advertisers an idea of the size of the audience tuned to each program. Networks and stations alike are dependent on audience research—on what some cynics refer to as "the numbers game."

Audience measurement information is provided by several independent research companies not owned or in any way controlled either by broadcasting stations or by networks. The research findings of these companies are published at regular intervals and made available to those advertisers, advertising agencies, networks, and stations that contract in advance for the service on a regular subscription basis. Most of the major research concerns provide *national* information on the number of homes tuned to each network program; several companies also provide *local* information concerning program and station audiences in individual cities. For each, national or local, two important measurement figures are reported: first, a *program rating*, representing the percentage of homes in which, on a given date, sets were tuned to a particular program; and second, a *sets-in-use* figure, indicating for each hour or half-hour period during the "rating week" the percentage of area homes in which radio sets or television sets were being used, regardless of the programs or stations to which they were tuned. Some concerns also provide *time-period ratings*, especially for radio, showing the average proportion of homes in which sets are tuned to each station during each half-hour period or 15-minute period of an entire week; in some cases, the securing of information is spread out over four to six weeks, and results for the different weeks combined or averaged.

PROGRAM RATINGS

In the commercial system of broadcasting we have in the United States, ratings occupy a position of tremendous importance. Network advertisers buy programs they think will attract large audiences and consequently will receive high ratings; if ratings prove to be low, they withdraw their support, and the program goes off the air. National spot advertisers use local rating figures to select the station in each community on which to place their advertising; the station that falls behind in the ratings race finds itself at a serious disadvantage in its efforts to sell programs or announcement time to advertisers. Program executives of networks are extremely sensitive to ratings; in selecting or developing new programs, they give strong preference to programs of types that have previously attracted large audiences, and if the rating of an existing program falls below its earlier level, they either do some frantic "doctoring" to bring the rating up again, or begin to look for a replacement to fill the time period. Even in the case of local stations, ratings are widely used as a guide to programming. Television stations buy syndicated programs on the basis of ratings those programs have received in other cities; both television and radio stations plan local program offerings with an eye to their rating potential and drop from their schedules the local presentations that fail to produce satisfactory ratings. Many radio stations have changed their whole pattern and philosophy of programming entirely as a result of consistently low time-ratings which resulted from the programming previously used.

Methods of Securing Rating Information

The companies that provide measurements of the size of listening audiences use a variety of methods in securing the rating information they report. One concern—the A. C. Nielsen Company—has installed "Audimeters" in each of some 1,150 television-equipped homes; the homes used have been carefully chosen to provide an accurate cross-section of all families throughout the nation from the standpoint of geographical location, community size, the socio-economic level of the family group, and the number of individuals in the household. The Audimeter, attached to the television set or sets in the home, records electronically on a moving tape the exact periods during which the set is in use, and the channel or station to which it is tuned. Tapes are replaced at two-week intervals; data from tapes covering each 14-day period are combined to give what is almost a minute-by-minute picture of television program selection and viewing throughout the broadcasting day. Prior to 1964, the Nielsen company also used Audimeters to provide national information on radio listening.

A second method of securing audience information, used by Pulse, Inc., is based on personal interviews with listeners in homes selected on a controlled random basis in communities in which audience measurements are to be supplied. Pulse interviewers call at a different group of homes on each day of the week, and ask members of the family who are available to indicate, on a "roster" or list of programs the interviewer supplies, those programs tuned in during each quarter-hour on the day of the interview or during the evening of the preceding day. All interviewing is done after six o'clock in the evening when most members of the family will be at home; out-of-home listening as well as that in the home is reported. Until 1962 Pulse provided ratings for both television and radio programs; since that year, however, the research organization has concentrated chiefly on radio and is the leading concern supplying local time-period ratings for radio stations in cities throughout the country. In a typical market, rating information in each report will be based on interviews in a thousand or more homes, and interviewing is usually spread out over a period of from four to six weeks to insure that results will not be unduly influenced by unusual conditions occurring in any one week. Pulse reports include the estimated number of individual men, women, teenagers, and children listening to each station in the market studied during the average quarter-hour in each time period during the day and evening.

The third important method of securing rating information is that of having housewives in a carefully chosen sample of homes keep *diaries* in which they record all television program listening in which members of the family engage during each day of a selected week. As when the roster or interview method is used, a completely new group of families is chosen to provide the information on which each rating report is based. The diary method is used by the third of the major program rating services, the American Research Bureau. ARB national ratings for network television programs are based on diaries kept in approximately 2,400 different homes—a new sample is used for each report—representing city and rural areas in all sections of the United States. The American Research Bureau also provides local television program ratings in all of the more important television markets and, since 1964, has supplied local rating information for radio in a number of major cities. Local ARB reports are based on diaries kept in an average of about 600 homes in each market, with one-fourth of these homes providing listening information for each week during a four-week period, with results combined in the rating figures released. The diary method is also used by the Nielsen company as a basis for local television rating reports in most major markets, as well as for "30-city" television ratings of network programs. A relatively new concern in the rating field, Media Statistics, Inc., uses diaries as the basis of local radio listening information in 30 or more of the country's most important radio markets. Mediastat reports, issued only three or four times a year, give elaborate breakdowns of the composition of the audience of each radio station by listener sex and age; at least in major cities, information is based on from 2,500 to 3,000 completed diaries in each market.

Naturally, when any of the three major methods of securing listening information is used, a considerable amount of time is required to tabulate results, so that rating reports cannot be released in printed form until three or four weeks after the end of the period covered in the report. But advertisers, networks, and stations sometimes need more immediate information, especially when new television programs make their debuts on network schedules. Such audience reports are available literally overnight from Arbitron, a service provided by the American Research Bureau, from Trendex, an independent research organization, or from Nielsen's Instant Audimeter Service. Trendex reports are based on use of the *coincidental telephone survey* technique. Telephone numbers are chosen at random from telephone directories in some 20 or 25 major cities; interviewers place calls to the homes so selected during the period in which a network program is actually being broadcast. When a phone call is completed, the respondent is asked whether the television set was in use at the time the telephone rang, and if so, to name the program to which the set was tuned. Arbitron reports the use of television sets in a carefully selected permanent sample of about

300 homes in New York City. Sets in each of the homes used are connected by special telephone lines with a central headquarters office, and electronic impulses carried over the lines enable an operator to record the number of sets tuned to each station on almost a minute-by-minute basis, and from this information to compute the rating for each network program. The coincidental telephone method is also used in providing Arbitron reports covering areas outside of New York City. Nielsen's Instant Audimeter Service uses a technique somewhat similar to that used by Arbitron, providing ratings for television programs heard in New York City.

The "Sampling" Principle

Although commercial rating services use a variety of techniques in securing listening information, all of the methods are alike in one respect: all are based on the principle of *sampling,* or of providing rating figures on the basis of information secured from a *sample* of the whole population. Since it would obviously be much too expensive to secure listening data every week or every month from every home in even a single community, the research organizations get information from a relatively small number of homes in the area studied. In most cases, these homes are chosen on a *random* basis—for example, by including in the sample only those householders whose names happen to appear at the tops of columns on pages in a telephone book or city directory. This smaller number of homes is presumably an accurate cross-section of all of the homes in the community. If the sample chosen actually is a good cross-section, then the program selection and listening behavior of families in the sample group should be representative of the program selection and listening engaged in by all the families in the community. So if a rating company finds that 15 per cent of the sample families tuned their sets to a specified program on a certain date, it is assumed that the program in question was similarly tuned in on that date by 15 per cent of *all* of the families in that community, and a rating of 15.0 is reported for that program.

Of course, the idea of sampling is not used solely by concerns engaged in radio and television research. The same principle is applied in national public opinion polls, the results of which are published in daily newspapers. Manufacturers of automobiles use information secured from a sample of the buying public to check reactions to proposed changes in the design of cars; samples of housewives are used to test new cake mixes or salad dressings. The federal government itself makes extensive use of sampling procedures for its reports on business conditions, or on total employment, or on changes in retail prices of consumer goods, or on the estimated size of the wheat crop for the coming year.

Interpretation of Ratings

By their use of carefully selected nationwide samples, each of the major rating organizations is able to provide its clients, at specified intervals, with a national rating for each sponsored network program. In most cases, national ratings are released once a month, at least during the "broadcasting season" extending from October through March or April. The Nielsen company issues two national television rating reports each month, on a year-round basis. Similarly, the organizations that give local radio or television listening information can, by use of local samples, provide local ratings for radio or television programs broadcast by stations serving each local area. In either case, the rating, as previously noted, is a figure representing the percentage of homes in the rating area considered, in which, on a specified date, television sets or radio sets were tuned to the program for which the rating is given.

At this point, several facts concerning ratings should be given special emphasis. First, ratings represent *percentages of homes, not of individuals,* since only on rare occasions would all of the members of the family in every household studied be at home and watching the same television program or listening to the same radio station. As a practical matter, the percentage of *individuals* living in the community who would listen to any program would always be considerably less than the percentage figure used as the program's rating; some members of each "listening" household will always be away from home while the program is on the air, or perhaps in a different part of the house where they are not actually "listeners" to the program. Second, television ratings at least are based only on those homes *which have receiving sets*. Research organizations estimate that at the beginning of 1965 approximately 93 per cent of all homes were equipped with television receiving sets—nearly 53 million of the nation's 56 million homes. In major cities, however, or other communities with local television service, probably 98 or 99 per cent of all families had television sets. In view of the somewhat higher incidence of radio set ownership throughout the country, radio ratings are usually based on the total number of homes in the area considered.

A third fact, and one that is highly important, is that *ratings may not be accepted as completely accurate* measurements. After all, they are based on information provided by only a sample of the whole population, and sometimes by only a rather limited sample. The best that statisticians will promise is that 95 times out of 100, a national rating of 10.0 for a network program, based on a national sample of 1,500 homes, will be not more than 1.5 rating points away from the actual percentage of homes from coast to coast that were tuned to the program in question. Similarly, a national rating of 20.0 can be expected to be within 2.0 rating points of the true percentage of homes with sets tuned to the program. Local ratings, based on much smaller samples, are less accurate. Assuming that the sample consists of 300 homes, for example, a reported rating of 10.0 will, in 95 cases out of 100, be within 3.4 rating points of showing the actual percentage of homes tuned to the program. Stated differently, with a rating of 10.0 reported by a sample of only 300 homes, the true percentage will be not less than 6.6, nor more than 13.4. These allowances, according to statisticians, must be made to compensate for errors due to chance in the selection of a sample that accurately represents the entire population.

The Values of Ratings

If program ratings are not completely accurate measures of the proportions of homes tuned to broadcast programs, why are they so extensively used? Simply because in a commercial system of broadcasting, some reasonably effective estimate of the size of each program's audience is needed, and ratings do provide what are at worst fairly close approximations. They allow broadcasters and advertisers to make comparisons between programs—to judge whether a given program is more attractive or less attractive to listeners than are other programs broadcast in comparable segments of the broadcasting day. They offer a reasonably accurate index to the relative popularity of various kinds of programs. They allow sponsors and program executives to determine whether programs in which they are interested are gaining in popularity, as compared with the situation a month or a year ago, or whether they are losing their attractiveness to listeners. Similarly, rating reports allow broadcasters to note the changes taking place in the tastes and preferences of the listening public by observing the rise or the decline in average ratings reported for programs of various types.

In addition, ratings give the sponsor of a program a basis for estimating the approximate number of homes his program—or the program including his commercial announcement—reaches each week, a figure roughly approximating the "circulation" figure of a magazine or newspaper. If, for example, his network television program has an average rating of 20.0, he knows that it has been tuned in by listeners in approximately 20 per cent of the nearly 53 million homes in this country that have television receiving sets, or in roughly ten million homes. A rating of 30.0 for the same program would mean that it was received in approximately 16 million homes—and even allowing for possible inaccuracies in the rating figure, the difference is quite a substantial one. Rating companies usually provide such "projections" of ratings in the form of a "total homes reached" figure for each program, in both their national and their local rating reports.

The major research companies in some cases also offer a special service to advertisers who sponsor five-times-a-week programs—a report on the *unduplicated* cumulative audience reached by the series in its various broadcasts throughout the week. A five-times-a-week news program, for example, might have an average rating of 6.0 for the five days it is broadcast, but by reaching different homes on different days the program might, in the course of a week, be heard at least once in as great a total number of homes as a once-a-week program with a rating of 15.0 or more.

Qualitative Information

Of decided value to advertisers, too, is information made available concerning the *kinds of individuals* included in the audience of each network television program. As early as 1940, the rating companies then in existence reported on the proportions of men, of women, and of children included in the audience of each network radio program. Similar information is now given in the local radio rating reports provided by Pulse, Inc., but with a separate category added for teen-age listeners. The American Research Bureau gives considerably more demographic information in both its national and local reports, including for each sponsored program not only a rating figure and an estimate of the number of homes in the survey area tuned to the program but also a fairly detailed analysis of the number and types of listeners included in the program's audience. The same type of information is given in local reports of the A. C. Nielsen Company. Media Statistics, in the various markets in which it operates, gives equally detailed information about the characteristics of the listening audience. It provides no ratings, or percentages of *homes,* for programs or for time periods, but its reports show, for each time period, the total number of individual listeners to each station, the number who are teen-agers between 10 and 17 years of age, and the number of adults in each of eight groupings on the basis of sex and age. One research organization some years ago issued periodic reports showing, for each network television program, the number of listeners in each 100 homes tuned to the program who were regular users of each of a variety of types of products from prepared cake mixes to filter cigarettes, and from safety razors or home permanents to instant coffee. The value of information of this type to advertisers is obvious, no less than of information concerning the age and sex of listeners tuned to specific stations or specific network programs.

Other types of qualitative information about audiences are supplied by a number of research organizations not offering a rating service. One such concern, the Home Testing Institute, reports the "TvQ scores" given network television programs by various types of listeners. A "TvQ score" is an index showing the percentage of listeners in various sex, age, and educational categories who *like* the program—consider it "one of their favorites." For each sponsored program, separate TvQ scores are given for men and for women on each of several age levels and in each educational group, as well as for listeners living in communities of different sizes and in different sections of the country. The Home Testing Institute contends that the TvQ score is not only an index to the degree of "liking" expressed for the program, but also serves as a fairly reliable measure of the amount of attention listeners are likely to give the program scored.

Variations in Program Ratings

Since ratings show the proportions of homes tuned to various programs, it is generally assumed that they also provide an accurate index to the *attractiveness* of those programs to listeners generally. On the whole, this is a reasonable assumption; at least, a program that receives an unusually high rating must be one that large numbers of listeners find interesting. But ratings are also affected by factors in no way related to the basic attractiveness of the programs themselves. For example, a television program broadcast during evening hours usually receives a much higher rating than one presented during the daytime; more people watch television at night than during daytime hours. In recent years, Nielsen national television rating reports for the month of January have shown average ratings for all evening programs ranging from around 18.0 to 19.5; during the same month, Monday-through-Friday daytime programs have had ratings averaging between 6.5 and 7.0. The season of the year is also very important, especially as it applies to ratings of evening television programs. People simply do not watch television as much in the evening during summer months as during the winter, partly because they spend less time in the house when the weather is warm, and partly because summer television schedules are largely filled with "reruns" of programs previously broadcast. In any case, ratings of evening network programs in July and August drop to an average of perhaps 12.5 to 13.0, as compared with the average of 18.0 or more in January—a decrease of nearly one-third. Ratings of daytime programs also fall off during the summer months, but the decline is moderate as compared with that for programs on evening schedules.

Ratings and competing programs.   A third factor with a decided effect on the rating of any program is the strength of the program's competition—the attractiveness or popularity of programs carried by other networks or stations at the same hour. If the program must compete with an unusually popular program pre-

TABLE 15

AVERAGE SETS-IN-USE FIGURES FOR RADIO AND TELE-VISION AT DIFFERENT HOURS OF THE DAY, MARCH 1963

Hour Beginning	Average Sets in Use		Hour Beginning	Average Sets in Use	
	Radio[1]	Telev'n		Radio[1]	Telev'n
6:00 A.M.	6.4	—	3:00 P.M.	7.1	24.5
7:00	12.5	5.7	4:00	7.0	29.7
8:00	15.0	12.6	5:00	8.7	33.2
9:00	13.4	14.7	6:00 P.M.	8.5	42.3
10:00	12.5	17.2	7:00	6.1	54.7
11:00	10.7	21.3	8:00	4.9	63.9
12:00 M.	10.6	25.7	9:00	4.2	64.9
1:00 P.M.	10.2	25.9	10:00	4.0	52.8
2:00	7.8	24.0	11:00	3.3	30.0
			12:00 mid.	no inf.	17.4

[1] Radio figures based on use only of "plug-in" radio sets in homes. Nielsen estimates that, in addition, battery-powered portable sets were used during winter months for a per-home average of a little more than 5 hours a week, and auto sets for a per-home average of nearly 3½ hours a week.

Radio sets-in-use figures computed from homes-in-thousands estimates for different hours in the national Nielsen Radio Index report for April 1963; television sets-in-use figures taken from the second national Nielsen Television Index report for April 1963. Reproduced with permission of the A. C. Nielsen Company.

sented at the same hour on a different network or different station, its rating naturally is lower than would otherwise be the case; if the competition is weak, the program receives a higher rating. Frequently a program benefits from its position in the schedule; if it follows an unusually popular program, there may be a substantial audience carry-over from the earlier show, resulting in a higher rating. Still another factor affecting ratings is the amount of promotion and publicity given each program by its sponsor or by the network. Sometimes a relatively weak program receives a fairly high rating simply as a result of the advance publicity it has received. However, publicity alone will not bring a continuation of high ratings to a program series lacking in basic listener attractiveness; after one or two experiences with the program, the listener will turn to the offerings of other stations or turn off the receiving set completely.

Factors affecting local ratings. Local television ratings are affected by the same factors, as well as by at least two others of considerable importance. First of these is the number of stations that serve the community. Sets-in-use figures do not vary too greatly from one community to the next, at the same hour and the same time of the year. If between eight and nine o'clock in the evening, the sets-in-use figure is 60.0 in a market with only two stations, that 60.0 figure will be divided between the two programs available; if the market is one with four stations, however, there are four programs among which to divide the 60 rating points the sets-in-use figure represents. A second important factor is the degree of "prestige" enjoyed by the station that carries the program in the local area. If the program is broadcast by a very popular station, one to which listeners tune in more frequently than to other local stations, the program's rating will probably be much higher than would be the case if the same program were broadcast over a less popular station in the community.

Radio program and time-block ratings. With radio networks carrying few sponsored programs more than five minutes in length, it is difficult to draw conclusions concerning the ratings of radio network programs. However, at least on the local level, the same factors operating in television affect both total radio listening and the ratings received by programs or by time-blocks on radio stations. Hour of the day is important, just as it is in television; in the case of radio, however, the greatest amount of in-home listening in practically every community comes between the hours of seven and eleven o'clock in the *morning*, when it generally exceeds television viewing over the same period. After-

TABLE 16

ESTIMATED AVERAGE HOURS PER DAY OF IN-HOME USE OF RADIO AND TELEVISION SETS DURING DIFFERENT MONTHS OF THE YEAR

	Average hours sets used per day			Average hours sets used per day	
	Radio[1]	Telev'n		Radio[1]	Telev'n
April[2]	1.58	5.24	October	1.53	5.06
May	1.67	4.30	November	1.50	5.59
June	1.62	4.54	December	1.50	5.48
July	1.50	4.25	January[2]	1.57	6.23
August	1.45	4.19	February	1.68	6.07
September	1.49	4.62	March	1.58	5.61

[1] Radio estimates are for average daily use of "plug-in" radio sets only, excluding auto radios and battery portables. In *Radio '63*, the Nielsen company has reported that during the winter of 1962–63, estimated use of auto radios amounted to 0.50 hours, and of battery portables, 0.72 hours, per radio home per day.

[2] Months of April through December were in 1962; of January through March, in 1963.

Radio figures from national Nielsen Radio Index for April 1963; television figures from second national Nielsen Television Index report for April 1963. Reproduced with permission of the A. C. Nielsen Company.

noon radio listening is substantially lower, and as a result of the competition from television, the amount of in-home listening to radio after seven o'clock at night is less than a third as great as that reported for early morning hours. The fact must be stressed, however, that the foregoing patterns are based on use only of "plug-in" radio sets. Auto radios and battery portables combined account for almost as great an amount of radio listening, and at some hours of the day their use may be considerably greater than the use of "plug-in" sets in the home.

Seasonal variations in radio listening are less important than in television; although in-home use of radio sets is somewhat less during summer months than in the winter, the decrease is probably offset by a greater amount of out-of-the-home listening during warmer weather. The average time-block ratings of any radio station are naturally affected by the number of stations that serve the community; if the total amount of listening done is divided among eight or ten stations, the proportion of homes tuned to any one of that number is necessarily much smaller than if signals of only three or four stations are available. Relative popularity of individual stations seems to be a much more important factor in radio than in television; a listener who tunes in a well-liked radio station tends to stay tuned to that one station as long as his set is in use, especially in view of the fact that distinct changes in program materials at 15- or 30-minute intervals have all but disappeared from radio.

RATINGS AND PROGRAMMING

As has already been noted, ratings provide much-needed information for advertisers who use radio or television; they are also of great value to program executives of networks or stations and to those who plan and develop new programs. This is especially true in television where program costs are extremely high; every program must attract an audience large enough to justify the very substantial cost of keeping it on the air. As suggested in an earlier chapter, individual programs tend to wear out, no matter how many listeners they attracted at the peak of their popularity. When a program's ratings show a serious decline, either the program's format must be changed to provide new elements to intrigue the listener, or the series must be taken off the air. And of course, whenever one program is dropped from the station's or the network's schedules, another program must be developed to take its place. The question of course is, what kind of program should that new program be? And should it be inserted in the weekly schedule in the same time period as the program it replaces, or should the entire schedule be rearranged to give the new offering a greater chance of success?

Use of Ratings in Selection of New Programs

The kind of program added will depend, of course, on what programs are already available and waiting, or on what programs can be developed and ready for broadcast in time to replace the one being dropped. But in choosing among the various programs that might be used, attention certainly will be given to the public's current tastes and preferences in the program field, as indicated by the types of programs most successful in attracting audiences. A study of the ratings received by programs over a period of time suggests that listener tastes in programs change considerably from one year to the next.

The nature and extent of some of these changes in the program preferences of listeners are indicated by the figures provided in Table 17. Figures in each case are averages of the ratings of the three most popular programs of the type named as given in January reports of the A. C. Nielsen Company. As the table shows, the "popularity scores" of some types of programs—news, panel quiz shows, and public affairs programs—remained relatively stable during the twelve-year period. Those of many other program types were appreciably lower in 1964 than in earlier years. The table shows rather clearly the reason for the inclusion in evening network schedules of large numbers of situation comedies, for the heavy use of adult Western dramas around 1960, for the decrease in the number of anthology dramatic programs since 1956, and for the complete disappearance from evening schedules of the once-popular boxing broadcasts. Program executives of television networks pay a great deal of attention to trends in the popularity of various types of programs in selecting the programs to be included in their schedules during each new season.

Scheduling Strategy

On the basis of information concerning program ratings over the years, three basic principles are generally applied in

TABLE 17

TRENDS IN NATIONAL RATINGS OF EVENING NETWORK TELEVISION PROGRAMS OF VARIOUS MAJOR TYPES

(Figures are averages of Nielsen ratings of the three highest-rated programs of each type named, for January of the year indicated)

	1952	1956	1960	1964
Comedy variety	49	30	25 [1]	28
Other evening variety	38	35	29	23
Musical variety	21	30	22	20
60 m. anthology drama	36	33	17	19 [1]
30 m. anthology drama	34	34	21	—
60 m. general drama [2]	—	—	31	26
30 m. general drama	27	31	23 [1]	29 [1]
Action-adventure drama [3]	30	29	20	20
Crime-detective drama	32	33	27	16
Mystery-suspense drama	24	22	22 [1]	20
Adult Western drama	—	26	40	29
Situation comedy drama	37	39	33	36
Quiz or game shows	34	39	23	15 [1]
Panel quiz programs	20	25	22	27
Human interest programs	18 [1]	30	18	19
News broadcasts	10	14	16	14
Public affairs programs [4]	5 [1]	17 [1]	16	15
Late-evening boxing	23	24 [1]	23 [1]	9 [1]

[1] Fewer than three programs of the type named were on the air during January of the year indicated.

[2] Program series featuring the same leading character in each week's presentation.

[3] In 1952, included programs with Western settings, of the *Roy Rogers* type, as well as other action programs.

[4] Documentaries, informative dramas, and interview or discussion programs presented in regular series form.

Figures compiled with permission of the A. C. Nielsen Company from ratings given in Nielsen Television Index reports for January of the years indicated.

the scheduling of programs: those of "block" programming, of "strip" programming, and, during the past six or eight years, of "counter" programming. Block programming refers simply to the scheduling of two, three, or even four programs of the same general type—or of types usually attractive to the same kind of listeners—in sequence, on the same evening, or during daytime hours. A network often presents three or four situation comedies in succession on one night of the week; on another night, it may offer a sequence of panel or audience-quiz programs or of programs of the action-adventure type. Each program in the series "helps" the others and in turn is helped by the others in attracting some particular kind of listeners. Strip programming refers to the presentation of programs in the same series at exactly the same hour, five days a week, so that those listeners who like the series can remember its broadcast time without difficulty. The strip programming idea is used for practically all Monday-through-Friday daytime programs as well as for evening news presentations. The third scheduling principle, counter-programming, is a method used to "counter" or combat some especially popular program carried on another network. Opposite the other network's program, those who plan the schedules insert a program of completely different type which will attract a different kind of listeners than the program to be "countered"—for instance, scheduling a Western to compete with a variety show, or a situation comedy to compete with a serious dramatic presentation.

Criticisms of Ratings

Although advertisers and program executives are thoroughly convinced of their values, ratings are often criticized by others interested in broadcasting. Entertainers whose programs receive unsatisfactory ratings protest that "you can't really measure popularity" by getting the "opinions of a few hundred listeners." Owners of radio stations also challenge the accuracy of rating figures which indicate a drop in radio listening to levels far below those of pretelevision days. They charge too, and with some justice, that radio is discriminated against in rating reports, which fail to include out-of-home listening. More serious are the criticisms of nonindustry people who can hardly be accused of personal bias. Congressional committees have conducted hearings questioning the accuracy of the figures reported by some of the rating concerns, especially in local areas; the Federal Communications Commission has made its own investigation of the methods used by the rating companies; the Federal Trade Commission has warned against unwarranted claims that ratings provide accurate measurements of audiences of programs or stations.

Although these nonindustry critics usually base their opposition to ratings on the contention that rating figures are not completely accurate, their real objection is that, because of their low rating potential, programs of types they would like to see broadcast are kept off the air. An often cited example is a program of concert music that was carried on television network schedules over a period of ten years, but which, in its last five seasons on the air, had January ratings ranging from 10.0 to as low as 6.0—in spite of being scheduled at the very desirable hour of 8:30 in the evening. The sponsor was satisfied, in spite of the low rating. The network, however, found it impossible to build up large enough audiences for programs that followed; and when the sponsor refused to move the program to a period later at night, the network dropped the program from its schedules. In other instances, equally desirable programs have been dropped by their sponsors when ratings fell below expected levels.

Admittedly, low ratings do keep many programs off the air, including some programs with above-average cultural values. A program with a rating of only 10.0 costs its sponsor twice as much for each home reached as does a program with equal time and production costs that can show a 20.0 rating. In the circumstances, advertisers can hardly be expected to continue their support for low-rated programs, regardless of the cultural advantages such programs may offer. Nor can a network company afford to retain a low-rated program when its presence seriously weakens the audience-attracting abilities of adjacent programs and prevents those programs from finding sponsors. But the fault in such cases, if any fault exists, does not lie in the system of ratings, as such; ratings are merely a measurement of the approximate size of the audiences reached by programs. So if the situation produced by low ratings is in any way an undesirable one, the fault lies not in the system of measurement, but in other existing conditions—perhaps in the prevailing level of culture of the American people, which makes them unwilling to tune in those programs that the critics of ratings believe should be broadcast.

In any case, ratings for programs will continue to be reported, and the rating companies will continue to "count the vote" that the listening public casts for each network or local program. Probably, in the future, more attention will be given by advertisers to the *kinds* of listeners reached; it may be quite possible that a relatively small audience of the "right kind" of people may be more valuable to certain sponsors than a much larger total audience that includes only a small proportion of listeners of the special type that the advertiser wants to reach. With more qualitative information available concerning audiences of programs, network executives and representatives of advertisers may be able to select more intelligently than in the past those programs that will be tuned in by listeners of types most needed by the advertiser.

10

BROADCASTING AND
ITS CRITICS

In the little more than forty years of its existence,
broadcasting has become a significant element
in our national life. Primarily an agency of mass
entertainment and by far the most important
source of entertainment for most of our people,
broadcasting is also an agency of mass information, especially in the field of news and public
affairs. Apparently most listeners are reasonably
well satisfied with the kind of entertainment and
information that stations and networks provide,
as evidenced by the amount of time devoted to
radio and television listening. And most Americans would agree that on the whole, broadcasting
offers a service of the utmost importance to our
society.

But broadcasting is not perfect; like other
agencies or institutions, it has its shortcomings.
And like our newspapers and our magazines, our

schools and colleges, or our system of government, broadcasting is often the object of criticism. Included among its critics are many educators and sociologists, men in public life, and writers for newspapers and magazines. Committees of Congress conduct investigations into the effects of certain programs on children. Even rank-and-file listeners find aspects of broadcasting that are not to their liking and voice their complaints to friends and neighbors or to operators of broadcasting stations.

Some of the criticisms of radio and television are of minor importance. Listeners complain when a favorite program is taken off the air, or when two well-liked programs are broadcast by different stations at the same hour. They complain about the extensive use of reruns of television programs, especially during the summer months. Some object vigorously when a broadcast of a favorite entertainment program is canceled to make way for an important news special. But other criticisms are more serious and point to what many intelligent people consider basic flaws in the manner in which broadcasting operates in this country. These more important criticisms fall into three major categories. First, many critics believe that radio and television offer too few worthwhile programs—too few cultural programs or other programs of outstanding quality. Second, many object to the content of certain programs, and in particular to the excessive use of sex and violence. And finally, there is widespread criticism both of the number and of the kinds of commercial announcements included in schedules of radio and television stations.

Of course, it is possible that some critics of broadcasting expect too much—expect more of radio and television than they do of other agencies of entertainment or information. Possibly, too, they fail to take into account the practical realities of the broadcasting situation—the fact that broadcasting is a commercial enterprise, engaged in providing entertainment for a mass audience. But most of the critics are honest, intelligent men; their objections are entitled to serious consideration, just as attention should also be given to the many values which radio and television offer the American listener.

CRITICISMS OF THE QUALITY OF PROGRAMS

Complaints concerning the quality of broadcast programs come from the more intellectual elements in our society—from educators, writers for serious magazines, men and women who are leaders in public life. They see broadcasting as an agency with a tremendous potential for raising the cultural standards of the American people and for creating an appreciation of the best in music, art, and literature. But they feel that this potential is not being realized; that radio and television offer too few broadcasts, for example, of complete operas, or of symphony orchestras, or of dramatizations of the great masterpieces of English and Western European literature. They believe, too, that present-day television has produced few really outstanding programs; that it has developed little that could probably be classed as "great literature" or as a significant contribution to the art of the theater. They regard the offerings of most radio stations as little more than "musical trash," lowering rather than raising the public's standards of taste in the musical field. As for network television, most would strongly endorse the criticism expressed in 1961 by the then Chairman of the Federal Communications Commission when he characterized television's program offerings as "a vast wasteland . . . of game shows, violence, audience participation shows, formula comedies about totally unbelievable families, blood and thunder, mayhem, violence, sadism, murder, Western badmen, Western good men, private eyes, gangsters, more violence, and cartoons."

The Case of "Cultural" Programs

With respect to what the critics refer to as "cultural" programs, their charges have an obvious foundation in fact. Programs in the field of literature, art, or serious music make up a very small part of the total offerings of our commercial radio and television stations. To be sure, some large-city radio stations—especially independent FM stations—do provide substantial schedules of classical and semiclassical music. But these stations are relatively few in number, and broadcasts of operas, of symphony concerts, and of other types of serious music have practically disappeared from national radio networks. Television networks provide a total of not more than perhaps 30 or 40 hours a year of what can technically be labeled as cultural programs, most of them one-time "specials" or programs presented on an irregular basis. During an entire season, national networks may schedule three or four complete operas, perhaps half a dozen broadcasts by symphony orchestras, and not more than one or two programs of classical ballet, although short segments of more modern forms of ballet are sometimes inserted in regular variety programs. During recent years, only one program of what might be considered "serious" music has been included in regular network schedules, and that program only on an alternate-week basis. Occasionally special broadcasts are devoted to dramatized adaptations of great novels or to presentations of the classics of the theater. One of the latter, a television version of *Macbeth* presented as a *Hallmark Hall of Fame* offering at a reported cost of nearly half a million dollars to the sponsoring company, is said to have been seen by more viewers than the total number of people who have ever seen the Shakespearian tragedy performed on the stage since the play was written more than three centuries ago.

Although a few outstanding programs of this sort are presented, the total volume of cultural offerings included in each season's television network schedule is decidedly small. Broadcasting in this country is not primarily an agency of cultural enlightenment, as may be the case in some European nations; the costs of presenting cultural programs are not borne by the government, nor paid from moneys derived from special taxes collected from owners of receiving sets. Because American broadcasting is commercial, it is essentially a *mass* medium, dependent for its economic success on the attracting of large audiences for the programs it presents. And cultural programs, regardless of their social values, usually attract only a very small segment of the total listening public. Audiences for such programs are usually not more than one-third or at most one-half as large as those for entertainment programs of equal costs. So it is quite understandable that advertisers, interested in reaching the largest possible number of people for each dollar they spend on radio or television, are not often willing to sponsor an opera broadcast, or a program featuring a symphony orchestra or a ballet company, or even a presentation of a classic of the theater. Nor are the executives of network companies so interested in raising cultural standards as to be willing to carry any appreciable number of such programs without sponsorship, and pay the costs out of network funds. As their contribution to public enlightenment, the network companies prefer to spend their money for presentations in the areas of news and public affairs, which are provided in this country in far greater numbers than in nations with government control of broadcasting—and which also attract larger audiences and consequently have greater advertiser support than do broadcasts of operas or of symphony orchestras or of classical ballet. In the circumstances, there seems to be little likelihood that American commercial television or radio will ever become the agency for the dissemination of "culture" that some of its critics would wish.

Quality of Entertainment Programs

Charges that broadcasting offers few entertainment programs of outstanding quality are also supported, to some extent, by the facts in the situation. Since 1955 or 1956 radio programming has shown little originality or imagination; with networks no longer a source of important radio programs, radio's offerings have been low in entertainment values—at least for most adult listeners—if only because of the general lack of program variety. Of course, the situation is largely a result of the economic problems faced by radio networks and by most radio stations in recent years, problems created by the rise of television and, in some degree, by the licensing policies of the Federal Communications Commission. A station operating at a loss or with a profit margin of only four or five thousand dollars—and that has been the situation in which nearly two-thirds of all radio stations have found themselves in recent years—can hardly be expected to produce outstanding programs. But some part of the responsibility for the low state of radio programming generally must also attach to the managers of most radio stations for their follow-the-leader attitudes and their wholesale acceptance of "news and music" programming with so little effort made to develop more imaginative local program forms.

But objections are not directed at radio alone. Critics of broadcasting charge that television has produced few really outstanding programs, programs that might properly be classed as "great literature" or as "significant contributions to the art of the drama." Probably it is true that few television programs have been "great" in this sense; few, certainly, can be regarded as having lasting literary values. But that situation is not one peculiar to television. Of the more than 4,600 new plays presented on Broadway between 1900 and 1950, how many can properly be classed as "great"? Or of the 35 or 40 original plays produced in New York each season since 1950, how many have been "significant contributions to the literature of the theater"? Or of the approximately 2,500 new novels or books of fiction published in this country each year, how many have had lasting literary values? Great works of art or of literature are infrequent, and in other fields no less than in television.

But if few television programs can be considered "great" or "significant," television has produced a substantial number which must at least be rated as "good"; some have been exceptionally good. Few critics would question the technical excellence or the entertainment values of such programs as *Studio One,* or the *Kraft TV Theater,* or the *Philco Television Playhouse,* or in more recent years the *DuPont Show of the Week,* or the *Dick Powell Theater,* or *Naked City,* or the *United States Steel Hour,* or in the field of problem drama, *The Defenders.* Television has produced a number of excellent variety shows, musical programs, even situation comedies. And it is worthy of notice that even the British Broadcasting Corporation, so highly regarded by the critics for its offering of "worthwhile" programs, has seen fit to include in its schedules a very substantial number of American-produced program series ranging from variety to serious drama, and from situation comedies to crime shows and Westerns. Presented on the BBC network on a regular basis have been such regular series as the *Perry Como Show, Arrest and Trial,* the *Dick Powell Theater, Naked City,* the *Lucy Show, The Defenders,* the *Danny Kaye* variety series, *Dr. Kildare,*

Violence—such scenes have caused great concern over the possible relation between television violence and juvenile delinquency.

Entertainment—Scene from a network variety show

Wagon Train, Bewitched, the *Dick Van Dyke Show, Get Smart,* and *The Man from U.N.C.L.E.,* as well as many American-produced documentary programs. Perhaps American television has produced few programs worthy of the designation of "great art," but the television industry has provided American listeners over the years with a rather impressive number of programs of superior quality.

Of course, not all programs are "superior." A majority are of no more than ordinary quality, even as entertainment. Some are poor, even bad—a fact that is recognized by a majority of television viewers, whose refusal to listen results in the cancellation, within twelve months, of three out of five of the new evening program series scheduled by national networks each year. But in view of the tremendous demands on television, the situation could hardly be otherwise. The entire Broadway theater is called on to provide less than 100 hours of new material each season. Hollywood produces only about 150 feature films or a little more than 300 hours of new motion picture material each year for showing in motion picture theaters. But the three national television networks are expected to provide from 200 to 250 hours of programming *each week,* and even allowing for the extensive reruns of filmed dramatic programs in evening schedules, that means that the networks are called upon to supply from 8,000 to 10,000 hours of new program material during a twelve-month period—at least 20 times as many hours as the output of the Broadway stage and the motion picture industry combined. Under the circumstances, it is less than reasonable to expect that all or even a majority of the programs offered by television will be more than mediocre in quality; there aren't enough outstanding producers or idea men or writers or entertainers to make it possible. Television programs could be better than they are, to be sure; improvement is always to be hoped for, and perhaps networks will attempt to provide a greater number of significant programs as listener demand for such programs increases. But the fact that many programs are mediocre today, and that some fall below even that standard, is hardly a legitimate basis for general criticism of the quality of television programs. More attention should be given to the really good programs that television provides.

CRITICISMS OF PROGRAM CONTENT

A second major group of criticisms of broadcasting are those relating to the content of programs. Complaints in this field come from a wide variety of sources. Teachers criticize the use of slang or of poor English by radio or television entertainers, as setting a bad example for children. Religious groups object to the use of barroom scenes in Westerns, and to matter-of-fact drinking by characters in other dramatic programs. Italians protest to the networks against the use of Italian names for characters in gangster or crime dramatizations; Negro organizations object vigorously to the portrayal of Negroes as comedy characters, or as working in menial capacities. But the most widespread criticisms of program content, coming from organized listener groups, from sociologists and psychiatrists, even from committees of Congress, center in two primary areas: the emphasis laid on sex and the consequent use of materials which listeners consider vulgar or indecent, and introduction of scenes of violence in programs.

Sex, Vulgarity, Indecency

The extent to which criticisms of vulgarity or indecency are justified is difficult to determine; standards of acceptability vary widely from one individual to the next. But it cannot be denied that broadcast programs occasionally do include materials of borderline type. Radio stations have carried recordings of popular musical numbers with obviously suggestive lyrics. At least one station in recent years has been denied license renewal because of the use of off-color humor by one of its disk-jockey personalities. Dramatic programs on television have used themes involving illicit sex relations; documentaries have presented frank discussions of prostitution, homosexuality, and abortion. Comedians in variety shows have sometimes used jokes with double meanings; female entertainers have appeared in costumes that many viewers felt were unnecessarily revealing; dance routines have included the "bumps" and "grinds" ordinarily associated with low-grade burlesque performances. In one or two cases, the themes or language used in network dramatic programs have been of such a questionable nature that the regular sponsors of the program series have refused to allow their names or their advertising to be used in connection with those particular broadcasts.

In fairness to those who operate our radio and television stations, it must be said that the use of obviously offensive material is the exception; certainly not the rule. Serious violations of requirements of good taste have been extremely rare. The record of radio and television has been especially good when compared with that of other agencies of entertainment—with the seeming preoccupation with illicit sex which characterizes the theater of today, with the undisguised vulgarity of night-club entertainers, with the themes of homosexuality and prostitution used in many of our most successful motion pictures, with the use of four-letter words and the detailed descriptions of sex situations in many of our best-selling novels. But broadcast programs are heard in the home; audiences include impressionable youngsters as well as adults, and the standards applied by radio and television should be considerably more rigid than those common in nightclubs or theaters. Broadcasters recognize their responsibilities in such a situation and have attempted to eliminate from programs any elements that listeners might find offensive or not in good taste. As a result, although individual standards differ and lapses do occur, such lapses are infrequent; only in rare instances have materials been used that offer a legitimate basis for criticism on grounds of vulgarity or possible indecency.

Excessive Violence

Critics of the use of violence in television programs, however, find more frequent occasions for complaint. Violence and suspense are standard elements in crime-detective, adventure, and Western dramatic shows. Men engage in bare-knuckled fist fights, they fight with clubs or knives, they fight with guns. Viewers see barroom brawls involving a score or more participants; they see beatings, floggings, attempted lynchings. We have murders and killings by the score; we hear murders being plotted; occasionally we see gangsters mowing down their enemies with machine guns. Such acts of violence are not the exception, but almost the rule; evidence presented before a Senate subcommittee indicates that during a one-week period in 1960, programs carried by the seven television stations in Los Angeles included no less than 114 murders, 128 attempted murders, and 49 "justifiable" killings, in addition to nine kidnappings, two suicides, three attempted rapes, and six situations in which men were subjected to physical torture.

Nor has the use of violence decreased in more recent years. In fact, the show-business weekly *Variety* was moved to comment in December 1965 about the use of sadism and torture in prime-time network television programs. After citing several instances, the article continued that "all three networks are now loaded nightly with more dramatic shows that have more violence and mayhem than was ever dreamed of by Sen. Dodd [1] when he was breathing fire about the medium in Washington hearings."

Those who criticize the use of violence in television programs believe that susceptible viewers—children in particular—are definitely harmed by what they see. Some may have a tendency to imitate, and themselves use violence in their dealings with others. Or in the case of other viewers, the portrayal of violence, brutality, and torture may be a source of psychological injury, creating morbid fears or causing serious emotional disturbances. Many psychologists and psychiatrists support this view. However, other equally reputable psychologists take an exactly opposite position; they state that exposure to scenes of violence on television provides a release for children's natural aggressive tendencies, and contend that there is little danger of psychological injury because viewers are always in some degree aware of the fact that what they see is fiction—that it isn't "really so." If the latter belief is a correct one, it may be that television's news broadcasts and documentary programs, to which critics have raised no objection, may in fact be more disturbing to sensitive viewers than are portrayals of violence in crime and adventure dramatic shows, especially when such

---

[1] Senator Thomas J. Dodd, Democrat, of Connecticut, Chairman of the Special Senate Subcommittee on Juvenile Delinquency.

news and documentary programs show the mangled victims of automobile or airplane accidents or portray the effects of starvation in famine-ridden countries or the brutality of guards in prison camps.

But the basic fact remains that television's dramatic programs do include numerous scenes of killing, brutality, and violence, and that no one actually knows whether sensitive viewers may be injured by exposure to such scenes, or not. There may be valid grounds for complaint, at least against the use of extreme brutality, or actions that create unreasoning fear, or the too-frequent portrayals of acts of violence in broadcast programs.

Self-Regulation by Broadcasters

Most broadcasters are very much aware of the problem, and have attempted to guard against possible injuries resulting from the programs they put on the air. Criticisms of the content of children's programs on radio resulted in the adoption, in the middle 1930s, of sets of basic program standards by each of the networks, and of an industry "code of good practices" by the National Association of Broadcasters. The standards adopted prohibited the use in children's programs of kidnapping situations, the overuse of violence, or the inclusion of other materials that might create undue suspense. Equally important, networks set up Continuity Acceptance departments to check all program scripts in advance and to make sure that possibly harmful materials were eliminated.

Network and industry codes have been revised from time to time, with new sections added to deal with new problems that have arisen. Each network has its own code of program practices, outlining types of material not to be included in network programs. In addition, networks and most television stations are subscribers to the Television Code of the National Association of Broadcasters, adopted in 1952 and amended frequently since that time. Radio stations belonging to the NAB have their own Code of Good Practices, differing somewhat from the Television Code but covering most of the same points.

Restrictions provided in Codes. Provisions of the NAB Television Code are fairly typical of standards outlined in the Radio Code and in code provisions of the various networks. It urges that programs emphasize "the commonly accepted moral, social, and ethical ideals" characteristic of American life, and foster "respect for parents, for honorable behavior, and for constituted authority." It prohibits the use of "profanity, obscenity, smut, and vulgarity," attacks on religion or improper references to any religious rite or faith, or the use of "words derisive of any race, color, creed, or nationality." It warns against the depicting of the use of liquor, except in situations essential to plot; it urges that law enforcement officers be portrayed with respect; and it urges strongly that criminality must be presented as undesirable and that techniques of crime may not be presented in such detail as to lead to imitation.

With respect to portrayals of "sex and violence," the Television Code includes the following:

Illicit sex relations are not treated as commendable. Sex crimes and abnormalities are generally unacceptable as program materials. The use of locations closely associated with sexual life or sexual sin must be governed by good taste and delicacy. . . . The costuming of all performers shall be within the bounds of propriety and shall avoid such exposure or such emphasis on anatomical detail as would embarrass or offend home viewers. The movements of dancers, actors or other performers shall be kept within the bounds of decency, and lewdness and impropriety shall not be suggested in the positions assumed by performers.

Material which is excessively violent or which would create morbid suspense or other undesirable reactions in children should be avoided. . . . The use of horror for its own sake will be eliminated. The use of visual or aural effects which would shock or alarm the viewer, and the detailed presentation of brutality or physical agony by sight or sound, are not permissible. . . . Particular restraint and care should be exercised in crime or mystery episodes involving children. Exceptional care should be exercised with reference to kidnapping or threats of kidnapping of children, in order to avoid terrorizing them.[2]

---

[2] From the Ninth Edition of the NAB Television Code, published in April, 1964.

Of course, not all television stations subscribe to the Television Code, and fewer than half of all radio stations subscribe to NAB's Radio Code. But it must be stated that with amazingly few exceptions, code subscribers and nonsubscribers alike uphold the *principles* laid down in the codes, as far as they relate to program content. Broadcasters know that they are dependent on the goodwill of the listening public; if only for selfish reasons, they can be expected to make a vigorous attempt to eliminate from their programs any materials likely to offend any appreciable number of listeners.

The problem of interpretation. But codes of practice are statements of general principles; they cannot possibly cover every situation that may arise. Interpretations are required; network or station officials must use their own judgments in making these interpretations. For example, the Television Code bans the use of material that is "excessively violent." This could hardly be held to prohibit the use of any violence whatever; no one argues that every suggestion of violence be eliminated from television programs. But how much violence and what types of violence may be regarded as permissible, and at what point does the use of violence become "excessive"? Is a fist fight "excessively violent," but a gun fight in which one participant is killed, permissible—or is it the other way around? If a war dramatization shows soldiers presumably being killed in battle, is that a portrayal of "excessive violence"? Obviously, decisions must be made on a case-by-case basis by those who produce programs or by network Continuity Acceptance departments; in the final analysis, the whole question of what is suitable for broadcast and what is not depends on the good judgment and good taste of those individuals responsible for the application and interpretation of program standards.

But individuals differ in their interpretations of the same general principles. What is condemned by one person may be considered quite acceptable by another, regardless of the language used in network or industry codes. So it is entirely understandable that we find some programs on the air open to honest criticism from some viewers because they contain too much violence or suspense, or place too great an emphasis on sex, or present other materials these viewers consider objectionable or in bad taste. Broadcasters certainly do not wish to offend their listeners, but judgments of station managers, of program producers, or of network Continuity Acceptance department members may not always coincide with the judgments of individual listeners on what materials may properly be put on the air.

CRITICISMS OF ADVERTISING

No feature of broadcasting is more irritating to rank-and-file listeners than the use of advertising messages in radio and television programs. Most people in the United States realize that, under the system of broadcasting used in this country, broadcasting is made possible by revenues received from sale of time to advertisers. But listeners are critical of broadcast advertising; far more critical, in most cases, than they are of advertising carried in newspapers and magazines. Some object to the advertising of certain types of products over the air; others charge that some advertising messages are fraudulent and misleading; many believe that much of the advertising on radio and television is lacking in good taste; and large numbers of listeners object to the quantity of advertising matter inserted in broadcast schedules.

Some Americans, of course, would like to do away entirely with advertising on radio and television. During the early 1920s, Secretary of Commerce Herbert Hoover convened a series of four national Radio Conferences to consider problems affecting radio. Secretary Hoover himself told the 1924 Conference that "the quickest way to kill broadcasting would be to use it for direct advertising." The 1925 Conference concluded that any "direct advertising" would be objectionable to the listening public. But radio had to be financed; the existing political climate precluded any possibility of its being supported by taxation, so in spite of the feelings of those who took part in the Hoover conferences, radio became "commercial," relying for its revenues on sale of time to advertisers. The regulatory acts of 1927 and of 1934 placed no restrictions on broadcast advertising, and today only a handful of critics would suggest that advertising be eliminated completely and that radio and television should be financed—and presumably operated—by the government.

But while the American people accept the *idea* of advertising on radio and television, they are entirely willing to criticize the manner in which advertising is provided. In 1947, a nationwide study of listener attitudes found that although 70 per cent of the respondents interviewed felt that radio was doing an "excellent" or at least a "good" job of serving the public, one listener in four believed that radio advertising was "boring and repetitious," or "noisy and distracting," or that it "claimed too much for the product," or was often "in bad taste." [3] Since the advent of television, the critical attitude of listeners toward commercial announcements has apparently become even stronger. A listener study of television conducted in 1960 found 40 per cent of the respondents feeling that "commercials are generally in poor taste" or annoying, and 63 per cent believing that "most commercials are too long." [4] However, three out of four listeners did agree that "commercials are a fair price to pay for the entertainment you get," although many complained that the advertising announcements on television were too numerous, that they interrupted programs too often, and that in many cases they were boring and dull and sometimes misleading and dishonest.

Objections to Dishonest or Misleading Advertising

Criticisms of fraudulent or misleading advertising are less common today than in earlier years, perhaps because relatively few of the commercial announcements carried by radio or television stations in recent years actually have been dishonest or misleading. Certainly the problem is less serious today than it was in radio's early years when some stations advertised "cures" for alcoholism, or operations to restore youthful vigor to men of advanced years, or even cures for cancer. Improvement is

---

[3] Paul F. Lazarsfeld and Patricia L. Kendall, *Radio Listening in America*. Prentice-Hall, Inc., 1948.

[4] Gary A. Steiner, *The People Look at Television*. Alfred A. Knopf, 1963.

a result partly of the efforts of legitimate advertisers and of the broadcasting industry itself, partly of the activities of various government agencies.

Code provisions on misleading advertising. Broadcasters naturally have been concerned over the problem of misrepresentations in advertising. The first Code of Commercial Practices of the National Association of Broadcasters, adopted in 1929, provided that matter barred from the mails as fraudulent or deceptive should not be broadcast, nor should statements or claims known to be false, deceptive, or greatly exaggerated. The present Television Code of the NAB urges that "great care should be exercised to prevent the presentation of false, misleading, or deceptive advertising," or of commercials which, "by copy or demonstration, involve material deception as to the characteristics, performance, or appearance of the product." The Code bars the use of any "claims that a medical product will affect a cure," or copy in which such words as "safe," "without risk," or "harmless" are used indiscriminately. It also includes a "men in white" ruling, barring the appearance in medical commercials of physicians, dentists, or nurses, or of actors presumably representing such physicians, dentists, or nurses, since such appearances might lead the viewer to believe that the product has the endorsement of the medical profession. Similar provisions are included in the NAB Radio Code. These restrictions on possibly fraudulent advertising have been vigorously applied by most stations and especially by the national networks.

The Federal Trade Commission. Even more important, probably, have been the activities of the Federal Trade Commission since 1938, when its powers were expanded by Congress explicitly to include a consideration of fraudulent advertising. At intervals, every network and every radio and television station is required to submit to the Trade Commission a copy of the text of every commercial announcement broadcast during the preceding week; these announcements are checked by the Commission's staff for possible violation of federal laws. As a rule, about 2 or 3 per cent of the commercials submitted are "set aside for further study"—less than half as large a proportion, incidentally, as of advertisements printed in newspapers or national magazines. If the Commission finds that either a printed or a broadcast advertisement is in fact fraudulent or misleading or that it makes unsupported or exaggerated claims, action is taken directly against the advertiser responsible, rather than against the newspaper, magazine or broadcasting station that disseminated the objectionable advertisement. Particular attention is given to claims in the advertising copy about what the product will do, its "harmless" qualities, or its endorsement by prominent authorities. Cease and desist orders have been issued by the FTC against claims in the advertising of most of the cigarette companies and many, if not all, of the companies manufacturing cosmetics and pharmaceuticals, with the result that we no longer hear commercials stating that there is "not a cough in a carload" of a particular cigarette, or that "most doctors recommend" a certain headache remedy, or that use of a given face cream will "make any woman look 20 years younger."

A form of television advertising under scrutiny of the Federal Trade Commission in recent years involves the use of special production effects in commercial announcements. Producers of television and magazine advertisements contend that a certain amount of artifice is necessary to show a product to the best advantage; because of the heat generated by studio lights, for example, certain food products melt, or become lifeless and unattractive in appearance. So in filming a commercial, mashed potatoes or cream cheese may be used instead of ice cream, or double-strength gelatin in place of the standard variety, or dry ice may be used to produce "steam" in showing what is presumably a piping-hot dish of food or cup of coffee. The Trade Commission realizes that problems exist, and is willing to accept a reasonable amount of such "dishonesty" in photography, whether for commercials for television or for those prepared for use in "slick" magazines. But the Commission does object when the use of such camera trickery apparently gives a product certain qualities it does not actually possess, or when it is used to make the advertised product look better than that of a competitor when in fact there is no discernible difference between them. While advertisements for a relatively small number of products have met with FTC disapproval on this ground, the Commission's interest in this form of misleading advertising has caused networks and advertisers to exercise a great amount of caution in dealing with filmed commercials for television. In 1962, the American Association of Advertising Agencies adopted a new "creative code" listing a number of questionable visual techniques, which its members are pledged to avoid in preparing such commercials.

Objections to Bad Taste in Advertising

A common criticism of radio and television advertising is that many commercial announcements are objectionable and violate the requirements of good taste. Substantial numbers of listeners object to the advertising of certain types of products. Members of militant religious groups are opposed to the advertising of beer, wines, or "hard liquor" on broadcast programs. In past years, many listeners objected on moral grounds to the advertising of cigarettes; more recently, cigarette advertising has been under attack on the basis of the relationship between excessive cigarette smoking and the incidence of lung cancer. Other products that many feel are inappropriate for radio and television advertising include laxatives, depilatories, deodorants, and articles of intimate wearing apparel. Individual listeners frequently object, too, to the advertising of bars and taverns, of race tracks, of motion picture theaters featuring "art" films, and of personal loan companies charging high rates of interest.

Even in cases where the product or service is itself entirely acceptable, the commercial announcement may be offensive or in bad taste. An insurance company's use of a "suppose you were to die tomorrow" theme would be disturbing to many listeners, as would the use of a similar "scare" technique in advertising medical products. Objection has been made to the appearance of scantily clad women in televised commercials for shampoos and beauty preparations. Many listeners have complained about the lack of taste in the advertising used for certain headache remedies or antacids, especially in filmed commercials in which the pain-relieving properties of the product are demonstrated through use of animated diagrams of the purported sufferer's head, stomach, or lower digestive tract. Criticisms are frequently made of the irritating qualities of commercials. They interrupt the entertainment—an obvious fact, and it certainly is annoying when a tender love scene in a dramatization is suddenly interrupted by a commercial for a tooth paste, a detergent, or a breakfast cereal. Frequently commercials are loud and raucous; some members of the Federal Communications Commission have even charged that the sound or "noise" level of filmed or recorded announcements has been intentionally raised above that of the surrounding program material.[5] And there has been widespread objection from listeners to the use of "hard sell" techniques by announcers, both network and local.

Code restrictions on bad taste in advertising.   Of course, violations of good taste in advertising are not the concern of federal laws. But broadcasters themselves, and most advertisers, have attempted to deal with the problem. Most radio and television stations refuse to carry advertising for a variety of products and services generally accepted without question by nearly all newspapers and magazines. The Television Code of the National Association of Broadcasters lists as "not acceptable" the advertising of "hard liquor," of trade schools that imply promises of employment, of "tip sheets" and racetrack publications, of fortune-telling and astrology, of organizations that promote betting or lotteries, or of "particularly intimate products which ordinarily are not freely discussed" in social groups. Networks have even longer lists of products for which advertising is not accepted. The National Broadcasting Company, for example, will not carry advertising for matrimonial agencies, cemeteries, mortuaries and funeral homes, for products with offensive trade names, for books or pamphlets dealing with self-diagnosis or self-medication, or for dangerous or habit-forming drugs. The network also refuses to accept advertising for physicians or dentists, or advertising intended to promote the sale of specific stocks or bonds.

Not all radio or television stations live up to the provisions of industry codes; a few are willing to carry "hard liquor" ad-

---

[5] In December 1965, NBC asked advertising agencies and producers of filmed and taped commercials to avoid elements that contribute to loud commercials, and to submit announcements to be used on the network early enough to permit prescreening and loudness checks.

vertising, and a larger number have accepted advertising for certain medical products specifically banned by the NAB Television Code Authority. Even the codes themselves do not prohibit the advertising of many products to which there has been listener objection—cigarettes, beer and wine, laxatives, deodorants, and the like. The reason is obviously economic; producers and distributors of these products are heavy buyers of radio and television time, and refusal to accept such advertising would cost the broadcasting industry hundreds of millions of dollars in revenues each year. So industry codes hold that this type of advertising is acceptable "when presented in the best of good taste" and in conformity with state and federal laws.

As to the question of good taste in commercial announcements themselves, the Television Code provides that "disturbing messages should be avoided; every effort should be made to keep the advertising message in harmony with the content and general tone of the program in which it appears." All three television networks have adopted more specific standards governing taste in commercial announcements. The Columbia Broadcasting System, for instance, stipulates that advertising for "cold or headache remedies or for antacids must emphasize pleasant aftereffects, not symptoms;" that "use of live models in advertising foundation garments" is prohibited unless the models are fully clothed, and that "in advertising personal products, no negative or scare copy" may be used, and "no visual devices depicting bodily functions, pain, discomfort, or unwanted hair."

Improvements in television commercials. In spite of such provisions, we still have commercial announcements that television and radio listeners find irritating. In fact, in the Steiner study already referred to, no less than 40 per cent of the men and women interviewed in 1960 believed that commercials *generally* were annoying and in poor taste. The situation may have been somewhat improved in recent years; at least, some of the more irritating medical commercials have been taken off the air, and the use of "hard sell" advertising has definitely decreased. On television at least, there has been a noticeable increase in the number of commercials tastefully, even artistically, produced.

The rapid expansion in the number of network color programs has had a marked effect on television commercials; by 1965 at least 80 national advertisers were providing filmed commercials in color, with the result that in many cases commercial announcements were rivaling the surrounding program materials in attractiveness. In fact, the television editor for *Newsweek* magazine is lavish in his praise of the quality of some of television's present-day commercials. "While TV's proudest dramatic shows look like B pictures from the 1930s," he says, "the best commercials are stunning showcases of advanced photography, editing, direction, writing, music and sound, all squeezed with ruthless discipline into a one-minute format." [6] But in spite of the willingness of many major advertisers to spend more money for production of advertising materials, there are still many commercials on the air that listeners find objectionable and that some believe to fall far short of the ordinary requirements of good taste.

Objections to the Quantity of Advertising

Undoubtedly the greatest source of criticism of broadcast advertising is found in the quantity of advertising matter included in radio and television programs. Some radio stations reportedly schedule as many as 200 commercial announcements a day; television stations have been known to devote as much as 25 per cent of their broadcasting time, at certain periods, to advertising and other nonentertainment materials. Some critics have described the typical broadcast program as a seemingly endless series of commercial announcements, interrupted occasionally by short segments of entertainment. Certainly listeners and viewers are acutely aware of the amount of advertising carried today on radio and television schedules—an amount decidedly greater than was permitted on radio stations before the advent of television.

Reasons for increased number of commercials. Several factors have contributed to the increase in the number of commercials

---

[6] *Newsweek,* April 26, 1965, p. 93.

carried by broadcasting stations. One is the decline in single sponsorship of programs and the extensive use of "spot carriers" and other programs with participating sponsorship, with more advertising announcements per hour of program time than are included in programs presented by a single sponsor. On television networks, the change has come about as a result of the increasingly high cost of network programs, as noted in an earlier chapter. On radio and television stations, it is in part at least the result of economic conditions within the industry—conditions which cause large numbers of stations to operate at a loss and to try to deal with their financial problems by including an ever-increasing number of spot announcements in their schedules.

Also contributing to the increased number of commercials carried by television stations has been the willingness of networks to provide longer "chain-break" periods between network programs. Rules of the Federal Communications Commission require each station to identify itself—to announce its call letters and location—at 30-minute intervals throughout the broadcasting day. Originally, each television network program was shortened by 30 seconds to provide time for these required identifications—a practice carried over to television from radio. Since the identification announcements themselves could be given in four or five seconds, stations used the remaining time to present short commercials for local or national spot advertisers; because of their preferred positions between network programs, these short announcements could be sold for premium prices. Since around 1958, as a result of pressure from their affiliates, all three television networks have increased the between-program intervals, first to 40 seconds and later, at certain times during the day and evening, to as much as 70 seconds. Consequently, in addition to the advertising spotted *within* network programs, television listeners are exposed to an average of nearly two minutes in each hour of local commercial material inserted in "chain-break" periods *between* programs.

That the too-frequent use of commercial announcements interferes with most listeners' enjoyment of programs can hardly be questioned. The situation is aggravated by the insertion in practically all network television programs of a tremendous amount of what advertisers refer to as "clutter"—billboards,[7] promotional materials for other programs, public service announcements, and lengthy lists of credits for entertainers, writers, directors, technicians, even makeup artists and hairdressers. When these materials are included in addition to the regular commercial announcements, the time left for entertainment in a 30-minute network program is often cut to as little as 21 or 22 minutes, and it is readily understandable that listeners complain about the "overcommercialization" of broadcast programs. Even national advertisers and advertising agencies have protested against the excessive amount of "clutter" in network television programs and the reduction in the amount of time devoted to entertainment.

Weakened code restrictions on quantity of advertising. Broadcasters are undoubtedly aware of these objections from advertisers as well as listeners, but the industry has done little to correct the situation. To be sure, the Television Code Authority of the National Association of Broadcasters did recommend in 1964 that "clutter" be held within bounds, and that in particular names of technicians and other noncreative personnel be not included in program credits. But restrictions on the number of commercials used in television programs have actually been relaxed, rather than made more severe. As originally adopted in 1952, the Television Code limited the time to be used for advertising to a maximum of seven minutes in hour-long sponsored programs, and to not more than twelve minutes in each hour of programs with participating sponsorship, with an additional minute allowed in each case for chain-break local advertising. But in 1963, the code was amended, and new limits on commercial materials established—ten minutes and 20 seconds for each program hour in prime time, including chain-break announcements, and 16 minutes and 20 seconds, including chain-break commercials, during each hour of programming at other times during

---

[7] "Billboards" are short visual and aural announcements inserted in the opening and again in the closing of television network spot carriers, identifying the participating sponsors of the program or the products advertised. Usually about eight seconds is allowed for each advertiser or product.

the day or late evening. In prime time periods, the code includes as "commercial material" such items as billboards, public service announcements, and promotions for other programs, as well as regular commercial copy. In nonprime time, the limits apply only to regular commercial announcements; other "clutter" materials are not counted.

Restrictions on the amount of commercial advertising carried by radio stations have been similarly relaxed. The Radio Code adopted by the National Association of Broadcasters in 1948 provided that, not counting advertising in station breaks, not more than three minutes of commercial material should be included in any sponsored 15-minute period of broadcasting time. In 1954, this restriction was dropped. Later, however, the Radio Code was amended to provide that in participating programs, advertising matter should not exceed an *average* of 14 minutes per hour, computed on a weekly basis, with not more than 18 minutes of advertising presented in any one hour, or more than five minutes in any one 15-minute period. And when in the summer of 1963 the Federal Communications Commission proposed to adopt a regulation that would officially limit the amount of radio and television advertising to the maximums provided in industry codes, broadcasters resisted so strongly that after a few months the Commission withdrew its proposal.

So regardless of criticisms, the amount of commercial advertising carried by broadcasting stations has not been reduced. Nor is it likely to be reduced appreciably in the future, unless economic conditions in the broadcasting industry are greatly changed. After all, in recent years from 30 to 40 per cent of all radio stations and nearly one-fifth of all commercial television stations have been operating at a loss. Any major reduction in station revenues would force a considerable number of stations into bankruptcy; and stations that are already losing money, or operating on a very small profit margin, are not likely to be willing to cut the number of commercials they broadcast when such a reduction would result in a corresponding loss of revenues. Of course, in theory, stations could reduce the number of commercial announcements without loss of income by raising the rates charged for advertising time. But in practice, an increase in charges for broadcasting time would mean that adver-

tisers would turn to other media to bring their sales messages
to the public—to newspapers and magazines, or to billboards,
handbills, or direct mail advertising—and that stations would
find themselves in even more serious financial difficulties. Individual radio or television stations with high rates of earnings
can afford to hold the amounts of advertising they carry to
levels well below the limits set in industry codes, and many
"prestige" stations in major markets already follow such a policy.
But unless economic conditions change materially, there is little
possibility that similar actions can be taken by the majority of
stations or, in view of their high costs of operation, by the
television networks. The problem of "too many commercials"
is one not easily solved.

VALUES OF CRITICISM

As long as we have broadcasting in this country, there
will probably be many intelligent men and women who are less
than satisfied with the types of entertainment or information
provided in broadcast programs. Some will object, as many do
now, to the relative absence of cultural programs from network
schedules or to the scarcity of programs they regard as meeting
high standards of artistic merit. Others will criticize the types
of materials included in certain programs, or will be irritated
by the amount of advertising broadcast by radio and television
stations.

In many cases, certainly, these criticisms of broadcasting
will be justified. As stated earlier in this chapter, broadcasting
in this country is far from perfect. Probably it will always fall
far short of what many regard as the ideal in programming. But
even with the imperfections evident in broadcasting today, most
American listeners apparently believe that the good qualities
outweigh the bad. They seem to be reasonably well satisfied
with the offerings of broadcasting stations—or at least, with some
of those offerings. Their attitude is compellingly demonstrated
by the time they devote to radio and television listening—by
the fact that in our millions of radio- and television-equipped
homes, radio sets are in use for an average of more than an

hour and a half a day, and television sets for more than five hours a day, with the average total time devoted to television viewing increasing every year. It is obvious that the great majority of listeners are finding some programs at least that meet with their approval, and that are providing entertainment or information of a type pleasing to them.

If radio and television are satisfying a majority of listeners, should those who are not satisfied—educators, newspaper columnists, magazine writers, and ordinary rank-and-file listeners—continue to voice their criticisms of programs or broadcasting practices which, in their judgment, should be improved? By all means. Reasonable and intelligent criticism is desirable and helpful, particularly when it takes the form of suggesting specific improvements or when it is aimed at weaknesses in programs where improvement is really possible. Of course, those who criticize should ask for changes which broadcasters have the power to effect—it does little good to urge that programs generally be made "better" or "more interesting" when broadcasters are already using every means at their command to make their programs more attractive to listeners. And it should be remembered, too, that honest criticism should include the commendation of good programs as well as calling attention to the faults and shortcomings found in other programs or in the broadcasting industry. But honest, intelligent criticism can be helpful in at least two important ways.

Criticism and Standards of the Listening Public

First of all, the fact that criticisms of programs are expressed by intelligent men and women will have some effect, at least, on other intelligent listeners. It is probably true, as the great amount of time devoted to radio and television listening would indicate, that most rank-and-file listeners are reasonably well satisfied with the program service they already receive. At the same time, it's probable that many are not *completely* satisfied; they may have the vague feeling that programs could be better, but they don't know in just what way they might be better. They have no clearly formulated standards on the basis of which they can evaluate programs. If through public criticism, even a relatively small proportion of listeners could be encouraged each year to develop such standards and to be even a little bit more discriminating and critical in their selection of programs, the long-range effect might be to bring about a considerable change in the kinds of programs that large numbers of listeners *want*—and when the wants and desires of important segments of the public change, broadcasters will certainly make an effort to satisfy those changing wants and desires through the programs they provide.

Effects on Broadcasters

A second value of criticism lies in its effect on broadcasters themselves. Some broadcasters, to be sure, resent criticism; they feel that when their programs are criticized, those who object are in effect attacking them as individuals, and questioning either their judgment or their integrity. But a majority of all broadcasters, certainly, welcome honest criticism of their efforts; the opinions expressed by interested listeners give them an idea of what other listeners may be thinking, and a little closer contact with the public and the public's wishes than would otherwise be possible. After all, a commercial broadcaster has a dollars-and-cents reason to want to satisfy the listeners in his community. But what he actually knows about his listeners' likes and dislikes and their program standards and tastes is limited very largely to what he is able to infer from the figures provided in program rating reports. So if even a few critics—writers for local newspapers, leaders of local organizations—object to the content of one of his programs, he knows that at least some part of the local audience is displeased. Almost certainly he will check the program in question to decide for himself whether there are really valid grounds for objection. And if objectionable features are to be found in the program, he will make an effort to see that those features are eliminated.

Perhaps few program series are ever taken off the air completely because of objections raised by a few local critics. But numerous instances could be cited in which operators of local stations have taken corrective action with respect to program elements that have occasioned criticism. In other cases, local station managers, aware of objections to a network program, have registered their own protests against the program to officials of the network, and if objectionable materials were not eliminated, have dropped the network program from their own local schedules.

Even more important, criticisms expressed against programs broadcast today tend to be remembered when ideas are being considered for programs a year or two in the future. If use of an unsavory character or of an objectionable situation in a program arouses a storm of criticism, station managers and network heads do not soon forget that fact, and it influences their future selection of programs. On the other hand, if a program or program series wins high critical acclaim, broadcasters naturally tend to use the qualities offered by that program as a yardstick in evaluating other program ideas brought to their attention.

Ratings give an index to the number of listeners who tune in a program, but they do not tell the broadcaster *why* that program attracts listeners or drives them away from the receiving set. If radio and television are to serve the public, it is important that station operators know what things the public wants and to what things the public objects, and public criticisms of programs, combined with letters from listeners praising or condemning the things that broadcasters do, give at least an idea of the feelings of those members of the public interested enough to make their feelings known.

11

NEWS AND
INFORMATION

One of the outstanding features of American
radio and television is the emphasis placed on
providing news and information for listeners.
Critics of broadcasting may object to the caliber
of entertainment programs or to the excessive
number of commercial announcements, but rarely
do their criticisms extend to the activities of networks and stations in the fields of news, public
affairs, and information. Although broadcasting
functions primarily as an agency of entertainment, American radio and television perform an
exceedingly useful service in providing information for listeners and in contributing to the development of an informed and enlightened public.

It is axiomatic that in a democracy, citizens
who participate in the political process should
be well informed. To most, American democracy implies the personal involvement of every

citizen in the various processes of government and asks for his participation to a greater degree than is expected in most other democratic countries. The intelligent American voter is not satisfied merely to help select his nation's and his community's political leaders; he expects to have a part in the shaping of public policy as well. He considers it his duty, and the duty of other intelligent citizens, to keep abreast of current affairs, to debate and discuss political issues with his neighbors, and to form opinions on public questions that may range from the need for higher wages for local garbage collectors to the most effective means of enforcing an international ban on the use of atomic missiles. Once he has formed an opinion and made that opinion known, he expects his elected representatives to give effect to his wishes by their votes in the city council, in the state legislature, and in the Congress of the United States. For as we usually interpret it in this country, democracy is government by public opinion. And naturally, the soundness and intelligence of opinions formed by the voting public depend on the extent and the nature of the information received by individual voters and on which their collective decisions are based.

Sources of Public Information

In any society, the public depends for most of its information about public affairs on the various mass media of communication—newspapers, magazines, radio, television, motion pictures, and books. But the effectiveness of any single medium of information is limited by certain obvious factors. Printed media can be effective only if people know how to read and have the money to buy printed materials. As a result, in countries with high illiteracy rates and with low average family incomes, the printed media—books, newspapers, and magazines— are remarkably inefficient as media of *mass* communication. Even in countries with high average individual incomes and high levels of technical literacy, such as the United States, the effectiveness of printed media in providing information at all levels of society is highly debatable. Americans are literate, but devote little of their time to reading. Studies of reading habits suggest that the average adult reads no more than three or four books a year, and that he devotes an average of not more than 30 to 35 minutes a day to magazines and newspapers; other studies indicate that his newspaper reading is largely limited to the comic strips, stories in the sports section, and the headlines on the front page of the paper. And of course, even in a nation as prosperous as our own, not all families have access to magazines or books or even daily papers. It has been estimated that only about 70 per cent of all homes receive a daily newspaper; aside from "best sellers" in fiction, very few books are sold to more than two or three thousand readers, and the most popular weekly news magazines or other "magazines of opinion" are not usually read in more than a million homes. It is an interesting fact that of all of the magazines and journals available to American readers, one of those with the largest average circulation in recent years has been *TV Guide*, the publication that lists the programs to be seen on television during the coming week.

Advantages Offered by Broadcasting

Radio and television also have limitations as agencies for the conveying of information, but as compared with printed media, they have certain evident advantages. First, with receiving sets in about 95 per cent of all American homes, radio and television can reach listeners on every educational, cultural, or economic level. Again, because of the existence of national networks, radio and television can ignore geographical barriers; the materials in network programs reach listeners in every section of the United States. Third, in news broadcasting or in their coverage of special events, radio and television have a distinct *time* advantage over the printed media; broadcasting stations can provide up-to-the-minute news, almost as it happens, while there is a necessary delay of several hours before a newspaper can bring a news story to its readers—and of several days or even several weeks before a magazine's coverage of news events reaches the public. And finally, the average radio or television listener in this country may make a choice among programs offered by several different radio and television stations, so that he has available a variety of sources of information and the possibility of hearing expressions of a variety of different points of view. It might also be added that broadcast information is presented by *people* and by means of the human voice; on television, viewers *see* the speaker, and what he says is supported by photographic evidence. Whether on television or over radio, broadcast information has a *personal* quality and a sense of "realness" the printed media cannot offer, with the result that people find it easier to give attention to materials on radio or television than to read the same materials in their daily newspapers.

As an agency of mass information, broadcasting is capable of bringing the listening public a wider variety and a greater quantity of information than can be provided effectively by any other medium. The question is, how well does broadcasting actually perform in satisfying the public's need for information —how much information actually is broadcast, and what kinds of information are provided? To answer this question, it is necessary to analyze the activities of networks and stations in the fields of general information, of news and public affairs, and of presentations of ideas and opinions of national and local leaders on the issues confronting the nation or the local community.

GENERAL INFORMATION

Broadcasting is primarily a medium of entertainment; most programs on radio and television are designed to entertain the listener. But stations and networks also provide information, some of it in the field of news and public affairs, but also a not inconsiderable quantity of general information on a wide variety of subjects.

Local Informational Programs

Much of the general information offered by radio stations relates directly to listener needs. Every radio station gives up-to-the-minute weather reports a dozen or more times a day— short, capsule announcements of current temperature readings with the weather forecast for the rest of the day and for the

a

A study in contrasts: (a) a radio control room; (b) a television control room requiring more people, more equipment, and greater complexity

b

day following. In fruit-growing areas in Florida and California, stations broadcast special frost warnings at frequent intervals; in areas where tornadoes are frequent, radio assists the local weather bureau by broadcasting emergency tornado warnings; during winter months, stations give information about road conditions when icy streets or heavy snowfalls make automobile driving hazardous. In times of weather emergencies in any part of the country, listeners depend on radio to learn about plans for the closing of schools or whether factories and local industries are suspending operations.

Most high-powered radio stations and regional stations serving farm areas carry daily programs of farm information—prices being paid at livestock and produce markets, details of pending farm legislation, advice on marketing or on the planting of crops or the times when fruit trees should be sprayed. An even larger number of stations offer regularly scheduled "women's interest" programs with information on buying foods, planning menus, home decoration, women's fashions, vacation traveling, or the planning of household budgets, as well as interviews with interesting local people or visitors to the community. Some radio stations carry programs giving the time and place of meetings of local organizations; others give names of those admitted to hospitals; several large-city stations give regular reports on traffic conditions on congested streets or freeways during the afternoon rush hours, using information relayed from helicopters or airplanes circling over the city.

In addition to "service" programs of the types named, practically every radio station presents religious programs on Sunday, some in cooperation with local churches, others from tapes or transcriptions provided by religious organizations. Some schedule programs of story reading for children. Many stations broadcast weekly taped or recorded "reports" from Congressmen, or from the governor of the state, or from the mayor of the local city, to keep listeners informed of the activities of national and local governments. A number of stations in larger cities devote from two to five hours a day to blocks of 60-minute "talk" programs on each of which an expert on some subject presents a ten or twelve minute talk and then is available for another 40 or 45 minutes to answer questions phoned in by listeners. Frequently appearing as guest speakers on such programs are ministers, physicians, social workers, artists, landscape gardeners, attorneys, marriage counselors, architects, judges of juvenile courts, tax consultants, school administrators, and other experts who can provide information of interest to listeners. Although only a small portion of radio stations devote more than an hour or so a day to informational programs, the fact that the average listener has access to a number of stations makes local radio an important source of general information.

Local television stations also contribute to the listener's stock of information, although on television the emphasis usually is different from that on radio. Nearly every television station schedules three or four local weather programs a day, ranging from five to eight minutes in length and giving much more detailed information than is supplied on radio about the meteorological conditions that affect the weather. Many television stations carry regular early-morning programs of farm information; at least a hundred stations employ full-time farm directors to supervise such programs. Television stations also broadcast a number of religious programs each week; in addition to offerings of the national networks, these usually include at least one program produced in the station's own studios and two or three filmed or videotaped presentations—some using the dramatic form—supplied by various religious organizations.

Many television stations include a daily "women's interest" program in their schedules; most of these programs feature interviews with interesting local people or with visitors to the community, especially those who are authorities on such subjects as home decoration, hair styling, or women's fashions in clothing, or who are widely known actors, writers, musicians, entertainers, or men or women in public life. Nearly every television station presents some sort of program for children on weekdays. Sometimes these are syndicated programs, largely on film, that require little or no local production effort. But most stations in larger markets also present children's programs that are locally developed and locally produced, and in many cases such programs are planned to include a considerable amount of information of types particularly appropriate for children.

Since 1959 or 1960, many of the larger television stations

have been producing local, filmed documentary programs, usually broadcast at intervals of two or three weeks. Subjects of these documentaries range from new methods of teaching used in local schools to the experiences of a convict after his release from a state prison, or from the procedures followed in a modern children's hospital to the varied services offered by a local social agency. Some stations also carry documentary programs made available by nearby state universities; a few provide instructional programs on such subjects as driver education or fire prevention, sometimes produced in cooperation with local school systems.

Network Informational Programs

Aside from news, the informational materials made available by radio networks in recent years have been limited almost entirely to short, five-minute talk features that affiliates can tape off the network line and insert in their local programs of recorded music. Television networks, however, offer a variety of informational programs to their affiliates, some on a regularly scheduled basis, others as "special" broadcasts. Since the early 1950s when many stations carried the documentary series *Victory at Sea*, dealing with war in the Pacific, network schedules have included such outstanding historical re-creations as *Crusade in Europe*, *The Valiant Years* and *Air Power*, and an increasing number of programs of general information.

Perhaps typical of network offerings in recent years are programs presented during the 1964–65 season, some as regular once-a-week features, others on alternate weeks, and a few on a less frequent basis. Included in the 1964–65 listings were such historical series as *FDR*, a biography of former president Franklin Delano Roosevelt; *World War I*, a documentary treatment of the "war to end war"; *The Great Adventure*, dramatizing outstanding events in American history; and *Profiles in Courage*, dealing with crises in the lives of the nation's political leaders. NBC's *Wild Kingdom* showed films of wild animals in their native habitats and their adjustments to life in captivity; the CBS series *Camera Three* dealt with the fine arts, poetry, or drama. Three weekly programs offered information for primary or elementary school children: *Discovery,* using a combination of live talent and films; *Exploring,* primarily in documentary form; and *Mr. Wizard,* making use of simple scientific experiments to explain the principles of chemistry and physics.

Programs presented on the documentary *Twentieth Century* series dealt each week with subjects ranging from historical events to current social problems; the weekly *ABC-Scope,* as well as the less frequently scheduled *CBS Reports, Chronicle,* and *NBC News Specials,* usually gave background details explaining current news events but also included documentary presentations of a general informational nature. Even the four weekly offerings in the field of religion—*Directions, Lamp Unto My Feet, Look Up and Live,* and the NBC series using different titles at different times during the year—were usually programs of general information, which used the dramatic, the documentary, or the discussion form to deal with current social problems. In addition to these, the Columbia Broadcasting System provided its affiliates with the six-day-a-week, 30-minute program series *Sunrise Semester,* presenting outstanding college instructors in lectures on literature, drama, and the humanities. And the NBC *Today* program, although emphasizing news, devoted from 45 minutes to an hour each morning to interviews with authorities on subjects ranging from foreign travel to air pollution, and from new advances in medical science to obedience training for dogs. During the 1964–65 season, the three television networks combined were presenting a total of at least 15 to 20 hours a week of programs of a general informational nature carried on a reguarly-scheduled basis—these in addition to the networks "hard" news offerings.

Hardly less important are the informational "specials" produced by the three national television networks. Not counting broadcasts of sports events, special news programs, or coverage of news events, broadcasts in connection with political conventions or the 1964 political campaign, or the considerable number of one-time entertainment programs, the three national networks during 1964 presented a total of approximately 120 hours of special broadcasts of an informational nature—an average of two to three such programs each week. Nearly all were filmed documentary programs; subjects covered a wide range of areas of interest or of importance to the listening public. Included were programs on "Smoking and Health," "Boxing's Last Round," "The Orient Express," "Life Along the Mississippi," "Emergence of the United States as a World Power," "The British 'Establishment' in Transition," "Today's Cowboys," "The American Carnival," "Explorers before Columbus," "The World of Witchcraft," "The Louvre," "Sophia Loren in Rome," "Breakthroughs in Medicine," "The River Nile," "The Adopted Child," "Election Year in an Average Town," "The French Army," "Cuba and Castro Today," "The Woman in Politics," "The Development of Printing," "Leonardo da Vinci," and, of course, scores of others on an equally wide range of subjects.

There can be little question that television makes an important contribution to the public's stock of general information.

Incidental Information

The informational programs that stations and networks provide are undoubtedly important, but it would be a mistake to assume that only by tuning in these programs does the radio or television listener add to his store of information about the world. Included in any person's stock of what we call general knowledge are thousands of bits of unrelated information that have come from personal experience, from casual reading, from conversation with friends, or from a variety of other sources. And certainly included among these sources of general knowledge or general information are those broadcast programs—television programs in particular—presented not to give information, but to entertain.

Listeners pick up some odds and ends of information by listening to musical programs. They get information from materials presented in quiz programs or daytime "game shows"—in fact, when respondents were asked to name their favorite "educational programs" in a radio listening study some years ago, two-thirds of the programs named were radio quiz shows. But a much more important source of general knowledge are the dramatic programs that fill most of the evening schedules of television networks. From *The Defenders* or *Perry Mason*, the listener gets at the very least some idea of courtroom procedures. He acquires an understanding of hospital routines from broadcasts of *Ben Casey* or *Dr. Kildare;* he learns something of the problems of high school teachers by watching *Mr. Novak;* such programs as *Dragnet* or *Robert Taylor's Detectives,* on network schedules a few years ago, gave an excellent insight into the routine activities of police departments in large cities. Those who watch the various "adult Western" programs on television get impressions about life in the "old West"—impressions not always accurate in detail, to be sure, but reasonably correct in the broad pictures presented. Even situation comedies and daytime serial dramas deal with *people,* and with the way men and women are likely to react in times of stress. Thanks to television, the viewer in Keokuk or Kalamazoo knows the patterns of living in the crowded tenements of New York City; he has seen with his own eyes the snowcapped peaks of the Rocky Mountains, the wheat fields of Kansas, the sunny beaches of Florida and southern California, and the clouds of dust created by a cattle drive in Texas. He has had almost first-hand experience with the congested traffic conditions in Paris or Mexico City or on Los Angeles freeways; he has seen the ski slopes of the Swiss Alps and has wandered through the corridors of luxury hotels on the Riviera; he has visited Disneyland and Coney Island and an hour later has taken a boat ride through the jungles of the Amazon or flown in an airplane over Spain. Every program offers a new experience, and every experience contributes to the listener's stock of general knowledge. Few would question the fact that the American people today are better informed about the world than any other generation in our nation's history—and television has contributed in no small degree to this wide dissemination of information among listeners at every social and economic level.

NEWS AND PUBLIC AFFAIRS

Without question, however, broadcasting's greatest contribution to public enlightenment has been in the field of news and public affairs. From the time they were first organized in the late 1920s, radio networks gave their listeners weekly reports on happenings in Washington. By the autumn of 1930, one

In 1925 KGW, Portland, Oregon, used this car to broadcast to people on the streets through loudspeakers the KGW signal picked up by a receiver in the truck. Before long some enterprising individual reversed the process, and mobile broadcasts were made from transmitters mounted in practically all kinds of vehicles.

A helicopter equipped with a color television camera

One station's mobile fleet

a

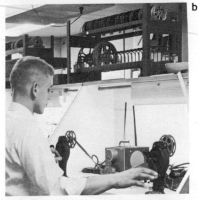

b

c

A few of the many people who work behind the scenes to produce a local newscast: (a) reporter-photographer team, (b) film processors and editors, and (c) news writers and editors.

network was providing its affiliates with a five-times-a-week, 15-minute, early-evening news program, and since that time emphasis on news and public affairs has steadily increased. In recent years, so excellent and so complete has been radio and television news coverage that when in 1964 interviewers for the Elmo Roper research organization made a study of the American people's source of news, 58 per cent of the respondents stated that they got "most of their news about what is going on in the world today" from television, and 26 per cent indicated that they depended primarily on radio for news.[1] The importance of television in particular in providing news first hand to the American people was dramatically illustrated on the 22nd of November, 1963, when millions of Americans sat silently before their television sets watching the events which followed the assassination of President John F. Kennedy. Ten minutes before the first announcement was made that the President had been shot, television sets were in use in approximately 23 per cent of all homes in the United States, according to the A. C. Nielsen Company. An hour later, the proportion of homes with sets tuned to reports of the tragedy had doubled, and between 6:00 p.m. and 10:00 p.m., the events in Dallas held the attention of viewers in from 65 per cent to 90 per cent of all American homes. Television allowed its viewers to see things while they were happening in a way no printed news medium could even attempt to equal.

News on Radio

Fortunately, tragedies like that of November 22nd, 1963, are the rare exception. But radio and television provides reports on news for their listeners in less spectacular fashion on regularly

---

[1] Newspapers were named by 56 per cent of the men and women interviewed, since many of the respondents named more than one medium as the most important news source. However, in the same study, when asked which medium they would be most inclined to believe if conflicting reports of the same news event were given by radio, by television, by newspapers and by magazines, 41 per cent indicated that they would believe the television account, while only 23 per cent had a greater faith in the accuracy of the account given by newspapers. Report of the study was released by the Television Information Office in March 1965.

scheduled news programs, day after day and year after year. Practically every radio station, no matter how small, carries a dozen or more news programs in its daily schedules. Since the middle 1950s, radio news has usually been presented in short, five-minute capsules at hourly intervals; many of the major radio stations also scheduled 15-minute news summaries at some time in the early morning, at the dinner hour, and again late at night, and several carry a similar program at noon. Network affiliates frequently schedule their short, capsule programs of local news immediately following the programs supplied by the networks. For national and regional news, most radio stations subscribe to a news wire service from the Associated Press or United Press International. Local news is often limited to what can be learned from routine telephone calls to public officials, police and fire departments, hospitals, and mortuaries. On at least two-thirds of all radio stations, most of the short, five-minute newscasts are given by whatever staff announcer happens to be on duty, and in the same language in which it comes from the wire of the news service to which the station subscribes.

Larger radio stations and those in major cities, however, tend to give much more attention to local news. Practically all have full-time news directors, in many cases men with newspaper training. On larger stations the news director may be assisted by a staff of as many as five or six men who serve as reporters in gathering local news, rewrite wire news copy, and present most of the station's regular news programs. Many radio stations have regular correspondents in outlying communities or in the capital city of the state. Some make extensive use of taped interviews with people involved in news events, including audio taped telephone calls to public officials in other cities. In many cases, the coverage of local news by large-city radio stations is on a par with that of local newspapers, at least with respect to stories of major importance. And of course, radio stations have the advantage of being able to interrupt programs at any time to bring their listeners accounts of local events which warrant such action—airplane disasters, fires, or police emergencies.

News is heavily emphasized by radio networks; in fact, the service provided to affiliates consists largely of news broadcasts. Five-minute news summaries are presented by national networks ten or a dozen times each day, in addition to two or three longer news or commentary programs. Radio networks also provide extended coverage of special events of national importance, from orbital flights of our astronauts to the national conventions of major political parties and from presidential press conferences to government reports on military actions abroad. Network and local station coverage of news on radio is so complete that in the Roper study cited in an earlier paragraph, more than one-fourth of all respondents stated that they depended primarily on radio for "news about what is going on in the world today."

Local Television News Programs

Television coverage of local news in most markets is even more complete than that provided by the larger radio stations, although news programs are presented at less frequent intervals. Nearly all television stations have included local news programs in their schedules almost from the time they first went on the air; by the late 1950s many had strong news departments. But local news operations have been expanded even further since 1960; on most stations, both the number and the length of news programs have been increased with a corresponding increase in the number of employees who devote full time to the gathering, editing, and presentation of news. A questionnaire study by *Television* magazine in the autumn of 1964 indicated that more than half of all stations reporting had half-hour local news programs tied to network news in their early evening schedules; many others had programs of similar length at ten or at eleven o'clock at night, and a large number also carried shorter local news programs during the early morning or at noon.

Budgets for news programs and the number of staff employees vary widely, according to the competitive situation and the station's economic position. However, of stations covered in the 1964 *Television* survey, more than half employed five or more men on a full-time basis to handle news programs, and in major markets such as New York, Chicago, or Minneapolis, as many as 30 or 40 employees might be included in the news department of a single station. In addition, in four out of five stations, including practically all of those in smaller markets, the regular news staff had the assistance of part-time help, either double-duty station employees or in some cases freelance newsmen living in the community. News budgets are limited on most of the smaller outlets, but of television stations giving budget information in the *Television* news survey more than half were spending at least $100,000 a year on local news coverage, and nearly one-fourth had budgets of more than twice that amount.

Practically every commercial television station subscribes to the wire news services of either United Press International or Associated Press as a source of national and regional news; a considerable number also receive the sports news service provided by Western Union. But since television is a visual medium, most stations also arrange for some type of news photo service. Both AP and UPI offer a facsimile service to provide news "stills" to television stations; most small-market outlets depend on the pictures provided by one of the two companies for the visual materials they use with their national news stories. A number of stations subscribe to the service of UPI Newsfilm or of other concerns that ship newsfilm to subscribers by air express. A more rapid type of newsfilm service, however, is provided by the television networks; each network offers subscribing affiliates filmed coverage of eight to ten stories a day, delivered by closed circuit over network lines during hours when no network program service is provided, and videotaped by stations for inclusion in their local newscasts. The NBC News Program Service, started in 1959, had more than 75 station subscribers at the end of 1964; CBS and ABC provide a similar service to many of their affiliates.

But locally produced news programs give major emphasis to local news events, especially since most stations also carry network news programs. To provide pictorial coverage of local happenings, members of the news staff of each station are equipped with motion picture cameras; a television newsman is often a combination reporter-interviewer-cameraman in covering local news. Most stations use silent film cameras; if sound is wanted, it is recorded separately on audio tape. Stations in larger markets, however, usually have one or more 16 mm. sound

Growth of WFAA, Dallas, Texas:
(top) humble beginning in a radio
"shack" atop the *Dallas Morning
News* building in 1922, (center)
"glamorous" penthouse studios of
the 1940s, (bottom) today's $3.5
million communications center for
AM, FM, and television

cameras available. Far more film footage is shot, of course, than is actually used. One station in Omaha reported to *Television* magazine that its newsmen shoot an average of 500,000 feet of newsfilm a year. Naturally, stations using film in news programs must have facilities for processing the film, and members of staffs of station news departments must devote a good many hours to editing and selecting the sequences to be used on the air.

As a result of their less flexible schedules, television stations are not as likely as radio outlets to break into their regular programs to give on-the-spot coverage of local news happenings. Except in cases of major disasters or emergencies, reporters and photographers are dispatched to the scene of a local news event, and their accounts and pictures are inserted in the station's regular news programs. But when a news event of outstanding importance occurs, stations in the locality cancel their regular programs to provide listeners with immediate coverage. In addition, special news programs are frequently arranged to present the filmed highlights of a state political convention, or of an unusually important meeting of the local city council, school board, or zoning commission. Evening network programs are often canceled to allow the station to broadcast a local basketball game or high school football game, especially when state championships are at stake. Most television stations provide a considerable amount of special coverage of local news events; usually, however, on a complete-program basis.

Although television outlets have no difficulty in finding sponsors for news programs, costs of producing local news shows are high, and many stations lose money on their news operations. But station owners recognize the fact that a television station's prestige and its "image" in the community are strongly affected by the quality and extent of its news service, with the result that over the past ten years there has been a steady increase in television's coverage of local news.

News on Television Networks

If the element of prestige is important in the field of local news, it has become an even stronger factor in the news activities of national television networks. With nearly all of the major network entertainment features produced by outside "packagers," news and public-affairs programs offer almost the only remaining opportunity for a network organization to develop its own "personality" or to give an outlet for the creative abilities of its executives and employees. As a result, competition between network news departments is unusually keen; each network organization attempts to outdo its rivals in the thoroughness of its newsgathering activities, in the personal authoritativeness and attractiveness of the men who present the news, and in the development of special programs in the area of public affairs. To support its news and public-affairs operations, the National Broadcasting Company's news department had an annual working budget in 1963 of $30 million and, including the *Today* show, provided more than a hundred hours of network programming each month. In the same year, CBS spent approximately the same amount for its news and documentary programs; the American Broadcasting Company's news department had a somewhat more modest budget. But news expenditures have increased since 1963, and budgets have expanded accordingly. A news story in *Variety* in September 1965 announced that for 1965–66 NBC had earmarked approximately $53 million for its news department and that production costs of *Today* and of the network's sports operation would bring the total to more than $60 million for the year. The same source estimated the annual budget of CBS News at around $45 million and that of ABC News at $21 million for the same broadcasting year. It is hardly surprising that television networks have for years lost money on their news and public-affairs operations; the news organization of one network company had a reported deficit in 1962 of nearly $12 million.

The three network companies combined employ nearly 1,500 people in their news and public affairs departments. Not all of these employees are concerned with the gathering and presentation of news as such, of course; network news departments are responsible for most of the informational programs mentioned earlier in this chapter and for network activities in the broadcasting of sports, for weekly discussion or interview programs, for news documentaries presented in regular series or as one-time documentary "specials," for appearances of candidates during political campaigns, and for "live" coverage of important special events, as well as for the network's regularly scheduled daily news programs. Sports broadcasts fill a considerable portion of each network's Saturday and Sunday afternoon schedules. In addition, during 1964, the American Broadcasting Company used more than 35 hours for special broadcasts of the Winter Olympics in this country and the Olympic Games in Tokyo, and NBC devoted 17 hours to coverage of the Olympics as well as broadcasting all of the World Series baseball games. It might be noted that almost every hour used for these special broadcasts of sports events called for the cancellation of one hour of regular, sponsored programming; revenues derived from sale of the sports broadcasts to advertisers were not as a rule large enough to pay costs of producing the specials and also to cover the amount of lost revenue from entertainment programs that were canceled.

Regularly scheduled news programs. Of course the chief function of a network news department is to provide a news service for the public, and television networks supply excellent coverage of national and international news. During the winter of 1964–65, NBC and CBS each scheduled 30-minute, early-evening news programs five days a week; ABC had a 15-minute, early-evening program, and another presentation 10 minutes in length at eleven o'clock at night. CBS presented *News with Mike Wallace* for 30 minutes each weekday morning, and a 30-minute, early-afternoon news program on Saturdays. NBC offered a 60-minute program on Sunday afternoons devoted primarily to interviews with people involved in current news, and news reports and news interviews filled about half of the time in NBC's five-day-a-week, two-hour *Today* program. In addition, each of the networks scheduled several short, 5-minute news summaries during the daytime hours on weekdays. In all, in a seven-day period, the three networks made more than 70 news programs available to their affiliated stations, accounting for a weekly total of approximately 18 hours of broadcasting time.

News "specials." The regular news programs of the television networks have the advantage already noted of bringing news to the public without the time delay required for the printing and distribution of daily newspapers; they also have the advantage of allowing viewers to *see* newsworthy events recorded on news film. But they are subject to one serious disadvantage; in a single 30-minute period, a television news program can deal with no more than ten or a dozen news happenings and can give little more than the highlights even of those. So networks supplement their regular news reports with frequent news "specials," sometimes documentaries to provide detailed background information about an important news situation and sometimes "on-the-spot" coverage of significant news events as they happen. Some of these special news programs are presented in such regular network series as *CBS Reports, ABC-Scope,* or *NBC News Specials.* More often, however, time for special news reports is provided by canceling regularly scheduled entertainment programs, and such cancellations are much more frequent than most viewers realize.

To illustrate, during the calendar year 1964 the National Broadcasting Company's television network carried a total of approximately 150 hours of news specials—in addition to some 50 hours of general-information and sports specials. The fact that 1964 was a presidential election year raised the total time to levels above those for ordinary years; a little more than 74 hours of the network's programming represented coverage of the Republican and Democratic national conventions, eleven hours went to preconvention news conferences with candidates for the Republican presidential nomination and to special reports on presidential primaries in various states, another eleven hours were used for the network's own convention previews or analyses of the progress of the campaign, and eight hours were required for the network's special coverage of the election returns on the night of the presidential election. But even with the pressures of a national political campaign, the National Broadcasting Company presented approximately 47 special broadcasts dealing with news events not related to the political campaign— the President's message to Congress, several Presidential press conferences, the earthquake in Alaska, the crisis in South Vietnam, the Ranger VII moon flight, the Bobby Baker hearings before a committee of the United States Senate, the Panama riots, the crisis in Cyprus, the deaths and funeral services of General Douglas MacArthur and former President Herbert Hoover, the Warren Commission report on the assassination of Presi-

dent John F. Kennedy, and other happenings of similar importance. In all, NBC devoted a total of 40 hours to such news
specials; in almost every case, the presentation of these programs,
as well as the network's news broadcasts relating to political
events, required the cancellation of regularly scheduled entertainment programs.

Although the summary deals with special programs presented by one network, both the Columbia Broadcasting System
and the American Broadcasting Company in 1964 provided substantially the same sort of coverage of both political and nonpolitical news events, in addition to their regularly scheduled
news programs. In view of the record, it is hardly surprising
that the three networks spend a combined total of more than
$100 million a year to provide information about national and
international happenings for television viewers.

IDEAS AND OPINIONS

Broadcasting has contributed in no small measure to the
listener's stock of general information and to his knowledge and
understanding of important events taking place throughout the
world. But to meet his responsibilities as an intelligent citizen,
the listener must also be acquainted with ideas—with the opinions
of national and local leaders on the vital issues that confront
the American people or the people of his community. Newspapers and national magazines provide a valuable forum for
opinions on public questions, but broadcasting also makes its
own contribution in presenting points of view concerning the
issues of the day. Often the views of the nation's leaders are
set forth in news or documentary programs, in interviews, or
in two-sided forums; occasionally programs are presented that
attempt to give a cross-section of the opinions held by ordinary
citizens, and a considerable number of broadcasters voice their
own views in editorial presentations.

Broadcast Editorials

In the early days of radio, editorials by station licensees
were relatively common; indeed, some stations apparently were
operated for the sole purpose of giving their owners an oppor-

tunity to express their sometimes decidedly extreme views on political matters, on religion, or even on the evils of chain stores. But as radio became commercial, editorial expressions became less frequent; advertisers were not interested in using the facilities of stations whose owners' outspoken opinions aroused the resentment of large numbers of listeners. In addition, the expression of editorial views was discouraged by the Federal Radio Commission, which refused to grant license renewals to what were regarded as "propaganda stations." The Federal Communications Commission took a similar position, and in its *Mayflower* decision in 1941, as noted in Chapter 7, the regulatory agency flatly banned all editorial presentations by the owners of radio stations. In 1949, however, the Commission abandoned its earlier position; in a new ruling on editorializing, the agency held that a licensee had the right to present his views over the facilities of his station, but warned that the station owner who expressed editorial opinions on controversial issues should also provide time for supporters of opposing points of view. In recent years, members of the Commission have actively encouraged the practice of editorializing by station licensees; one or two members have even suggested that for a licensee to operate his station "in the public interest," he is practically obligated to take an editorial position on issues affecting the welfare of the community.

Encouraged by the favorable attitude of the Federal Communications Commission, an increasing number of radio and television stations now present editorial opinions on various community matters or on national or local issues. A survey of broadcasting stations reported in *Broadcasting Yearbook* for 1966 indicates that more than 60 per cent of all AM radio stations and 55 per cent of all television stations editorialized during 1965. Their editorials were usually presented by the station manager or by the station's news director. In some cases, the opinions offered were the joint product of a committee of station employees—the manager, the news director, and one or two other responsible staff members; on most stations, however, editorials presented the views of the station manager or of the licensee himself. The *Broadcasting* survey indicated that about one-sixth of the radio stations and nearly one-fourth of all television stations carried editorial comment on a regularly scheduled daily or weekly basis; operators of other stations expressed editorial opinions less frequently, waiting, as one station manager put it, until "something comes up that is important enough to justify an editorial."

It must be admitted that only a small proportion of editorials on radio or television stations deal with highly controversial issues. Stations urge their listeners to contribute to the local Community Chest or to register and vote; they deplore the increase in juvenile delinquency; they call for more vigorous enforcement of traffic laws. Sometimes they may endorse or oppose the adoption of a specific ordinance by the local city council or express disapproval of some action of a zoning commission. Or perhaps a radio or television station may campaign vigorously for the installation of traffic lights at street intersections near schools, or for modernization of the city's fire-fighting equipment, or for the elimination of a hazardous grade crossing on a heavily traveled street. Most broadcast editorials deal with purely local conditions. Rarely does a station take a definite stand on any highly controversial issue, as is evidenced by the fact that not more than once or twice a year is an editorializing station asked to provide time for a reply to an editorial the station has presented.

Particularly is this true when listeners in the community have strong feelings with respect to some local or sectional issue. Not many licensees of Southern stations have been willing to take an editorial stand either for or against school desegregation or on restrictions placed on voting rights of Negroes in the South, although many have deplored the violence that has accompanied civil rights demonstrations. Nor have many station owners editorialized on partisan political issues. Some stations have endorsed individual candidates for local offices, but only a very small number are known to have urged their listeners to support a particular candidate for the Presidency or for election to the national Congress. Radio and television stations are not usually identified, as are most newspapers, as having Republican or Democratic leanings, as being liberal or conservative, or as being consistently pro-Administration or anti-Administration.

The same is true of national radio and television networks. Networks simply do not editorialize—at least in any direct manner. On only one or two occasions in broadcasting's history has any network official gone on the air to express his personal views or those of the corporation he represents, and then only to discuss some matter affecting broadcasting. A few news commentators on radio networks do take recognizable editorial positions on national issues, but their comments reflect their personal views, not those of the networks on which they appear. The same is true of local commentators on a few radio and television stations in large cities and of one or two of the news analysts employed by television networks. The opinions expressed are their own; not the editorial expressions of their employers.

Documentaries as Editorials

A documentary program is presumably an *objective* "report in depth" of a single topic of general concern or importance. But even the most unbiased documentary may have an editorial effect. A documentary special that actually shows illegal gambling establishments in operation in a large city certainly has some effect on viewer attitudes and an equally evident impact on the zeal of city officials in seeing that laws are properly enforced—probably a much more marked impact than any number of editorial statements by the manager of a television station. Network documentary programs on civil rights issues have done much to produce an awareness of the problem throughout the nation and to create a national public opinion in favor of federal legislation. Programs showing conditions in prisons or mental hospitals have sometimes helped to bring about improvements; the same has been the case when local documentaries have dealt with problems of slum clearance, drug addiction, or wars between juvenile gangs in large cities. On one or two occasions, networks have presented documentary programs which have reflected an obvious editorial purpose, at least on the part of the program's producer—Edward R. Murrow's CBS program of some years ago on treatment of witnesses in hearings of the Senate Committee on Un-American Activities, for example, or possibly the Howard K. Smith program on ABC entitled the "Political Obituary of Richard M. Nixon."

The deliberately slanted or editorial version of the documentary is, fortunately, not too common. Most broadcasters tend to be scrupulously fair in dealing with public issues, and when a documentary program is used to support one side of a controversy, it is almost impossible for opposing points of view to be presented with equal effectiveness. But even an objective documentary program may often have an unintended editorial effect. It is manifestly impossible in a 60-minute or a 30-minute program to include *all* of the significant facts concerning a complex problem such as race relations or foreign policy; a selection must be made. And the process of editorial selection, of determining which facts to include and which to leave out, of deciding which aspects of the problem under consideration are to be given special emphasis—the very elements which make for the effectiveness of the documentary form tend to affect the listener's conclusions concerning the problem.

Broadcasting as a Public Forum

In addition to their editorial programs, radio and television provide a public forum for the expression of the views of community leaders. In most cases, these views are presented on regularly scheduled news programs and in "news specials" dealing with important events or problems of the day.

Controversy is an important element in news. When national leaders disagree about vital issues, the public is interested; when those leaders express their varying opinions, their statements are included in radio and television coverage of the news. If the President of the United States or the Secretary of State expresses an opinion concerning our country's foreign policy, that opinion is included in the regularly scheduled news programs—usually with opposing comments by minority leaders in Congress. Similarly network news programs report the views of advocates of additional federal subsidies for public education, or of increased expenditures for foreign aid, or of changes in Social Security legislation; they also include the opinions of those who disagree. The same is true with respect to views on local issues. Local news programs include the opinions of those who favor or who oppose the adoption of state or city income taxes, or bond issues for the construction of new school buildings, or salary increases for city firemen. Inclusion of statements of opinion has been facilitated by the use of audio tape on radio and the widespread use of filmed interviews or statements on television news programs.

Controversy on regular programs. A number of radio and television stations in major cities carry regular forum or discussion programs in which the advocates and opponents of proposed state or local projects can present opposing views in face-to-face situations. National television networks schedule weekly programs of the "press conference" type in which national leaders or representatives of foreign governments answer pointed questions posed by members of a panel of newspapermen and network news personalities. Special programs on free time are provided for such newsworthy happenings as Presidential press conferences, and less frequently for leaders of the minority party in Congress to voice opposition to some major Administration proposal. But national networks prefer to handle expressions of opinion in regularly scheduled news or interview programs—understandably, since the grant of a half-hour period for a special sustaining network program of opinion means the cancellation of a regularly scheduled commercial program and a resulting loss of $60,000 or $70,000 in network revenues. Local stations, with few exceptions, follow the lead of the networks in preferring to limit expressions of opinion on public issues to their news programs or to either regular or special programs in which advocates of opposing points of view appear in a face-to-face situation.

Controversy on paid time. Although radio and television stations are reluctant to provide free time for programs in which only one side of a controversial issue is to be presented, nearly all stations will *sell* time for such one-sided presentations. Almost without exception, stations sell time for appearances by candidates for national or local office during political campaigns. In addition, most stations are willing to make paid time available for public utilities companies to argue for franchise renewals or to justify higher rates, or for state or local medical societies to express their opposition to government health insurance. Many stations—radio stations in particular—are also willing to sell time for taped or recorded commentary programs, scheduled on a regular weekly or daily basis, in which featured speakers give their views on various social, economic, or political questions. Some of these programs are sponsored by religious organizations, others by ultraconservative groups, some by labor organizations.

Stations that sell time for one-sided, controversial presentations have sometimes found themselves in an embarrassing position as a result of the "fairness doctrine" of the Federal Communications Commission. This doctrine, referred to in Chapter 7, was laid down originally as applying to stations whose owners expressed editorial views, the Commission holding that those who editorialized should show "fairness" by making time available for the presentation of opposing points of view. Since 1958 or 1959, however, the regulatory body has emphasized the need for "fairness" with respect to all discussions of controversial issues and in a 1963 ruling, already referred to, held that when time was sold for the presentation of one point of view on a public issue, the licensee of the station which sold the time could not reject the presentation of the other side "and thus leave the public uninformed" simply "on the ground that he cannot obtain paid sponsorship for that presentation." One result of the Commission's ruling is that local political organizations have in a number of cases demanded free time to reply to sponsored programs in which attacks have been made on policies of the Administration in Washington.

Broadcasting in Political Campaigns

Radio and television play an important part both in national and in local political campaigns. During the early months of presidential election years, candidates for the Republican and Democratic presidential nominations are given wide exposure on network news programs and those of the press conference or interview type. Network coverage of primary election campaigns includes additional appearances of leading candidates before the microphone or the television camera, so that by the time the national political conventions are held the listening public has had dozens of opportunities to become acquainted not only with each candidate's views on major issues, but with nearly every facet of his personality as well. Broadcasts from the conventions themselves, including coverage of meetings of platform and credentials committees, allow the listener to learn far more about the actual principles each party organization supports than is possible from formal platform statements. And during the eight or nine weeks before the election, candidates for the nation's highest office are seen and heard repeatedly over network facilities, not only in special broadcast programs on time paid for by political organizations but on news specials documenting the progress of the campaign and on the networks' regular news programs.

Candidates for election to Congress or to state and local offices appear less often than do the presidential aspirants, but most of them are given a chance to present their views over local radio and television stations. Nearly all candidates buy time for special programs designed to reach listeners in their respective areas. In addition, stations donate time to candidates for the more important offices, and voters are given ample opportunity to form individual judgments about the qualifications and the personal strengths or weaknesses of the men who seek to represent them in Congress or in the state legislature or to serve as city or county officials.

Costs of political broadcasts. In every national election, each of the two major political parties spends millions of dollars for radio and television time. During the 1960 campaign, Republican national, state, and local party organizations spent a total of nearly $7.56 million for programs and spot announcements; Democratic expenditures in the same campaign amounted to approximately $6.2 million. Two years later, with no presidential election involved, Republican expenditures for broadcast time totaled about $7.52 million, while a little more than $11.98 million was spent in behalf of Democratic candidates. Payments for time during the 1964 campaign were more than those for the two earlier years combined; including about $10 million spent by candidates for nomination in primary elections, a total of slightly more than $34.6 million went for programs and spot announcements in behalf of candidates for major and minor political parties. Of this total, only $4.2 million went to national networks; the remainder represented expenditures for time on individual stations, according to a staff report of the Federal Communications Commission. On national television networks, both major parties made extensive use of short, five-minute program segments inserted immediately following entertainment programs; on CBS, these five-minute periods were sold at a rate of approximately $15,000 each when scheduled during evening hours, and half that amount when inserted between daytime network programs.

Free time for candidates. In each of the three campaigns considered, candidates probably appeared as frequently on news programs or on time donated by stations as on time purchased in their behalf by political organizations. During the 1962 campaign, at least, radio stations broadcast a total of 2,074 sustaining programs on which rival candidates for the same office appeared; television stations scheduled 737 such programs. In addition, television stations provided some 3,364 quarter hours of free time for appearances of individual candidates, and AM radio stations an additional 12,297 quarter hours. These figures do not include taped or filmed statements by candidates used on regular news programs.

Although stations often invite candidates to appear over their facilities without charge, network organizations are careful to avoid giving time for free programs to candidates for the offices of President or Vice-President after their nomination by party conventions. Section 315 of the Federal Communications Act provides that "if any licensee shall permit any person who is a legally qualified candidate for any public office to use a broadcasting station, he shall afford equal opportunities to all other such candidates for that office in the use of such broadcasting station." Consequently, if during the course of a campaign a network were to make sustaining time available to the Democratic party's presidential nominee, it would be required by law to provide an equal amount of free time not only for his Republican rival but also for the presidential candidates of perhaps ten or a dozen minor parties—the Socialist party, the Socialist-Labor party, the Prohibition party, and in the 1964 campaign at least even such splinter organizations as the Spiritualist party and the Vegetarian party. In 1960, a special Act of Congress waived this provision of the Communications Act as it applied to candidates for the offices of President and Vice-President of the United States. This allowed the national networks to bring their listeners a series of four hour-long "Great Debates," or confrontations between Republican candidate Richard M. Nixon and Democratic candidate John F. Kennedy, and also to present both candidates on other sustaining programs filling more hours of network time than the total amount purchased by the two major parties. However, the 1960 waiver applied only to that year's campaign; in 1964, Congress failed to act on a similar proposal, so no time for special network programs was donated to candidates for the Presidency, although filmed excerpts from the campaign speeches of both major party candidates were extensively used on network news programs and on numerous network "specials" reporting the progress of the campaign.[2]

Although the national networks do not provide free time for presidential candidates in the period following their nominations by national conventions, the network organizations usually arrange for the appearances, on sustaining programs, of the leading contenders for the presidential nomination of each major party during the months *before* the conventions. Up to the time of the actual convention vote, these aspirants are technically candidates for their party's *nomination,* rather than for election to the Presidency; as a result, the problem of splinter party candidates does not exist. Similarly, since with few exceptions the various minor parties do not nominate candidates for state and local offices, stations usually have no minor party difficulties when they offer free time to Republican or Democratic candidates for Congress or for the office of governor of a state or mayor of a city. As a result, radio and television stations often allow nominees of the two major parties to present their views

---

[2] As noted in Chapter 7, a 1959 amendment to the Communications Act exempts appearances of candidates on regular news programs or news interview programs from the "equal opportunity" provision of Section 315 of the Act, so that even the use of a complete speech by a candidate in a news program or news special would not require the providing of equal time to other candidates for the same office.

on a sustaining basis, instead of limiting the unsponsored appearances of such candidates to brief items in local news programs.

THE VALUES OF BROADCAST INFORMATION

From the facts presented, it is obvious that stations and networks provide an impressive amount of broadcast information for their listeners. Most station licensees undoubtedly believe that a broadcaster, having been granted a government-created monopoly in the use of a particular channel, has a responsibility that goes beyond the providing of entertainment. Most of them also feel that the carrying of informational programs enhances the image of their stations in the communities they serve. In any event, nearly every station includes a substantial number of informational programs in its schedule, some taken from network lines, others produced by the station itself.

Quantity of Broadcast Information Available

Only in the area of news, of course, do national radio networks offer much in the way of information. News is also the most extensively provided type of information on radio stations, although most radio broadcasting outlets carry many other programs that give specialized information to listeners. Television networks and television stations are considerably more active than their radio counterparts in providing news and other information; each of the television networks devotes an average of from 12 to 18 hours of broadcasting time each week to regular and special news presentations, to programs of general information, and to programs giving the views of national and local leaders on important public issues. Television stations provide perhaps six or eight hours of locally produced programs of similar types each week, in addition to carrying the network offerings, bringing the total weekly time used for information on the average television station to an impressive 18 or 20 hours. During election years, the time used to present information is substantially increased as a result of network coverage of political conventions and network and local time used by candidates for public office.

Audiences for Informational Programs

Not only do broadcasters devote a considerable amount of time to the presentation of information, especially in the areas of news and public affairs, but many of their informational programs reach large numbers of listeners. Not all informational programs have large audiences, to be sure; most listeners to radio and television prefer entertainment to information, and some informational programs attract relatively small numbers of listeners. The news-interview program *Meet the Press,* for example, presented each week on the NBC television network, is heard each week in an average of only two or three million homes. Documentary series do somewhat better; during the winter months *CBS Reports* and *NBC News Specials* find listeners in as many as five or six million homes, and in January 1965 *The Twentieth Century,* scheduled at an hour when it faced no competition from entertainment programs on other networks, was watched each week by an estimated twelve to fifteen million viewers in from six to seven million television-equipped homes. During the same month, the early-evening news programs on the three television networks were tuned in each night in a combined total of nearly 20 million homes, and reports of national rating services lend credence to the National Broadcasting Company's claim that its *Huntley-Brinkley Report* has a larger circulation than any other agency in this country or in the world for the dissemination of news to the public.

The importance of broadcasting and particularly of television in keeping men and women informed about important events is perhaps most strongly indicated by the number of listeners reached by some of television's special news programs. Mention has already been made of the millions of people who watched the television coverage of events following the assassination of President John F. Kennedy. But other, less tragic, events have also attracted large audiences. According to estimates of the A. C. Nielsen Company more than 92 per cent of all television homes were tuned to some portion at least of the 1960 Democratic and Republican national conventions, for an average listening time of more than 15 hours per home. An equally high proportion of television sets were tuned to the networks' coverage of election returns the following November. The 1964 presidential election perhaps engendered less interest, but over the seven-hour period from 7:30 P.M. until 2:30 A.M., on election night, television sets in an hourly average of more than 24 million homes were tuned to reports of the 1964 election returns, with listeners in an estimated 45,000,000 homes hearing some portion of the broadcasts provided by the various networks. Nearly 40 million listeners in 22 million homes ·watched the inauguration of President Lyndon B. Johnson in January 1965, and additional millions watched the inaugural day parade that followed the ceremonies, according to reports of the American Research Bureau. Television coverage of the space flight of astronaut John Glenn in February 1962 attracted listeners in 39,900,000 homes; the Gordon Cooper orbital flight in May 1963 was watched in 91 per cent of all television homes, with viewing time averaging more than two and a half hours. More recent space flights by other astronauts have attracted equally large audiences. And the American Research Bureau estimates that at least 70 million people watched and listened to all or some part of President Lyndon B. Johnson's Message to Congress in March 1965, calling for federal legislation to insure voting rights for Negroes. The message, carried by all three television networks as were the other news events mentioned, reached listeners in a total of 35.2 million homes—nearly 58 per cent of all television-equipped homes in the nation. Television has repeatedly demonstrated its ability to bring news of important events to audiences of millions of American viewers; radio supplements this service by making accounts of those news happenings available to listeners who do not have access to television sets at the time the events take place.

Reaching the Mass Audience

Of course, audiences for such special news programs are exceptional; the average news or public affairs or general information program presented by a television network is probably heard by not more than eight or ten million people. And the criticism is made that the audiences of such programs are made up largely of the more intelligent and better-educated elements in the population, while those most in need of information devote most of their listening time to rock 'n' roll music on radio or to watching television Westerns. While there may be some basis for this criticism, audiences of informational programs are by no means limited to the intellectual elite in our society. To begin with, some programs have considerably more than eight or ten million listeners; at least 40 million people listen to television network news programs every night, for example, and certainly not all can be classed as "intellectuals." Even when audiences are smaller, it is hardly reasonable to assume that exactly the same eight or ten million people listen to a documentary dealing with birth control that heard a program on the military situation in Southeast Asia on the preceding evening or that will give their attention a day or two later to an exposé of political corruption. The total number of individuals who tune in and listen to *some* informational programs, at least, is decidedly more than 10 million—probably closer to 50 or 60 million, possibly even more. And many of that total number are men and women with limited educational attainments. The information provided in broadcast programs reaches people on nearly every economic and social level.

It is probably true that the American people are better informed than are the people of any other nation in the world. Many factors have played a part in creating such a situation; our books, our newspapers and magazines, our libraries, our churches, our system of public education, the training our children receive in the home. But certainly, radio and television have also made a contribution, and a most important contribution, to the enlightenment of the American people.

12

EDUCATION AND
CULTURE

Although broadcasting makes a significant contribution in providing news and information to
the American people, its service in supplying
educational or cultural programs is far less impressive. Advertisers naturally want their programs or their advertising messages to reach the
largest number of listeners possible, and the
so-called cultural programs—those that deal with
art or literature or that present the works of great
composers—generally fail to attract substantial
audiences, with the result that the number of
cultural programs offered is definitely limited.
Similarly, commercial broadcasting provides
little programming that might be described as
educational in character—programs providing instruction on a systematic basis either for adults
or for children. Information may be given on a
variety of subjects, but rarely is a program series

presented in an attempt to provide a thorough treatment of any selected body of knowledge. With school enrollments increasing, with shortages of trained teachers and properly equipped classrooms, and with horizons of knowledge rapidly widening, educators believe that there is a need for broadcast programs that can supplement the instruction provided in the public schools or that have value in the field of formal adult education. Commercial broadcasting stations can hardly be expected to provide such programs, at least not to the extent that educators think necessary.

From the earliest days of radio, many influential groups of Americans have believed that education and culture should receive the same attention in broadcasting in this country that they are given in Europe, and that if commercial broadcasting stations are unable to provide programs to meet our educational and cultural needs, some other means must be found to make such programs available. The only satisfactory solution to the problem, in the opinion of many who are convinced of the need for such programs, is to be found in the creation of a second broadcasting service, independent of our present commercial system, supported by educational interests, and operated for the sole purpose of providing cultural, educational, and informational programs for listeners. Anything less, they argue, would be an unsatisfactory compromise, incapable of meeting either the cultural and educational needs of the public or the practical requirements of successful commercial operation.

Early Educational Stations

The idea of such a "second service" had its beginnings in the early 1920s when scores of schools and colleges applied for licenses for radio stations. According to records of the Department of Commerce, authorizations were granted between 1921 and 1925 to 153 educational institutions. Not all of the stations authorized were actually constructed; some that did go on the air suspended operation within a year after receiving their licenses, so that by the end of 1925 probably not more than a hundred school-owned stations were attempting to provide service. Even these stations lacked adequate financing, and after the creation of the Federal Radio Commission in 1927 only a limited number could buy the equipment needed to meet the Commission's engineering requirements. So the number of noncommercial educational stations steadily decreased. Some were sold to commercial operators, others surrendered their licenses voluntarily, a few were taken off the air by the Radio Commission in favor of commercial stations promising a better or a more consistent service. But a number of college- or school-owned stations did survive. At the beginning of 1935 a total of 31 noncommercial educational stations remained on the air, 19 of them operated by tax-supported state colleges or universities. Only five of the educational stations were licensed for full-time operation; the others shared time with commercial stations and were allowed to broadcast for only two or three hours a day. About a dozen religious stations also operated on a noncommercial basis, most of them limited to broadcasting religious services on Sunday mornings. By 1940, the number of noncommercial educational stations had dropped to 26, and only a handful of these survivors were being adequately financed by the schools to which they were licensed.

Pressures for Educational Reservations

During the 1920s, nearly all radio stations operated on a part-time basis, sharing frequency assignments with other stations in the same general area. This arrangement created serious problems for the then-existing educational stations; the commercial broadcasters with whom time was shared naturally wanted to increase their authorized hours of operation at the expense of their noncommercial neighbors. In 1930, after several educational stations had almost literally been pushed off the air, a National Conference on Radio and Education, convened by the United States Commissioner of Education, demanded that Congress should adopt legislation reserving 15 per cent of all broadcasting facilities for the exclusive use of educational institutions. Congress asked the Federal Radio Commission to study the proposal, and if it saw fit, to recommend suitable legislation. The Radio Commission showed little interest in the 15 per cent idea, however, and made no recommendation. Four years later, the idea of educational reservations came up again, this time in the form of a proposed amendment to the Federal Communications Act then under consideration by Congress. The amendment failed to receive the necessary support, and the proposal was not incorporated in the Federal Communications Act of 1934.

The Federal Communications Commission, however, took a more favorable attitude than had the earlier Radio Commission toward the idea of reserving facilities for noncommercial use. In 1945, the Communications Commission set a precedent by designating 20 channels in the Frequency Modulation band as "educational" channels, to be used only by noncommercial educational stations. Seven years later, the Commission followed up this action by reserving a total of 242 specific channel assignments for the exclusive use of educational television stations, 80 of the assignments on channels in the VHF band of frequencies and 162 on UHF channels.

The Federal Communications Commission's decision to reserve these educational channels was largely a result of the activities of various interested educational groups. The National Association of Educational Broadcasters was a leader in the movement to secure educational reservations in the early 1930s; the same organization, backed by the United States Office of Education, had much to do with the Commission's action in setting aside Frequency Modulation channels for educational station use. Five years later, the NAEB and the United States Office of Education were responsible for the formation of the Joint Committee on Educational Television, representing such important educational groups as the American Council on Education, the Association of Land-Grant Colleges, the National Association of State Universities, the National Council of Chief State School Officers, and the National Education Association. Under the guidance of the Joint Committee, dozens of educational leaders appeared at hearings before the Federal Communications Commission to urge that specific reservations be made for the educational television stations that might later come into being. There was little opposition to the idea, and the result was that when the Commission's Sixth Report and Order was issued in April 1952, channels in 242 communities were set aside for noncommercial use. The Commission's 1965 revision of its allocations table for television more than doubled the number of reservations of channels for noncommercial use—from the 242 assignments in 1952 to a total of 604 reservations in 559 different communities, including two assignments each in 45 major cities. Of the noncommercial channel assignments in the 1965 allocations table, 102 were in the VHF band and 502 were UHF stations.

Educational Radio since 1945

At the end of World War II, some 35 standard-band stations were operating on a noncommercial basis, including several licensed to religious organizations. During the next ten years, the number of noncommercial AM stations increased slightly, but during the 1950s and early 1960s some of the educational stations went off the air and one or two were changed to commercial outlets. As a result, by January 1966, only 32 AM stations were still operated on a noncommercial basis. Of this total, 16 stations were supported by tax-supported colleges or universities, five or six others were licensed to private colleges or other educational agencies, and one was owned by a municipality. The remainder were operated by seminaries, local churches, or other religious organizations. All but two of the university stations had daytime power of 5,000 watts; however, only four were licensed for full-time operation and some were allowed to broadcast for no more than two or three hours a day.

Although the number of educational AM stations has shown a slight decrease since 1945, there has been a tremendous expansion in the number of noncommercial radio stations using the FM band. In January 1966 a total of 269 noncommercial FM stations were on the air, all but 20 on frequencies reserved for education. Of the total number, 84 were licensed to tax-supported colleges and universities; 104 others were operated by private colleges, and 60 served the needs of local public school systems. The remainder were licensed to various state agencies, to private educational groups, or in a few instances to religious organizations. About two-fifths of the noncommercial FMs were low-powered 10-watt stations, costing little to construct or operate. But nearly 25 of the educational FM stations used power of 50,000 watts or more, and nine or ten were authorized to broadcast with 200,000 or even 300,000 watts power, including stations licensed to religious organizations or to private corporations.

Programs provided by educational radio stations vary widely. Many of the noncommercial stations are relatively well financed and have competent program staffs; other stations, especially the 10-watt FMs, have very limited budgets, and in some cases are operated entirely by students. A few stations owned by local boards of education limit their programming activities to the presentation of instructional materials for use in the classroom. Other stations aim their programs at a general audience. As is the case with commercial radio stations, recorded music forms the backbone of program schedules. The educational stations, however, make little use of current popular recordings—at least of the types used by "top 40" commercial stations. Instead, most of them provide listeners with programs of show tunes and "middle of the road" music, with substantial amounts of time each week devoted to broadcasts of classical and semi-classical music. Some stations also present programs of jazz and folk music. Most of the educational radio stations use an hour or more a day to present talk programs, ranging from educational lectures to discussions of public controversial issues. College- and university-owned stations usually carry play-by-play broadcasts of local sports events, especially those involving teams representing their own institutions. Some educational radio stations owned by state or private colleges, like those licensed to local school systems, offer instructional programs for use in classrooms of elementary and secondary schools. Although the larger university stations include news broadcasts in their daily schedules, most of the smaller educational FM outlets give almost no time to current news, probably because their operating budgets are too small to cover the costs of a wire news service.

Little is known about the audiences reached by educational radio stations; such stations are not usually mentioned in local rating reports of commercial rating services, and in any case, the number of listeners to most of the educational stations is probably small. But educational radio stations are providing a "second broadcasting service" in radio, and one of particular value to those listeners who are interested in serious talks or in music of somewhat better quality than that provided by most commercial radio stations.

THE RISE OF EDUCATIONAL TELEVISION

Although the number of educational radio stations has increased tremendously since the opening of the FM bands in 1945, much more significant has been the rapid development of educational television. Hardly had the Federal Communications Commission's Report and Order of 1952 been released when plans were being made by educational institutions to construct stations on channels which the Commission had reserved for the exclusive use of educational television outlets. By the end of 1953, only two educational television stations had gone on the air, one of which suspended operation during the following year; by the end of 1954, however, eight additional stations had been constructed. During the next four years, the number of educational outlets had increased to 34, and by the beginning of January 1966, a total of 105 noncommercial television stations were in operation, 61 using VHF channels and the remainder assigned to channels in the UHF band.

Rules of the Federal Communications Commission provide that noncommercial educational stations may be licensed only to "nonprofit educational organizations upon a showing that the proposed stations will be used primarily to serve the educational needs of the community." Under this rule, licenses have been issued to a variety of types of organizations. Of the 105 stations in operation in the autumn of 1965, 28 were licensed to tax-supported state colleges and universities, two to privately owned colleges, 16 to state boards of education or state educational television commissions, 22 to local boards of education, junior colleges, or local vocational schools, and two to other local agencies. Perhaps of greatest importance, however, were the 35 stations licensed to local nonprofit educational associations organized for the express purpose of operating stations in their communities; most of these stations were located in major cities and were reasonably well financed, although depending primarily on public contributions for support.

Factors Encouraging Expansion

A number of factors have contributed to the rapid development of educational television since 1954 or 1955. One has been the concern of college and university administrators over expanding college enrollments. With little chance that faculties and physical plants could be expanded rapidly enough to keep pace with the increased numbers of students, officials of some tax-supported institutions saw in television a possible method of coping with the problem. In this they were encouraged, as were public school administrators, by findings of dozens of research studies investigating television's effectiveness as a classroom teaching tool; in nearly every instance researchers reported that while instruction by television was not significantly *more* effective than that provided by teachers in a face-to-face situation, television instruction was at worst *no less* effective than that provided by conventional methods, at least in some subject-matter areas. As a result, many university and public school administrators saw television as a means of providing instruction for students without adding large numbers of highly qualified instructors to teaching staffs.[1]

In the case of community stations, the motivating factor was probably different. Community leaders who were active in the development of these stations expected them to use a part of their time to broadcast programs for use in public school classrooms, but they were interested primarily in the possibilities which educational television offered in the area of adult education and in the providing of cultural programs. Probably many organizers of community groups hoped that the educational television stations to be built would be able to devote several hours a week to broadcasts by symphony orchestras, to operas, to seri-

---

[1] In recent years, a large number of colleges and universities have installed closed-circuit television systems to provide in-school instruction for students, often with classrooms in a dozen or more buildings linked by coaxial cable with the originating television studio. Similar systems are also in use in many high schools and elementary schools. Where the school buildings to be served are scattered over a large area, however, as in major cities or when schools are located in several different communities, open-circuit or "broadcast" television is required.

ous drama, to programs dealing with art or literature, and to other cultural materials not provided by commercial television.

Financial Assistance

An important factor in the rapid growth of educational television has been the financial assistance given prospective licensees of educational stations by outside agencies. In cities in which educational stations have been constructed by community groups, funds for construction and operation of the educational outlets came largely from public subscriptions; local business concerns were often heavy contributors. In many communities commercial broadcasters donated money or equipment to help get the new educational stations on the air. In one case, the owner of a commercial outlet in a two-station market bought the rival commercial VHF station in that city and turned it over to an educational institution—channel, transmitter, antenna tower, studios and technical equipment—with the understanding that the station would be operated on a noncommercial basis. In many other communities, commercial broadcasters have donated amounts ranging from $50,000 to as much as $250,000, or have provided studios, antenna towers or equipment worth thousands of dollars. Contributions of commercial stations and networks to new educational stations between 1955 and 1965 probably totaled $15 million or more.

Even more important has been the financial support provided the infant educational television stations by foundations— the Ford Foundation in particular. The Fund for Adult Education, using money provided by the Ford Foundation, made substantial grants of money to early educational stations for purchase of equipment. At least 30 new stations received donations of $100,000 or $150,000 each from the Fund, with the proviso that a part of the money received be used to buy equipment for kinescope recording. Later, Foundation money was made available for the purchase of videotape recording equipment; educational stations were among the first to install such equipment. But probably the most important contribution of the Ford Foundation and the Fund for Adult Education, in terms of long-range development of educational television at least, was the financing of the National Educational Television and Radio Center,[2] an agency organized to produce educational and cultural programs on film or videotape for distribution to noncommercial educational stations. By the end of 1965, the Ford Foundation had contributed more than $96 million, either directly or through organizations it financed, to help establish educational television. Other foundations had contributed smaller amounts toward the construction or support of individual educational stations.

The growth of educational television has also been aided by actions of the federal government. The National Defense Education Act passed by Congress in 1958 authorized the spending of up to $110 million a year for three years for the encouragement and improvement of the teaching of mathematics, the sciences, and foreign languages. Many of the grants approved by the Department of Health, Education and Welfare under provisions of this Act have involved research studies or other experiments in the field of educational television. In May 1962 Congress passed a second measure, this time authorizing the use of $32 million of federal funds for construction of educational television stations. By the summer of 1964, $8 million of this amount had actually been appropriated and made available; in each case, an amount equal to the federal grant had to be provided from state or local funds. And while no financial aid is involved, the construction of educational stations on UHF channels has been stimulated by the enactment by Congress of the law requiring all television sets manufactured after April 1964 to be equipped with all-channel tuning and be capable of bringing in signals of UHF stations as well as those of stations assigned to VHF channels.

Airborne Television Instruction

An experiment of unusual interest was inaugurated in 1961 by the Midwest Program on Airborne Television Instruction. Transmitters installed on DC-6B airplanes flying at high altitudes provided televised lessons in art, music, history, geography, mathematics, biology, chemistry and French to be received on

---

[2] In 1963 the last three words of the original title were dropped; the organization is now known simply as National Educational Television.

sets in elementary schools and high schools over an area including most of the states of Indiana and Illinois, and parts of Wisconsin, Michigan, and Ohio. Lessons to be broadcast were prepared and videotaped at Purdue University or at other universities cooperating in the project. The experiment was financed largely by the Ford Foundation and the Westinghouse Electric Company, in cooperation with Purdue University and CBS Laboratories, which helped develop the technique. In some cases, Airborne program materials were picked up and rebroadcast by regular educational television stations. According to some estimates, lessons provided by the Midwest program were used on a regular basis by elementary or secondary schools in more than two thousand communities.

Possibilities of an Interconnected Educational Network

Although National Educational Television performs most of the functions of a network organization for educational television stations, producing or buying rights to filmed or videotaped programs and supplying them to affiliated educational stations, many educational broadcasters have expressed a desire to have educational television stations throughout the country linked together permanently by A.T.&T. lines, in the same way as stations affiliated with a commercial network organization. They feel that educational stations would benefit greatly if programs originating "live" in New York or Washington or Los Angeles could be broadcast simultaneously on stations from coast to coast. A beginning of such an interconnected network was made in 1962 when noncommercial television stations in Boston, New York and other cities in Northeastern states were linked together experimentally in an Eastern Educational Network, with costs of interconnection paid by the Ford Foundation. Several states have set up state networks of educational television stations, and plans are under way in other states to link together the educational stations within their boundaries on a permanent interconnected basis.

The problem of establishing and maintaining a national interconnected network of educational television stations is, of course, one of finding money to pay the costs of interconnection. Commercial television network companies pay at least $12 million each to the American Telephone & Telegraph Company as annual rental charges on the lines used to carry network programs to affiliates throughout the country. The annual cost of providing a similar "live" network service for a hundred or more noncommercial stations would be almost as great. Some educators have proposed that the programs of an educational network might be sent out over A.T.&T. lines after midnight, when rates are appreciably lower, with programs videotaped off network lines by affiliated stations and broadcast the following day. But even this arrangement would cost several million dollars a year, an amount that noncommercial stations could hardly be expected to pay out of existing budgets. Unless some foundation or perhaps the federal government itself should decide to pay the costs of interconnection, it is probable that any national network of educational television stations will operate on the same basis as in the past, with programs on videotape or film shipped by mail to affiliated stations.

THE SECOND TELEVISION SERVICE

But with or without an interconnected network, the United States has a "second" television service, operated for the specific purpose of providing educational, informative, and cultural programs for listeners. More than one hundred noncommercial educational stations are already on the air—roughly one educational station for every six commercial outlets—and the number of stations has been increasing at the rate of six or eight each year. Educational authorities expect the number of noncommercial broadcasting facilities to reach a total of at least 130 or 140 before any appreciable slow-up takes place in the rate of growth.

Programming

Programs offered by educational outlets fall into two major classes. During school hours, a major part of the schedule of the typical station consists of instructional programs intended for use in classrooms of elementary and secondary schools. Frequently the same lessons are broadcast twice or even three times each day, to make them available for classes meeting at different hours. Most of these daytime instructional programs are locally produced; variations in courses of study from state to state and even from city to city make it difficult to make the same instructional materials fit lesson plans in use in different localities. In most cases, the specific sequence of materials used in each broadcast course is worked out by station producers in cooperation with committees of teachers from the local school system, or with assistant superintendents responsible for curricula. Instructors or "experts" appearing before the cameras in televised courses come, in most cases, from the instructional staff of the local school system, and are selected jointly by local school authorities and by representatives of the television station. Almost all of the instructional programs planned for classroom use follow the "lecture and demonstration" pattern, with a "master teacher" who appears on the program and who prepares and presents her own materials. This "extension of the classroom" technique is sometimes criticized as not making full use of the possibilities offered by television, but as yet no better method of instruction has been developed that can be used for subjects ranging from physical science to driver education—and one economically feasible for use by a single station. Apparently local school authorities feel that televised instruction is effective; in any event, the number of school systems using educational television programs in the classroom is steadily increasing.

The second group of programs provided by noncommercial educational stations includes those intended for out-of-school listening, usually by an adult audience. It is through these programs that educational television has its opportunity to offer instruction and inspiration for the general audience, and to serve the cultural needs of the community—to provide that "second television service" which is one of its major objectives. A limited number of cultural programs are provided by most stations, but a major part of the nonclassroom offerings consists of adult educational programs of the "how to do it" type, of roundtable or panel discussion programs, and of talks on a wide variety of subjects.

The published schedule of WNDT, the noncommercial VHF television station in New York City, for a typical week in

February 1965 is fairly representative of the offerings of educational stations throughout the country. The station was on the air Monday through Friday from 9:30 in the morning until 11:00 at night; like most other educational television stations, WNDT did not broadcast on Saturday or Sunday. Daytime hours were devoted largely to classroom instruction using programs developed in cooperation with the Board of Education of the city of New York. Schedules for the late afternoon and early evening during the five-day period included eight half-hour programs for young children, five half-hours of instruction in basic English for Puerto Ricans, three program periods providing instruction in advanced French, two programs dealing with gardening, two talks on French cooking, and three programs of vocal music. Programs scheduled later in the evening included a documentary on life in the "old West," two half-hour dramatic presentations by a Little Theater group, an hour-long British-produced dramatization of short stories by Guy de Maupassant, a 30-minute piano recital from Lincoln Center, interviews with a composer of "new music," a famous photographer and the art editor of a national magazine, and two presentations dealing with the art of motion pictures. The "prime time" schedule also included no less than eight panel discussion or "conversation" programs on topics ranging from Negro rights in Northern cities to conditions in Red China and to the responsibilities of American broadcasters, and at least a dozen talks or interviews on such subjects as narcotic addiction, the use of computers, oceanography, air pollution, current happenings in the religious field, recently published books, and chess masterpieces. Ten 5-minute periods were devoted to news, and five longer programs to news commentary. It might be mentioned that of the approximately 37 hours of nonclassroom programming, more than twelve hours consisted of repeats of broadcasts that had been carried on the station before, in many cases only a few days earlier.

The WNDT schedule is fairly typical of the offerings of educational television stations generally. Aside from instructional programs intended for classroom use in high schools and elementary schools, locally produced programming consists largely of talks, interviews and roundtable discussions presented by local educators. Most stations broadcast news on a regular basis, but except in a few major cities news is not a significant part of the daily schedule, since educational outlets are not usually able to pay the costs of a television news service or of on-the-spot coverage of local news events. Many of the stations licensed to schools and colleges broadcast local college or high school basketball or football games in an effort to attract more listeners. Occasionally educational stations present recitals by local musicians or musical groups, usually those connected with local schools, and a few have experimented with dramatic offerings by local amateur theatrical groups. But for the major portion of their musical and dramatic presentations, most of their documentary programs and even a considerable number of their roundtable discussions, talks and interviews, educational television stations rely on the filmed and videotaped materials provided by the educational television network, National Educational Television.

National Educational Television

The National Educational Television organization, or NET, as it is more commonly known, was created in 1952 as the National Educational Television and Radio Center. Financial support has come largely from the Fund for Adult Education, or in recent years directly from the Ford Foundation. The organization has engaged in a variety of activities, from lobbying in Washington to encouraging schools and local community groups to apply for licenses for educational stations; NET's main function, however, has been that of supplying programs. Practically all of the educational television stations in the country are NET affiliates and part of its "taped network"; for an annual membership fee of only $100, each affiliate is provided with five hours of new programming each week and an additional five hours of programs taken from the organization's program library. Additional programs from the NET library, which now includes nearly 3,000 separate programs, may be secured by affiliates on payment of a rental charge of $5.00 for each half-hour of material.

During the first ten years of its existence, the network secured most of its programs from member stations which produced them under grants from the network organization. Additional programs were purchased from the British Broadcasting Corporation and a few were produced by private contractors. In 1963, however, the Ford Foundation increased the amount of its annual subsidy to the educational network to $6 million, with the proviso that practically all of this amount was to be used to produce programs of high quality. Officials of NET, as a result, adopted the policy in 1964 of having nearly all of the network's new programs produced by independent professional program packagers instead of by affiliated educational stations. The network organization will probably continue to use programs produced by the British Broadcasting Corporation and occasionally programs secured from state-owned television systems in other countries.

Programs in the library of National Educational Television in the autumn of 1964 included perhaps a score of major dramatic offerings—plays by Shakespeare, Ibsen, Molière, Chekhov, and the like—nearly all of which were produced by the British Broadcasting Corporation and originally presented over its facilities. There were also a limited number of notable musical programs featuring such organizations as the Boston Symphony Orchestra and the San Francisco Opera Company. But due to their expense, such "big production" programs were in extremely short supply. However, affiliates do have access to a wide range of cultural and informational programs of many types including series featuring the Chicago Fine Arts String Quartet; presentations of folk music or American jazz; an impressive variety of documentaries produced by NET affiliates; interviews or "conversations" with American and foreign writers, dramatists, poets, artists, statesmen, and philosophers; political commentaries and news analyses—many of them provided by the BBC; programs providing instruction in French, Spanish, or other foreign languages; several highly imaginative and well-produced children's program series; and of course numerous programs used for classroom instruction in various fields.

But up to the present time, NET has been able to supply its affiliates with only a limited number of the more elaborate cultural programs—operas, symphonies, plays of outstanding literary merit—that proponents of educational broadcasting would like to see included on the schedules of educational stations.

Providing cultural programs of outstanding quality seems to be as much of a problem for educational stations and for NET as it is for commercial stations and networks.

The Problem of Finances

The rapid and steady increase in the number of educational television stations, however, has been a source of much gratification to those interested in the new medium of information and instruction. But educational television is faced with problems that must be solved, and one of the serious problems is that of securing adequate financial support. Television is expensive. Stations need substantial amounts of money to pay the costs of operation. Commercial stations sell time to advertisers to provide the revenues needed to pay salaries and buy equipment and produce programs for their listeners. But educational stations are noncommercial; by the terms of their licenses they are barred from selling time; they must find other sources of income. University stations and those owned by local school districts depend primarily, of course, on money provided by taxes, but the amount available from taxes is necessarily limited. Most university- and community-association-owned stations receive some payments from local school systems—the standard rate of payment seems to be one dollar per pupil per year—for providing instructional programs for classroom use; in a few major cities, these payments amount to as much as $100,000 or even $200,000 a year. Community stations depend for most of their income on donations by foundations or local business concerns, on annual fund-raising campaigns, even in some cases on such devices as "white elephant" auctions of objects sent in by listeners. In earlier years, a source of funds for some stations was the production of program series for educational network use under grants from the National Educational Television organization but NET's decision in 1964 to have most of its programs produced by independent professional concerns has largely dried up this source of revenue. A considerable number of stations receive some income from services rendered commercial stations in their community, including the videotaping of commercial network programs for broadcast at a later hour.

Operating budgets. As a result of their dependence on such sources of income, most educational television stations are seriously underfinanced. They simply don't have the money available to provide the type of service in the cultural field that they are expected to offer. Reports to the Federal Communications Commission show that not including the costs of selling time, the operating expenses of non-network-owned commercial television stations in 1964 averaged above $950,000 a year. In comparison, the income of the average educational television station in 1963–64 was only $368,000 a year, according to a study of educational stations made by the National Association of Educational Broadcasters.[3] As a result, the educational station must limit its hours of operation each week; it is forced to get along with a smaller staff than that of the commercial station in the same community —the average educational station in 1964 had only 26 full-time employees; salaries of employees are usually lower; and the station has far less money to spend in providing programs for listeners. In the words of Wilbur Schramm of the Stanford Institute for Communication Research, "the truth is that ETV from the start has been a shoestring operation, long on imagination but short on cash, high on ideals but low on salaries, strong on program standards but weak in money for talent and equipment."[4]

The same characterization may also be applied to NET and its predecessor organization, the National Educational Television and Radio Center, the main suppliers of programs intended for use by educational television stations. Prior to 1964, the Center, or NET as it became in 1963, had an annual budget of around $3.5 million, a considerable part of which went into nonprogramming activities. As a result of the substantially increased grant from the Ford Foundation NET's total 1965 budget was raised to more than $8 million, with perhaps three-fourths of the total spent for program production. But six or seven million dollars a year will not buy any great number of high-quality programs,

---

[3] *The Financing of Educational Television Stations*, April 1965, published by the National Association of Educational Broadcasters.

[4] Wilbur Schramm, Jack Lyle, and Ithiel de Sola Pool, *The People Look at Educational Television*. Stanford University Press, 1963.

when the average production cost of evening programs on commercial networks runs close to $140,000 for each hour of material broadcast and when the three national commercial television networks reported programming expenses for 1964 averaged more than $180 million each.

Program underwriting. The educational network organization in recent years has been forced to supplement its income from foundation grants by arranging for costs of certain program series to be underwritten by various professional groups or industrial concerns. These programs are of course not "sponsored"— the underwriting organization does not pay for time on stations which carry the programs—but credit is given the underwriting company by inserting in the opening and closing portions of each program the words "produced in cooperation with" or "produced under a grant from" the agency which paid the program's production costs. A well-known example of a series so underwritten is *The Age of Kings,* a cycle of eight Shakespearian plays produced by the British Broadcasting Corporation, with costs of American showings on educational television stations paid for by the Humble Oil Company. Other groups that have underwritten program series for NET include the American Medical Association, the National Science Foundation, the National Aeronautics and Space Administration, the International Business Machines company, the National Association of Manufacturers, and the brokerage firm of Merrill, Lynch, Pierce, Fenner & Smith.

Arranging this sort of semisponsorship of programs to be carried on noncommercial educational stations apparently has the blessing of the Federal Communications Commission which in March 1965 approved a program-underwriting plan submitted by WNDT, the educational television station in New York City. The WNDT proposal called for programs broadcast by the station between 8:00 and 10:00 P.M. five evenings a week to be underwritten during the 1965–66 season by fifteen commercial or industrial companies, each of whom would contribute $200,000 toward the production costs of those programs. Underwriting concerns would be identified during the programs in accordance with the Commission's sponsorship identification rules, and four such "identification of underwriting companies" announcements would be made during each two-hour period, with three of the underwriting companies given credit in each announcement. Of course the identifications would not be "commercial announcements" in the usual sense, but spokesmen for the National Association of Broadcasters, as well as one member of the Commission who voted against the proposal, contend that the plan is not in keeping with the spirit of Commission rules barring advertising on noncommercial educational stations. Even so, while program-underwriting might eventually become an important source of support for educational television, the National Association of Educational Broadcasters estimated that it was relatively insignificant in the 1965 financial picture, taking care of less than 2 per cent of the operating costs of the nation's educational stations.

The Problem of Quality

Lack of adequate financing of educational television stations creates a problem with respect to the quality of program offerings. Costs of power and equipment and technical operating expenses are just as high on an hour-for-hour basis for educational as for commercial stations. Consequently the educational station can stay within its limited budget only by holding personnel and program costs to a minimum. Almost always the educational television station has fewer employees than does its commercial counterpart, although the number of hours of local programming each week may be from twice to three times as great as the number provided by most commercial outlets. Salaries too are often lower than those paid for equivalent work by commercial stations, especially for top-level employees. As a result, there is a tendency for producers and writers and on-the-air personalities of greater than average ability to leave the educational field for work at higher pay on commercial stations. Simply because of its financial limitations, the educational station finds it difficult to compete with commercial outlets in securing or holding the services of competent and experienced program personnel.

Naturally, this weakness in production talent has its effect on the quality of programs developed and presented. Even more

serious is the fact that because of the lack of money, most educational stations cannot even attempt to put on the air the types
of locally produced cultural programs their operators would like
to provide and that should be provided by stations attempting
to offer a real "second television service." Locally produced programs of serious drama are out of the question; they cost far
too much both in time and money, even if top-notch scripts
could be secured and if the necessary professional quality of
dramatic talent were available in the community. The same situation exists with respect to serious musical programs; even in
cities that support symphony orchestras, the fees charged for
television appearances of such professional organizations are far
too great to be within the reach of the average educational station. As a result, educational television stations are forced to
depend for their cultural programs on those provided by the
National Educational Television organization. Some of the NET
programs have been excellent, but as already noted the network
has been able to supply only a very limited number of really
first-rate dramatic or musical programs or programs dealing with
literature or the dance or fine arts. Costs of outstanding programs are high, and the educational network organization does
not have unlimited funds at its disposal.

Although weak in the area of cultural programs, educational television stations do better in the field of information,
providing informative programs ranging over a wide variety of
subjects from elementary science to marriage customs in India
or to conditions among share-croppers in the South. Some of
these presentations are in documentary form, usually supplied
by NET. Others take the form of roundtable discussions. However, the great majority of the programs provided by educational
stations are low-cost "one-man" presentations—lectures by teachers or other authorities, or informal "conversations" with invited
guests. Such programs can be put together with minimum effort
on the part of the station's staff; there are no supporting entertainers, no special settings need to be constructed, little or no
rehearsal time is required, and in most cases no effort is made
to employ any special production techniques to make the program more attractive to listeners. In many cases, in fact, there is
little evidence of the use of much imagination or ingenuity on

the part of the producer of the program; the presentation is successful only in the degree to which the speaker who appears is able by sheer force of personality to hold listener attention during the time the program is on the air. And as might be expected, not all of those who appear on such programs have the vitality and color and the sense of showmanship the situation demands. The "one-man show" format is not the most effective for television use, but programs using the form can be produced more cheaply than those of other types, and most educational stations cannot afford to pay the additional costs required for other programs. Limited budgets do not make for high program quality, and until educational television is better financed than it has been in the past, a part at least of the programs presented by educational stations will fail to meet the standards of quality desirable in an effective "second service."

The Problem of Audiences

A third problem which the educational television station must face is that of attracting listeners for its programs. An educational station should reasonably expect to reach enough listeners to justify its costs of operation, just as a commercial station is expected to attract audiences large enough to satisfy its advertisers. Just how many listeners the educational station should reach is of course a difficult question to answer. But if educational television is to be a significant force in disseminating culture and providing education and organized information for the people living in the community, the number reached and influenced should be substantial; the greater the number who listen to each program, the greater the effectiveness of the station in attaining its educational and cultural objectives.

Unfortunately, with very few exceptions the audiences attracted by educational television stations are small, especially as compared with those of commercial outlets. Some educational stations are assigned to UHF channels in markets served by VHF commercial stations; naturally in such situations the educational station works at a serious disadvantage. But even the VHF educational stations have relatively few listeners. In part, the problem lies in the fact that when they turn on their television sets most men and women want to be entertained, rather than enlightened or exposed to culture. Possibly, too, the limited number of programs of outstanding quality on educational station schedules has something to do with the situation. Lack of station and program promotion is certainly a factor; with a limited budget, the educational station does not have the money needed to carry on an elaborate promotional campaign to make listeners aware of whatever attractive programs the station is able to provide. In addition, very few educational stations schedule programs intended primarily as "audience-builders," regardless of their instructional or cultural values. In any case, no matter what the cause, it is an accepted fact that educational television stations are almost never able to attract substantial audiences, even for their most outstanding programs.

Estimates of size of audiences. Educational broadcasters find some reason to be encouraged, however, by the results of a series of studies of audiences of educational television stations conducted in 1961 under the supervision of Dr. Wilbur Schramm of the Stanford Institute for Communication Research. As reported in *The People Look at Educational Television,* referred to earlier in this chapter, telephone or personal interviews were conducted with a cross-section sample of men and women in each of seven communities served by educational stations; respondents were queried with respect to the extent of their listening to the educational stations available. In three cities, Boston, Pittsburgh, and San Francisco, from 21 to 24 per cent of those interviewed were classed as "regular" listeners to the local educational station; an additional 31 to 40 per cent were classed as "occasional" listeners. Proportions of "regular" and "occasional" listeners were lower in the other communities studied; in Columbus, Ohio, where the educational station occupied a UHF channel in a community served by three VHF commercial stations, only 3 per cent of the men and women interviewed could be placed in the "regular" listening category. But the success of the stations in Boston, Pittsburgh, and San Francisco—each one a community-supported station with a much higher-than-average budget—lends support to the belief that a well-managed, adequately financed educational television station can attract a substantial audience and can make itself an important cultural and educational force in the community it serves.

Findings of the Schramm studies are possibly somewhat misleading, however, as a result of the system of classification used to identify "regular" and "occasional" listeners. Any respondent who reported listening to the educational station at any time during the seven days preceding the interview was considered a "regular" listener. In addition, a respondent who had not tuned in the station during the preceding week, but who could recall *ever* having listened to a program broadcast by the educational station, was classed as an "occasional" listener. Obviously, the proportions of men and women reported as "regular" listeners had no relationship whatever to the figures reported as "ratings" for commercial stations. In Pittsburgh, for example, where 24 per cent of all respondents were reported as being "regular" listeners to the educational station, the time these "regulars" spent listening to the station averaged only an hour and 13 minutes a week.

No figures are available showing the size of actual audiences tuned to programs on educational stations; the regular commercial rating services do not include educational television stations in their local rating reports. However, the American Research Bureau does report, for different periods of the day, the proportion of homes using television in which sets are tuned to stations "other" than the commercial outlets in the community; these "other" stations would of course include the local educational station as well as out-of-town commercial stations. A projection of these ARB figures for November 1962 in 20 major markets in which VHF educational stations were in operation indicates that the average "share of audience" for the educational stations could not have been more than approximately 1.5 per cent, and that the average rating for programs carried by educational stations would have been not more than 0.3 during daylight hours, or more than 0.9 at night. These figures are merely approximations, of course, but they do indicate that, on the basis of methods of measurement used for commercial broadcasting stations, the audiences reached by educational television stations are often discouragingly small. And if educational stations are serving only a small minority of the listeners in their communities, they are providing only to a very limited degree that "second television service" intended to bring education, information, and culture to the American listening public.

Audience-building programs.   Unfortunately, most operators of educational television stations seem relatively unconcerned over the failure of their program offerings to attract substantial audiences. They feel that the function of the educational station is to provide instructional materials for use in the classroom, and to make available educational and cultural programs to satisfy the needs of a cultured and well-educated minority. If listeners fail to take advantage of the service offered, they maintain that the station is not responsible. A few educational broadcasters take a different position; they would at least *like* to have their cultural and informative offerings heard by the largest audiences possible; they would also like to reach listeners with only average educational attainments and even the educationally underprivileged, as well as those with a university education. To that end, these station operators schedule some programs with the sole objective of attracting large numbers of listeners—in particular, broadcasts of sports events or even motion picture feature films— in the hope of acquainting more listeners with the availability of service from educational stations and creating some habit of listening to those stations. The policy followed by these educational station operators is similar to that of the British Broadcasting Corporation, which provides a substantial number of entertainment programs along with the informational materials on the BBC's second or "cultural" television network, simply to attract a larger audience. Obviously, American educational broadcasters are at a considerable disadvantage in this respect; not only does lack of adequate financing make it almost impossible to secure programs of sufficient appeal to attract large numbers of television viewers, but school administrators and community leaders tend to frown on such efforts to popularize what they think should be a serious educational effort.

Evaluation of ETV

America has a "second service" in television, provided by its constantly expanding system of educational television stations. Most experts seem to agree that these stations have operated with a reasonably high degree of effectiveness in providing instructional materials for use in our elementary and secondary schools. However, the educational stations have been much less successful in their efforts to provide an educational and cultural service for the adult television audience. High-quality programs have been offered too infrequently; the number of listeners attracted has been too small. As Dr. Schramm comments on findings of his studies of educational station audiences, "The loyalty that many ETV viewers feel toward the educational station, the fact that it had a personality for them and an importance, was clearly evident. At the same time, however, many of the viewers wished that the station had more money to hire needed personnel of high quality, to maintain professional standards of production, to keep on the air longer, to broadcast programs that would be sometimes a little more 'fun,' a little more 'interesting,' a little more 'challenging.' "

The basic problem is money—money to provide better programs, which in turn will attract larger audiences. Some progress is being made; educational television stations in several major cities have budgets of more than a million dollars a year. Even more important, the increased grant of the Ford Foundation to NET in 1963, combined with funds from other sources, gave that agency a total annual budget of approximately $8 million, with prospects of equally substantial financing in the future. With most of NET's funds spent for programming, there is every reason to expect that NET affiliates will have a larger number of outstanding cultural and informative programs available than in the past and that educational television will be able to offer a more attractive and more effective "second service" in providing organized information, education, and culture for American television viewers.

13

THE PUBLIC
INTEREST

It has been the intent of Congress, in providing
for the regulation of broadcasting, that radio and
television stations be operated in a way that will
serve "the public interest." Both the Radio Act
of 1927 and the Federal Communications Act of
1934 provided that station licenses are to be
issued if the licensing authority "shall determine
that the public interest, convenience or necessity
would be served by the granting thereof." But as
noted in an earlier chapter, neither Act of Congress attempted to spell out just what was
involved in "serving the public interest, convenience or necessity"; it was left to the Federal
Radio Commission and after 1934 to the Federal
Communications Commission to determine what
was to constitute "the public interest" in the
field of broadcasting.

As interpreted by the Federal Communications Commission, "the public interest" affects the number and distribution of stations throughout the country, the types of individuals or companies who are permitted to operate stations, and the preventing of monopoly in broadcasting. But in the opinion of the Commission, of federal courts, and of practically all of our national leaders, serving the public interest also involves programs. People listen to programs. They are influenced by what they hear or see in programs; it is through the programs provided by radio and television stations that broadcasting affects our society. On one aspect of the obligation of broadcasters as licensees of stations practically all Americans would agree: the broadcasting of materials that are definitely harmful to our society or to individual listeners is *not* in the public interest. Of course, differences of opinion exist as to what materials may be harmful, but the basic principle that socially harmful materials should not go on the air is accepted by broadcasters and by the listening public no less than by officials of government.

INTERPRETATIONS OF THE "PUBLIC INTEREST" IN PROGRAMMING

But what sort of programs *should* be broadcast? Is broadcasting solely an entertainment medium? Should substantially all programs be directed at the interests and tastes of a mass audience, or should stations also serve the special interests of the intellectual minority in our population? Should broadcasters give listeners the kinds of programs that listeners themselves want, or should an effort be made to raise public standards of taste? Exactly what is involved in "serving the public interest" in the programs that radio and television provide? And if radio and television programming can be improved—as the product of any human agency can be improved—what methods can be used to effect improvement?

On these and similar questions, national leaders have widely varying views. After more than four decades of commercial broadcasting in this country, we have not yet arrived at any consensus as to what constitutes the public interest in the types of programming offered, nor is there agreement on the desirability or effectiveness of steps that might be taken to bring about program improvement. It is not the purpose of this book to attempt to provide answers on either point. But leaders of the broadcasting industry, government officials, critics, educators, and other public figures have offered their views on the subject, and a review of some of the opinions expressed may show the complexity of the problem and perhaps help readers to form their own personal judgments concerning the requirements of programming "in the public interest."

Position of Regulatory Agencies

Almost from the time of its creation, the Federal Radio Commission gave its attention to programs. In granting licenses it frequently had to choose between two or more applicants for the same facility, and the type of programming to be provided was often the deciding factor. In 1929, the Federal Radio Commission in its *Great Lakes* opinion, referred to in Chapter 7, laid down its criteria for the evaluation of program service: [1]

There is a deeper significance to the principle of non-discrimination which the Commission believes may well furnish the basic formula for the evaluation of broadcasting stations. The entire listening public within the service area of a station, or of a group of stations in one community, is entitled to service from that station or stations. If, therefore, all the programs transmitted are intended for, and interesting or valuable to, only a small portion of that public, the rest of the listeners are being discriminated against. . . . The tastes, needs and desires of all substantial groups among the listening public should be met, in some fair proportion, by a well-rounded program, in which entertainment, consisting of music of both classical and lighter grades, religion, education and instruction, important public events, discussion of public questions, weather, market reports, news, and matters of interest to all members of the family find a place.

With so few channels in the spectrum and so few hours in the day, there are obvious limitations on the emphasis which can appropriately be placed on any portion of the program. There are parts

---

[1] Federal Radio Commission, *In the Matter of the Application of the Great Lakes Broadcasting Company*, Docket No. 4900, 1929. Reprinted in *FRC Annual Report* (1929). p. 43.

of the day and of the evening when one type of service is more appropriate than another. There are differences between communities as to the need for one type as against another. The Commission does not propose to erect a rigid schedule specifying the hours or minutes that may be devoted to one kind of program or another. What it wishes to emphasize is the general character which it believes must be conformed to by a station in order best to serve the public.

Two features in the Radio Commission's opinion stand out clearly: first, the need to provide a "well-rounded" and varied program service, including programs to meet the special needs and interests of all of the "substantial groups" included in the total listening public, and second, the listing of several specific types of programs which must be included in the schedule if the public's interests are to be served. However, the Radio Commission did not insist that all of the categories of programs named be offered by each individual station. In later decisions, it was made clear that the regulatory body was interested in the overall programming provided by the several stations serving each community.

The basic principles laid down in the *Great Lakes* opinion have been generally affirmed in decisions and public statements of the Federal Communications Commission ever since that body was created in 1934. In its public notice known as the *Blue Book* in 1946, the Communications Commission added a third requirement—the providing of "a sufficient number" of sustaining programs, combined with a warning against overcommercialization. As noted in Chapter 7, economic conditions in recent years have resulted in a lessening of the Commission's emphasis on the need for sustaining programs, and even in the relaxing of its standards as to the number of advertising announcements that may be included in the daily schedule, although the regulatory body still objects to overcommercialization. But the Federal Communications Commission still applies the same two basic principles concerning programming that were laid down by the Radio Commission in its *Great Lakes* opinion. The situation is summed up by Commissioner Lee Loevinger in an address before the Religious Broadcasters Association in January 1965: [2]

---

[2] Quoted in the *Journal of Broadcasting,* Winter 1965. p. 3.

By 1929 the Federal Radio Commission had promulgated a standard of program service which it thought would meet the tastes, needs and desires of all substantial groups of the listening public. This consisted of seven or eight elements including entertainment, religion, education and news. When the FCC succeeded the Federal Radio Commission it adopted and carried forward the same standards, and it has continued to use seven categories of programming as its test in judging both proposals and performance in this field. In 1930 the Commission promulgated a statement of programming policy in which it expanded what it called "the major elements usually necessary to meet the public interest, needs and desires to a total of fourteen. The fourteen elements listed were opportunity for local self-expression, development and use of local talent, programs for children, religious programs, educational programs, public affairs programs, editorializing by licensees, political broadcasts, agricultural programs, news programs, weather and market reports, sports programs, service to minority groups, and entertainment programming.

Although the program categories specified by the Commission are ostensibly "not intended as a rigid mold or fixed formula for station operation" they have in fact operated and been applied by the Commission as prima facie minimum requirements of acceptable programming. Even an uncontested application for an available broadcasting frequency in which the proposed programming omits any of the specified categories may be set for hearing by the Commission on issues in which the applicant has the burden of establishing that the proposed programming will serve the public interest, convenience and necessity.

In its new forms for applications for radio station licenses, adopted in 1965 and put into effect in 1966, the Communications Commission has reduced the number of program categories used. But the agency's insistence on use of categories is evidenced by its action in June 1964 in ordering a hearing on the application for a new UHF television station in Eugene, Oregon—the only application filed for the facility. One of the grounds given for the order was that the applicant had failed to specify the amounts or percentages of time to be devoted separately to "religious, agricultural, news, discussion, talks, or other programming," although the application did state that 30 per cent of the station's time on the air would be used to present "educational" and "public service" programs.

Broadcasters' Interpretation of Public Interest

Although broadcasters generally question the right of the Federal Communications Commission to regulate programming, most industry leaders accept the principle of providing variety and over-all "balance" in program schedules. While economic considerations make it necessary that most programs be aimed at a mass audience, to attract the largest possible number of listeners, some portion of the schedule is devoted to the interests of intellectuals and other minority groups. The industry point of view is well expressed in a statement by Robert W. Sarnoff, while Chairman of the Board of the National Broadcasting Company: [3]

NBC's concept of a television service in the public interest is one that gives reasonable satisfaction to the varying interests of the main audience elements; which does so by proportioning its program structure in general to the relative weights of these varying elements; which does not allow majority tastes to suppress a fair reflection of minority interests and does not frustrate majority interests by converting a mass medium into a specialized one.

We believe that broadcasters in a democracy have an obligation to lead the audience by providing information that will equip them for better citizenship, and by offering opportunities to enjoy the arts so as to broaden and cultivate taste. In leading the audience, however, the broadcaster cannot be so far ahead that his service is rejected by the majority, for that would defeat both the purpose of such leadership and the very nature of a mass medium. Essentially this is a doctrine of reasonable treatment of all segments of the public, so that each viewer or listener, in varying degrees, can find something he values in the broadcast schedule.

In a service based on these premises, popular entertainment, in a variety of forms, must predominate, because it is responsive to majority audience desires. In addition, a responsible service will include entertainment in the more cultivated arts which have not yet established mass appeal; and it will give significant recognition to nonentertainment programs in the field of news, information, public affairs and education, even though these appeal to smaller audiences.

No one of these program types has any special claim to serving

---

[3] Testimony before the Federal Communications Commission, January 29, 1962.

the public interest. It is the total proportioned blend of programming that serves the public interest, because only such a blend meets the varying and conflicting interests of the total public served by broadcasting.

The nature of broadcasting as a mass medium and its primary function to serve the interests of a mass audience have been stressed by another industry leader, Dr. Frank Stanton, President of the Columbia Broadcasting System. In Dr. Stanton's opinion,[4]

Television is a mass medium and not an elite medium. This means that we cannot turn our backs on the tens of millions of people and address ourselves exclusively to the tens of thousands. . . . While television can at times lead or make contributions to society, we cannot force people to like what they don't like or want what they don't want. . . . No unit in broadcasting can go too far too fast. It cannot run so far ahead of the public's wants as to lose its attention. . . .

It is a major part of our function to try to appeal to most of the people most of the time. This is an inescapable part of the nature of television . . . and a broadcaster who ceases to have the consent of his public, and to be a satisfactory servant to that public, would lose his support and disappear from the scene. . . .

Within the limits of taste and the avoidance of harm to any segment of our viewers, I suggest that a program in which a large part of the audience is interested is by that very fact a program in the public interest. On the other hand, that is not the whole of the definition of the public interest. Not for a moment do I suggest that a program in which only a minority is interested is by that fact contrary to the public interest. But I say it is wrong to insist that the only programs which are in the public interest are those which only relatively few people watch. And so I am convinced that we should reject the notion that in a cultural democracy it is wrong to appeal to most of the people most of the time. . . .

In searching for balance, we must remember that broadcasting is something like politics; it is the art of the possible. We can go only a little faster than people will let us. But by going a little faster, and yet keeping touch with the people, broadcasting will gradually become a vehicle for the thoughts and impressions, the achievements and aspirations of man.

---

[4] Testimony at a Federal Communications Commission hearing on network practices, February 1960.

Does Present Programming Serve the Public Interest?

The record of American broadcasting shows that radio and television have, in actual fact, provided a reasonable degree of "balance" in programming; while serving primarily the interests of the majority, they have provided a substantial amount of programming of interest to minority audiences, especially in the areas of news, information, and public affairs. But as Dr. Stanton has pointed out, broadcasters do plan their schedules with the purpose of reaching "most of the people most of the time"; the bulk of their programs are aimed at a mass audience. In large degree, this is simply the result of the economic factors governing broadcasting. Under our commercial system, radio and television depend for their revenues on advertising. Advertisers must reach mass audiences to build mass markets for the products they offer for sale. So operators of stations and program heads of national networks devote most of their time to programs that will attract the largest numbers of listeners possible—for the most part, programs of a light entertainment nature. In addition, commercial broadcasters with few exceptions believe that in order to serve the public interest most effectively, they need to reach, and to make their programs attractive and satisfying to, the largest possible proportion of the listening public. They agree with Dr. Stanton's statement that "a program in which a large part of the public is interested is by that fact a program in the public interest."

But some of our national leaders disagree with that basic philosophy. Among those who disagree was one of broadcasting's most distinguished news commentators, the late Edward R. Murrow, who found in the program staples of our national television networks "evidence of decadence, escapism, and insulation from the realities of the world in which we live." Mr. Murrow expressed his concern in a talk presented in October, 1958, before the national convention of the Radio-Television News Directors Association: [5]

I am frightened by the imbalance, the constant striving to reach the largest possible audience for everything, by the absence of a sus-

---

[5] Quoted in part in the *Columbia Journalism Review*, Summer 1965. p. 27.

tained study of the state of the nation. Heywood Broun once said, "No body politic is healthy until it begins to itch." I would like television to produce some itching pills, rather than this constant outpouring of tranquilizers. . . .

To a very considerable extent the media of mass communications in a given country reflect the political, economic and social climate in which they flourish. . . . We are currently wealthy, fat, comfortable and complacent. We have currently a built-in allergy to unpleasant or disturbing information. Our mass media reflect this. But unless we get up off our fat surpluses and recognize that television in the main is being used to distract, delude, amuse and insulate us, then television and those who finance it, those who look at it and those who work at it, may see a totally different picture too late. I do not advocate that we turn television into a twenty-seven-inch wailing wall, where long-hairs constantly moan about the state of our culture and our defense. But I would just like to see it reflect occasionally the hard, unyielding realities of the world in which we live.

Some of the most striking indictments of the program service provided by American broadcasters have come from heads of the government agency which regulates broadcasting. Early in May 1961, Newton N. Minow, then Chairman of the Federal Communications Commission, in a speech before the annual convention of the National Association of Broadcasters, took the industry strongly to task for underestimating the tastes and interests of the American people. Two or three lines of his statement have been quoted in an earlier chapter, but the importance of the Chairman's indictment of television programming more than justifies the use of a longer quotation:

I am the Chairman of the FCC. I am also a television viewer and the husband and father of other television viewers. I have seen a great many programs that seemed to me eminently worthwhile. Some were wonderfully entertaining; some were dramatic and moving; some were marvelously informative. When television is good, nothing —not the theater, not the magazines or newspapers—nothing is better. But when television is bad, nothing is worse.

I invite you to sit in front of your television set when your station goes on the air and keep your eyes glued to that set until the station signs off. I assure you that you will observe a vast wasteland.

You will see a procession of game shows, violence, audience participation shows, formula comedies about totally unbelievable families, blood and thunder, mayhem, violence, sadism, murder, western badmen, western good men, private eyes, gangsters, more violence, and cartoons. And, endlessly, commercials—many screaming, cajoling, and offending. And most of all, boredom. True, you will see a few things that you enjoy. But they will be very, very few. . . .

Why is so much of television so bad? I do not accept the idea that the present over-all programming is aimed accurately at the public taste. The ratings tell us only that some people have their television sets turned on, so many tuned to one channel and so many to another. They don't tell us what the public might watch if they were offered half a dozen additional choices. A rating never reveals what the acceptance would have been if what you gave them had been better—if all the forces of art and creativity and daring and imagination had been unleashed. I believe in the people's good sense and good taste, and I am not convinced that the people's taste is as low as some of you assume.

Four years later, Mr. Minow's successor, Chairman E. William Henry of the Federal Communications Commission gave a similar evaluation of the state of television programming. Although he recognized that by 1965 there had been an expansion in hard news programming and in coverage of spot news events, other programming, in his opinion, had shown little improvement.[6]

Four years ago, in this same city, this same gathering heard my predecessor call television a "wasteland." Among other things, he expressed a concern about violence, and about the unending commercials. But the heart of his charge was a lack of balance and a diversity of choice for the public—an overemphasis on sheer amusement and relaxation, a neglect of stimulation, ideas and information—an imitative barrenness.

Television entertainment (today) has changed very little. . . . Still present in daytime schedules are the same vast bulk of movies and cartoons, repeats from former network seasons, sob stories and game shows. They still sell the same vast bulk of soap, peanut butter and pain killers. Late afternoon is still the Children's Hour—still dominated by cartoons, slapstick, and adventure serials. In prime evening hours, feature movies have won a larger and larger place. Situation comedies have taken over from action-adventure shows; untouch-

---

[6] From an address before the annual convention of the National Association of Broadcasters delivered on March 23, 1965.

able mobsters have given way to unwashed monsters; and the newest innovation—the spicy night-time soap opera—has top priority on Hollywood's drawing boards. . . .

Entertainment "specials" bring some rare and wonderful moments. . . . (But) the over-all size of network public service has remained static or declined. Using the Nielsen rating service and its definition of public service programs (which excludes hard news), in the 1963–64 season only 210 network hours made the grade. Thus, the so-called barren season of 1960–61 had 22 per cent *more* network public service hours than the season just passed. In all the years from 1961 to 1965, the proportion of total network time devoted to public service programs—as defined by Nielsen—has remained about 4 per cent. Only about four out of every 100 programs fell into the public service category.

Put it all together and what have you got? At best, a mixed bag—some changes for the better, some for the worse.

Chairmen of the Federal Communications Commission are not alone in their criticisms of the quality of broadcast programming. As pointed out in Chapter 10, there are many writers, educators, and other important public figures who believe that the type of programs provided leave much to be desired. For the most part, their criticisms of quality of programs can be summed up under two major headings. First, the charge is made that in attempting to reach a mass audience, broadcasters are failing to provide a large enough number of those cultural and informational programs attractive to the intelligent minority in our population. And second, the criticism is frequently made that even in those entertainment programs designed to meet the needs and interests of the mass audience, standards of program quality are much too low. Both types of criticism were included in Chairman Henry's assessment of television programming.

Whether commercial radio and television stations offer a sufficient number of cultural and informational programs is a question not easy to answer. The so-called cultural programs are certainly few in number; on the other hand, networks and stations do offer a substantial amount of programs in the fields of news and public affairs, and a variety of other informational programs. But it is an interesting fact, in any case, that in urging that more time be devoted to programs to meet the needs and interests of the more intelligent segment of the public, most critics

—FCC chairmen included—apparently ignore the existence in this country of a large and rapidly growing number of educational stations, established and maintained to provide the very type of cultural and public service programs in which the critics are most interested. Samuel B. Gould, while serving as president of the company operating noncommercial educational television station WNDT in New York City, had the following to say with respect to the function of educational television: [7]

We recognize that certain types of programming cannot be sufficiently provided by commercial television because of its nature and economic needs. . . . The role that commercial television plays in our economy makes it mandatory that most programs be fashioned for a mass audience in order to satisfy the profit need. . . . Yet there is a minority audience to be served also. It is a large enough group to merit attention, but not from a commercial viewpoint.

Commercial television by its very nature cannot give primary attention to the needs and desires of minority audiences. The minority viewer is thus left with the alternatives of confining his television attention to a few programs rather inconveniently scheduled, or of ignoring the medium altogether. Yet he recognizes that television has very real possibilities for him in terms of cultural enrichment or even continuing education, possibilities he sees occasionally illustrated superbly by commercial television and that make his desire for additional programs of this sort all the more acute.

Out of these assumptions emerges the need for "educational" television and the definition of its real purpose. The need is for programs of an educational and cultural nature, presented regularly and at hours convenient to a maximum number of viewers. Its purpose is to provide an *additional* kind of television for audiences who are specialized in terms of their educational and cultural desires. . . . Educational television is and should be a part of the total pattern of television, adding a new dimension to that pattern.

As Mr. Gould points out, educational stations are a part of our total broadcasting resources. They exist, and they do provide a service consisting largely of cultural and informative programs, a majority of which are broadcast during prime evening hours. With more than 100 educational television stations on the air, including outlets in nearly every major city, and with more than 300 educational radio stations scattered from coast

---

[7] *Television Quarterly,* November 1962. p. 33.

to coast, most listeners throughout the country have access to the cultural and public service programs these stations provide. And when offerings of educational radio and educational television are considered in combination with the excellent public affairs programs presented by commercial television networks, it would seem that the needs of intelligent minority listeners are being reasonably well served—at least in the fields of culture and information. In evaluating the program service that broadcasting provides for American listeners, the *whole* of broadcasting must be considered.

As to quality standards of programming generally and the emphasis on entertainment programs, the American people seem, on the whole, to approve the types of programming that radio and television provide. Listening studies indicate that since 1960, radio listening has increased appreciably—perhaps as a result of the greater diversity of program material available on radio in recent years. And reports of the A. C. Nielsen Company show that the time devoted to television viewing in the average home was higher in 1964 and 1965 than ever before. Commissioner Lee Loevinger of the Federal Communications Commission sums up the situation as follows: [8]

Complaints have often been made that broadcasting—and particularly television—has mainly programs that are banal, boring and bad; that there are excessive commercials; and that there is a woeful lack of public service programming. It should be noted that these complaints have come principally from critics, intellectuals and the educated elite. (Studies have shown that) the public, at least, likes and is generally satisfied with television.

I do not deem it the proper role of government in a democracy to establish standards of taste or to dictate the intellectual or cultural level of expression in the mass media. Much television programming is trash, by my standards. But one man's trash is another man's treasure; one man's vast wasteland is another man's verdant vineyard.

But even assuming that the public is satisfied, does the programming provided by radio and television today adequately serve the public interest? Are standards in entertainment pro-

---

[8] In a speech before the Association for Education by Journalism at Lincoln, Nebraska, in August 1963. Quoted in part in *Variety*, September 4, 1963. p. 30.

gramming as high as they might be? There are many who believe
with Mr. Minow and Mr. Henry that broadcast programming falls
far short of the ideal, even as entertainment. They feel that too
many radio stations are little more than "glorified jukeboxes" offering a type of music which has little attractiveness for adult listeners, and that too many network television programs are aimed
too directly at juvenile tastes. Jack Gould, television critic of the
New York Times, believes that "the qualitative level of the entertainment phase of TV has shown relentless deterioration." [9] And
Hubbell Robinson, while Executive Vice President for Television
Programs for the Columbia Broadcasting System, commenting on
the need for more dramatic programs "with salt and grit" in them,
said: [10]

> If television entertainment is to be healthy and totally reward-
> ing to a total audience, its diet must contain those astringents as well
> as the bland and the innocuous with which it is currently sadly over-
> burdened. . . . To seek to escape totally from the world in which we
> live and with which we must cope seems to me ill-advised, and in
> the long run, fatal.

IMPROVEMENT IN PROGRAMMING

If radio and television programming can be improved, by
what means can improvement be brought about? In the long run,
of course, any raising of program quality must come from broadcasters themselves. But perhaps means may be found to *encour-
age* broadcasters to provide better programs. And naturally, since
we already have a federal agency empowered by Act of Congress
to license radio and television stations "in the public interest,"
it may seem at first thought that the stimulus for program improvement might well come from that government agency itself,
the Federal Communications Commission.

Program Improvement by Action of Government

Unfortunately for those who would turn to the government
for improvement of programs, that government agency is also

---

[9] See page 378.

[10] *Television Quarterly*, Fall 1963. p. 30.

prohibited by law from interfering, in any direct manner at least, with the programs offered by broadcasting stations. Section 326 of the Federal Communications Act of 1934 provides explicitly that the Act confers on the Federal Communications Commission no power of censorship over programs. Furthermore, the no-censorship provision of the Act is backed up by the First Amendment to the Constitution of the United States prohibiting government infringement on "freedom of speech or of the press," which the United States Supreme Court interprets as applying also to radio. The Federal Communications Commission can *suggest* improvements in programming in public statements addressed to broadcasters by its Chairman or by other members. It can indicate types of programs that its members consider desirable in the program section of its application forms. But neither the Commission nor any other agency of government has the power to control or to interfere, directly at least, with the programs provided by radio and television.

Even the use of indirect "pressures" by the Federal Communications Commission to effect program improvement raises a substantial moral and ethical question as to the function of government in our society. This is the contention of Professor Harry Kalven, Jr., of the University of Chicago Law School, and Maurice Rosenfield, executive director of radio station WAIT in Chicago, as set forth in an article referring to Chairman Minow's "wasteland" characterization of television: [11]

Mr. Minow's remark may mean that TV is a vast wasteland because it *does*, in fact, reflect the majority taste of the public. If this is the point, we have not so much a criticism of the broadcasting industry as a criticism of public taste. We are confronted with an intelligible issue: should the government interfere with radio and television broadcasting in an effort to improve the level of public taste? ... There is first the inevitable question of whose taste is to be substituted for the public taste. There is second the difficulty that we would not lightly accept this premise for government intervention elsewhere in our life. Should a government agency attempt the regulation of books, newspapers, magazines, movies and plays, so that we will buy, read or see better ones than we do now? Should it attempt to control the production of automobiles so that we will

---

[11] In *Fortune*, October 1962. p. 116.

prefer compacts to large, high-powered models? Should it attempt to regulate the allocation of resources so that our whole pattern of consumer preferences will be less unlovely—for example, more books and fewer refrigerators? The answer is no, and the argument for government interference with the radio and television taste level is a claim on behalf of sumptuary legislation. One does not need approve of all aspects of American taste today to reject a paternalistic government's attempt to improve it.

Even if we were to assume that the Federal Communications Commission has the legal *power*, whether by direct or by indirect means, to control programming on radio and television stations, it is extremely doubtful whether any actions taken by the Commission would have the effect of raising the *quality* of programs offered. The Commission might, for example, specify that certain general *types* of programs must be included in station schedules and that other types of programs be excluded. But this would not necessarily or even probably result in higher levels of quality or excellence in the programs put on the air. The difficulty is clearly pointed out by Aline Saarinen, of the National Broadcasting Company's news department, in her exposition of what she refers to as the "category" fallacy: [12]

It is not to difficult to score the number of people who said that they "liked" drama or music or sports or whatever. The fallacy lies in giving those results meaning, when the terms are so meaningless and generic. . . . Two people will say they love art. But one man's Picasso is another man's Norman Rockwell. By category, they are both art, but our information is meaningless as such. . . .

There is a very peculiar attitude in America today that anything called Culture is somehow morally good, uplifting, and a means of salvation. In such reasoning certain categories are prejudged as noble, and certain others as contemptuous. To apply this kind of reasoning is to ask whether the FCC would give good marks if a broadcaster produced a ballet, and bad marks if he produced a Western. It allows no room for the important consideration of quality. A ballet may be dull, the music mediocre, the production poor, and the whole thing bad television—of the type which might prejudice any but the most confirmed balletomanes against any more ballet viewing. A Western, on the other hand, might be superbly written, incisively acted, filled

---

[12] *Television Quarterly,* Winter 1964. p. 15.

with insight into human reactions and nature, imaginatively filmed, and may be very good television. Yet the category definition of "Culture" has missed the mark in judging the two efforts.

Other Suggestions for Program Improvement

The same difficulties that prevent effective government action aimed at the improvement of broadcast programs are also present in many other proposals made for the achievement of that objective. A number of suggestions have been offered, in some cases by witnesses appearing in hearings conducted by Congressional committees or by the Federal Communications Commission. Many of them call for direct governmental action; nearly all suggest expanded offerings of programs in certain "desirable" categories. Representatives of several important national organizations [13] have proposed that stations be required by the Commission to devote a fixed minimum proportion of their total broadcasting hours each week to public-service programs, with substantial amounts of such programming to be presented in prime time. Other proposals have involved the use of the government's taxing power to insure program improvement, one writer suggesting the granting of partial tax exemptions to television networks that offered stipulated amounts of public-service programming each week, and another recommending that the tax power be used to reduce the profits of broadcasters who failed to meet specified standards in the number of public-service programs provided.

John Fischer, editor of *Harper's* magazine, proposes that broadcasters pay rental fees on the channels they use, with the proceeds devoted to paying production costs of cultural and other public-service programs to be scheduled by national radio and television networks in desirable evening hours—presumably by government order. The whole operation would be supervised by a nonpolitical National Broadcasting Authority, made up of national leaders in the fields of education, culture and informa-

---

[13] The American Farm Bureau Federation, the American Association of University Women, and the National Education Association, among others.

tion.[14] The same "body of national leaders" proposal was embodied in an earlier suggestion of Senator William Benton of Connecticut, who in 1951 introduced a Senate resolution calling for the creation of a National Citizen's Advisory Board for Radio and Television. This Board, with the aid of a research staff, would make a continuing study of broadcast program service in the areas of culture and public affairs, and submit an annual report to Congress, with suggestions for program improvement. It is presumed that the Federal Communications Commission, in passing on license renewals, was expected to take into account the extent to which the Board's recommendations had been followed by station operators. A somewhat similar plan was also suggested in May 1965 by Representative Oren D. Harris of Arkansas, Chairman of the House Committee on Commerce; the function of his national advisory group would be to help formulate a "national policy for television" and to set policy guidelines and standards for the broadcasting industry.

Most of these proposals have the objective of requiring broadcasters to devote more time to certain types of programs. And in so doing, they fail to take into account one of the important "facts of life" with respect to broadcasting—a fact that is basic to any real improvement. As stated by Dr. Frank Stanton, President of the Columbia Broadcasting System, "we cannot force people to like what they don't like or want what they don't want." [15] Or as expressed by Robert Sarnoff, while Chairman of the Board of NBC,[16]

It is a mistake to assume that viewing can take place without the consent of the viewers—that a mass audience will just sit there and watch, regardless of what is on the screen. . . . Even if the government could force programs to its prescription, it could not force the public to watch the prescribed programs. Neither can the networks, the stations, the sponsors, the advertising agencies, the packagers. The

---

[14] *Harper's*, July 1959. p. 10.

[15] Testimony before the Federal Communications Commission, February 1960.

[16] In speech delivered before an NBC affiliates meeting in December 1961. Quoted in *Television Magazine,* January 1962. p. 48.

ultimate decisions on what the public sees can come only from the public itself, as long as it is free to watch or not to watch as it pleases.

And there is a second and equally important "fact of life" with respect to commercial broadcasters. That fact is that broadcasters will not present—they cannot *afford* to present—any appreciable number of programs that are not wanted, watched, or listened to by substantial numbers of listeners. We will get more high-quality programs, on commercial stations at least, only when the public makes it clear that it *wants* high-quality programs.

Developing a Discriminating Audience

Perhaps the problem of program quality does not lie in the fact that we have Westerns and adventure dramas and situation comedies on the air, but that we should have more Westerns with really adult themes, more dramatic programs that deal realistically with problems of everyday living, more situation comedies offering freshness and pleasant humor and good taste. We can get such programs only if the listening public, in greater numbers than in the past, tunes in the "quality" entertainment programs that are already available, and withholds its listening support from programs at best banal and frothy and at worst cheap and tawdry. Broadcasters and advertisers are alike in preferring to offer only those programs that give evidence of public approval in what serves as the ballot box of the broadcasting industry—the ratings that programs receive.

But for programs of high quality to achieve higher ratings, it will be necessary to induce the public, or at least substantial numbers of listeners, to be more discriminating in their choice of programs. And in the opinion of many critics, this in turn is possible only through the use of some continuing program of listener education. Program improvement would be facilitated, too, by the development of more effective channels of communication between intelligent and interested listeners and the operators of broadcasting stations in their communities.

One method of increasing the number of discriminating listeners might be to improve the type of radio and television criticism offered in our daily newspapers, with more attention devoted to the problems of the broadcasting industry and to the artistic and social merits of individual programs. One television critic, Ernest Kreiling, whose syndicated column appears in a number of papers throughout the country, takes newspaper publishers to task for their failure to provide this kind of in-depth criticism of broadcasting: [17]

American newspapers generally have failed to develop a significant body of informed, penetrating and effective criticism of television. As a working definition, television criticism means to report, interpret and evaluate, from a background of knowledge, the activities of the television industry, its programming and its responsibility in society—to alert and involve the viewing public so that it will demand, and get, the TV fare which is truly in its own interest. Such criticism calls for considerably more than sniping and pontificating at an industry which won't listen unless the viewer listens. It means actually motivating the casual viewer. And this requires involving him in discussions ranging from Gomer Pyle to E. William Henry, from Perry Mason to Canon 35, from the Farmer's Daughter to the Fairness Doctrine, from CATV to ETV, from Combat to COMSAT, from Hazel to Emmy, from obnoxious programs to obnoxious commercials, and from Nielsen to Sarnoff. This is the broad gauge genre of useful criticism that is so woefully lacking.

A similar view is expressed by Jack Gould, the authoritative television critic of the *New York Times:*[18]

The American press by and large is giving television a dangerous and short-sighted free ride in its columns. It has surrendered to the easy and inexpensive policy of dishing fan magazine pap and ignoring the evolution of a cultural medium of unrivaled social force. If the qualitative level of the entertainment of TV has shown relentless deterioration, the press shares part of the responsibility. On the 1,650 newspapers there are not more than ten critics who are paid to examine TV both esthetically and sociologically. The practical effect . . . is to let the TV junk go unprotested and leave the TV accomplishment inadequately cheered and encouraged. . . .

---

[17] From a monograph published in part in *The Bulletin of the American Society of Newspaper Editors,* September 1, 1965. p. 1.

[18] *The Bulletin of the American Society of Newspaper Editors,* September 1, 1965. p. 4.

The urgent need is for local criticism, criticism written in the same community where the paper is published. . . . The local broadcaster will not be responsive to criticism that talks of distant networks in New York and Hollywood. What makes him jump with joy or anguish is when he picks up the paper in his home town and sees his own station, his own call letters, either damned or praised. If the local broadcaster goes unreviewed day in and day out, is he not entitled to conclude that he must be doing something right? Certainly he has neither incentive nor cause to complain over the programming that the networks give, him, which is the national consequence of the local paper's indifference to its hometown TV.

Another type of agency that might be helpful in the development of a more discriminating listening public and that would provide an effective channel for communication between listeners and broadcasters is suggested by Dr. Walter B. Emery, Professor of Television and Radio at Michigan State University and formerly an attorney on the staff of the Federal Communications Commission. After discussing proposals for the creation of national Citizens' Advisory Boards, Dr. Emery suggests that such groups might well be organized on the local level: [19]

Back in the forties, a movement for the development of listener councils got started. I was always sorry the movement did not get very far. It would be helpful if it could be revived. Every community ought to have such a council, composed of thoughtful people with varied interests, conducting studies and making evaluations of programs and passing them on to broadcasters for consideration. There could be frequent conferences between management and representatives of the council that would be mutually helpful. Community needs and interests could be more clearly perceived by the broadcasters, and, at the same time, their problems of station operation and financial survival might be better understood by listeners who are not faced with meeting payrolls in a station every day, securing advertising revenue, and meeting other practical needs to keep the station on the air.

A final suggestion for the development of a critical audience for broadcast programs comes from a distinguished writer and critic of the mass media, Gilbert Seldes, a former Vice

---

[19] *The Centennial Review,* Summer 1964. p. 306.

President of the Columbia Broadcasting System and later Director of the Annenberg School of Communications at the University of Pennsylvania: [20]

> I do not give one hoot either for the FCC or a few intellectuals that criticize television. I want a minimum of five million people to be *actively* critical. One thing I want to do, for instance, is to have the material of broadcasting, particularly television, studied in a school —and not only if somebody puts on Shakespeare. I would sacrifice the reading of *Ivanhoe*, writing a report on *Ivanhoe*, if students in every school in the country would write a report about "Have Gun, Will Travel," or "Maverick." I want to go beyond that into colleges when you begin your study of the mass media. If we had a GI Bill which said, among other things, that one course you've got to take is The Mass Media, we would now have these five million families who would be critical of what they're going to have.

Whether any or all of the methods suggested will be attempted on any broad scale, and whether if attempted they will succeed in developing the discerning and discriminating audiences that must exist if program standards are to be very much improved, only time will tell. In the meantime, broadcasters will probably follow the recommendation of Dr. Frank Stanton, President of the Columbia Broadcasting System, of "going only a little faster than the public" in the direction of program improvement. As Dr. Stanton has said,[21]

> The fast way to growth or improvement in free societies is often the wrong way. The only sure way is through the increased acceptance by the public of what is good and the increased rejection of what is shoddy. This is sometimes a painfully slow process. But it is a process that has proved to be spectacularly productive. It invites experiment and innovation. It is the surest way to insure that television, with its great potential, will always be a medium serving, and drawing its strength from, a free people.

---

[20] From a talk presented in October 1961.

[21] In testimony before the Federal Communications Commission, January 23, 1962.

INDEX

A

ABC (*See* American Broadcasting Company)

Advertising:
announcements (*See* Commercial announcements)
before 1928, 38
in chain-breaks, 105, 289, 290–91
circulation, 247, 255
code limits on quantity, 290–91
restrictions on content, 286–87
cooperative, 109
costs, on TV networks, 103, 107, 170–73
criticisms, 281–92
in Europe, 14
expenditures for, 5, 101, 106
factors affecting amount, 288–92
Federal Trade Commission regulation, 283–84
from 1928 to 1941, 44, 46
lack of taste, 282, 285–88
listener appraisal, 282
local, 46, 81, 101, 108, 111, 147
misleading, 177, 185, 282–85
national spot, 46, 81, 101, 106, 107, 145, 147
network, 46, 81, 100, 103, 107, 147, 170–73
objectionable or harmful, 185–88
in participating programs, 29, 102, 103, 105, 108, 112, 288–89
quantity, possibility of reducing, 291–92
revenues (*See* Revenues)
network and station, 1930–45 (table), 46
sponsorship, types, 100–104
time, sale of, 100, 110–12
of unacceptable products, 285–87

Advertising (continued)
in wartime, 64
Advertising agencies, 51, 100, 112, 121, 173
Affiliated stations:
affiliation and programming, 73
and revenues, 146, 157
compensation arrangements, 167–69
contracts with networks, 168–69
of educational TV network, 347
FCC regulations concerning, 169, 186
network payments, 146, 147, 156, 168, 173
noninterconnected, 76, 119
number, radio, 41, 42, 49, 69, 142, 167
television, primary (table), 167
Airborne instruction, 342
Allocations, channel:
for FM stations, 183
for TV stations, 86, 182
American Broadcasting Company, 42, 64, 69, 76, 89, 117, 171, 316, 317
American Federation of Musicians, 53, 133
American Research Bureau, 250–51, 256, 356
American Society of Authors, Composers and Publishers, 52, 134
American system of broadcasting:
advantages, disadvantages, 24
characteristics, 22
competition under, 23
cultural programs, 24
programming under, 26–31
reflecting political inheritance, 11, 13
American Telephone & Telegraph Co., 41, 76, 117, 119, 131, 173, 343, 344
Application forms, 191, 363